"*The Power of Collaborative Leadership* makes Peter Senge's *The Fifth Discipline* come to life. For those who agree with the basic message of Senge, this is fascinating reading material. It clearly demonstrates that getting involved in organizational learning is a long and tough journey. It opened my eyes."

—**Ton Vervoort**, Philips International BV

"*The Power of Collaborative Leadership* takes us beyond process management, total quality management, and even transformational leadership to organizational learning. The authors draw the important distinction between traditional single-loop learning and much more robust double-loop learning, which can shake a corporation or a society to its very foundations.

They explain how the leadership that comes from true organizational learning distributes power throughout the organization, rather than concentrating it in a centralized hierarchy.

The Power of Collaborative Leadership is a thought-provoking and important contribution to management literature that every business leader should read, reflect on, and learn from."

—**Peter A. Darbee**, Senior Vice President,
CFO, and Treasurer, PG&E Corporation

"In *The Power of Collaborative Leadership*, Bert Frydman and Iva Wilson allow us to journey with them through their odyssey of learning within large, highly structured organizations faced with new market demands and rapid technological change. This book is an honest and personally candid accounting of their personal learning experiences and the challenges that all who greet life with an open mind and a desire to search out new frontiers must ultimately face.

This gift of a learning history will aid readers in their personal and professional journey toward greater competitive effectiveness. *The Power of Collaborative Leadership* will teach organizational leaders to apply the principles and insights that enable all employees to release their creative, life-affirming energy into the workplace."

—**Dave Morse**, Vice President,
Customer Sales and Services, Pacific Bell, SBC, Inc.

"The format of *The Power of Collaborative Leadership* is ideally suited for its purpose. The authors' reflections about their experiences, as interpreted by the ideas of organizational learning and human dynamics, are fascinating to read. As an ex-CEO, I found myself fully engaged with the authors' discussions. I only wish that I had the full benefit of this book while I was leading my own company, and I'm sure that many other executives will feel the same way.

I would strongly recommend this book to anyone who has taken an interest in organizational learning and who is thinking about introducing the concepts of OL to their work environment.

The Power of Collaborative Leadership will become a classic OL resource book that should benefit all who care about improving the quality of life and work in modern business organizations."

—**Peter M. Banks**, retired President and CEO,
ERIM International, Inc.,
and former Dean of Engineering, University of Michigan

"This book is every manager's story. Two senior execs who have been through it all—restructuring, reengineering, downsizing, and TQM—engage the reader in a rich dialogue. They argue that transformation is a must in today's world and ponder whether organizational learning is the way to go. They tried it in practice and learned a lot on the way. So will the reader!"

—**Arie de Geus**, author, *The Living Company*

"If you believe as I do that organizational learning is a requirement if one hopes to build and sustain a successful organization, this is a must-read. Frydman, Wilson, and Wyer provide real life insight into the challenges of establishing an organizational learning environment. They've been there, and their experiences are real. Now they have provided the opportunity for more organizations to join the journey to an environment where people can build futures."

—**Rich Teerlink**, retired Chairman and Chief Executive Officer,
Harley-Davidson, Inc.

"*The Power of Collaborative Leadership* is an extraordinary opportunity to 'participate' in a reflective conversation with today's foremost organizational explorers. Their process of learning and the practical integration of their collective experiences unfold before the reader."

—**David Marsing**, Vice President and COO,
Network Communications Group, Intel Corp.

"*The Power of Collaborative Leadership* goes beyond the usual touting of one's successes by taking a courageous look at failures as well, and providing rich insights into the pitfalls and the challenges of pursuing visionary aspirations in the face of pragmatic realities. Through candid reflections and thoughtful dialogue, the authors provide valuable lessons about what it takes to embark on a learning journey, both individually and as an organization. This book is a must-read for all leaders who are serious about transformative change in their organizations."

—**Daniel H. Kim**, Founding Member, Society for Organizational Learning; Co-founder, Organizational Learning Center at MIT; and Publisher, Pegasus Communications, Inc.

"Provocative and challenging! The authors offer readers a new perspective on how to lead an organization, how to involve employees, and how to get results through people involvement and learning. They give receptive leaders a new tool for the toolbox as Senge and Peters have done before them. You may not agree with all the concepts presented, but I am sure you will be a better leader after reading *The Power of Collaborative Leadership*."

—**Clifton L. Smith**, President and CEO,
Corning Asahi Video Products Company

"In *The Power of Collaborative Leadership*, the authors open their hearts with a great deal of courage. They share the doubts, uncertainties, disappointments, and frustrations encountered during their journeys, while still growing from such rich and volatile learning experiences. The reader gains invaluable insight on the dos and don'ts so fundamental to any business manager who strives to move an organization to a new level of performance through organizational learning"

—**Marcos Magalhães**, CEO, Philips Electronics, Latin America

The Power of Collaborative Leadership

The Power of Collaborative Leadership:

Lessons for the Learning Organization

Bert Frydman / Iva Wilson / JoAnne Wyer

Foreword by Peter Senge

Boston   Oxford   Auckland   Johannesburg   Melbourne   New Delhi

$\mathcal{R}$ A member of the Reed Elsevier group

∞ Recognizing the importance of preserving what has been written, Butterworth–Heinemann prints its books on acid-free paper whenever possible.

AMERICAN FORESTS
GLOBAL Butterworth–Heinemann supports the efforts of American Forests and the Global
RELEAF ReLeaf program in its campaign for the betterment of trees, forests, and our envi-
2000   ronment.

Library of Congress Cataloging-in-Publication Data

Frydman, Bert, 1945-
   The power of collaborative leadership: lessons for the learning organization/
   Bert Frydman, Iva Wilson, JoAnne Wyer.
      p. cm.
   Includes bibliographical references and index.
   ISBN 0-7506-7268-4 (alk. paper)
      1. Organization learning. 2. Leardership. I. Wilson, Iva 1938- II. Wyer,
   JoAnne, 1948- III. Title.

   HD58.82.F79 2000
   658.4'063—dc21

                                                    00-030350

British Library Cataloguing-in-Publication Data
A catalogue record for this book is available from the British Library.

The publisher offers special discounts on bulk orders of this book.
For information, please contact:
Manager of Special Sales
Butterworth–Heinemann
225 Wildwood Avenue
Woburn, MA 01801–2041
Tel: 781-904-2500
Fax: 781-904-2620

For information on all Butterworth–Heinemann publications available, contact our World Wide Web home page at: http://www.bh.com

10 9 8 7 6 5 4 3 2 1

Printed in the United States of America

We would like to dedicate this book to the people
of the Pacific Bell and Philips Display
Components for participating in these
experiments and making it possible for us
to learn and to write this book

Contents

Foreword

"Whoever does not understand history is doomed to repeat it." This familiar refrain has rarely been more timely, especially in the world of organizations and management.

In this era of profound change, it is hard to find organizations anywhere—businesses, schools, healthcare organizations, governmental organizations—that are not trying to reinvent themselves, develop e-commerce strategies, or dismantle old cultures to adapt to new realities. But their efforts are usually disappointing. The history of success of quality management, reengineering, or the more recent trend, knowledge management, is dismal. Typically, less than a third of these programs are even still alive a year after they are announced. Those that survive rarely achieve hoped-for impacts. Obviously, sustaining change in established institutions is not easy.

But what is even more disquieting is how little serious effort managers seem to muster to understand why change efforts fail. "Try and try again" seems to be the motto. Yet, repeating yesterday's errors is not likely to produce tomorrow's success. What hope can there be for learning if what is actually going on is that no one wants to talk about "failure." If it is not safe to explore what happened when highly visible change efforts produce disappointing outcomes, these problems will be repeated. Yet, undertaking such reflective self-examination takes time. Analysis can quickly become finger pointing. So, it is also easy to see how it may seem better to ignore disappointments, to declare victory and move on—even if that means the disappointments will likely be repeated, often by some new "change leader."

Ironically, learning from success fares no better. Because of the lack of appetite to study our history, when successful change does occur in some part of a larger organization, it rarely spreads. In fact, the innovators typically leave rather than deal with the internal politics and bureaucracy of their former employers.

For example, several years ago, a leading auto manufacturer brought out a new passenger car which eventually proved to be one of its most successful ever. It was a best seller for over 15 years. The team that developed the car became mythical within the industry. They developed extraordinary spirit and camaraderie. They broke lots of rules. They pioneered innovations in process and leadership methods. And, they all left the company within a year after the car was launched.

Recently, a major American electronics manufacturer introduced a dramatic new product platform, the first fully digitized product of its sort. The product is also almost completely remanufacturable; that is, when the customer is done, they can give it back to the manufacturer and new machines will be built from the old, thereby achieving both substantial cost savings and reducing environmental waste. The product has won many engineering awards, and after two years, its sales exceed all forecasts. Yet, its lead engineer, who also developed extraordinary teamwork through his innovative leadership, has also left the firm, and other members of the original product team have scattered.

In neither case was there any effort by the firm to understand why the innovators were so successful. If they broke rules, maybe the rules are wrong. If they created new practices, maybe others could learn from them. None of these larger changes has occurred, because there was no attempt to study or learn from the innovators. This pattern of failure to learn from highly successful but radical innovations occurs far more often than most recognize.[1]

I have come to the conclusion that the inability to learn from history is not just due to lack of will or political conservatism. Though these undoubtedly play a part, there are deeper issues. We simply do not know how to learn from history where change efforts are complex and their outcomes, both successful and unsuccessful, are threatening. Managers are action-oriented people. They are paid to produce results not insights. Even if they are reflective by nature, which many are not, they have little help in doing so, and very few models to guide them. And matters are getting worse, not better. With overwork and stress levels rising, what little predisposition for reflection and analysis exists is now swamped by a rising sea of day-to-day urgency. The search for quick answers results either in "Here's how we did it" books by retired or current CEOs, most of which offer little serious reflection or self-criticism, or in typical academic case studies that look at a complex change process from the proverbial "50,000 feet," summarizing everything in fifteen pages. More serious academic studies of change typically take a theoretical point of view that gives little sense for the feelings and thinking of those on "the field of battle." Overall, we lack a genre of reflective histories that both serious practitioners and academics alike would find valuable.

This problem has been very evident to those of us who have worked to develop the Society for Organizational Learning (SoL). SoL was founded to promote partnerships among practitioners, researchers, and consultants to build knowledge for fundamental change. Most of the corporate members are Fortune 100 companies. Over the past ten years, SoL members have undertaken many major change efforts, often with researchers closely involved. This has resulted in a series of learning histories and other reflective studies that, we hope, will contribute useful exemplars of what is possible when practitioners are committed to building transferable knowledge and researchers are committed to practical impact.[2]

I am very pleased that *The Power of Collaborative Leadership* has now arisen from the spirit of partnership and mutual inquiry within the SoL community. It is a rare book, one that actually captures "thinking in the moment" from experienced practitioners. It reflects the complexity of feelings and multiplicity of interpretations that coexist in complex change efforts. It shows how time is needed to make sense of things, and how that sense-making can continue to evolve for many years. It weaves theory and practice with integrity by delving deeply to explore non-trivial insights and potential guiding principles that emerge from experience. In short, it is a very exciting book for those of us genuinely interested in expanding our capacity to learn from history. For those looking for easy answers and quick fixes, it would better to look elsewhere.

In many ways, the uniqueness of the book arises from the three-way partnership that produced it. It starts with two very different managers, Bert Frydman and Iva Wilson. Bert and Iva have been involved in organizational learning efforts in large, well-established firms for many years. Both rose to hold positions of influence in their organizations. Both had a passion for innovation and believed deeply that their organizations had to change.

Yet, you can hardly imagine two more different personalities or styles of leading change. Bert is Canadian-American. Iva is Eastern European. Bert rose through the ranks, starting as a field technician. In a sense, he was always close to the mainstream of his organization. Conversely, Iva was always on the periphery of the mainstream. She was the first woman to earn a Ph.D. in engineering at a prestigious German university. In virtually all of her engineering managerial positions, she was the first woman.

Eventually, she became the highest-ranking woman manager for a global electronics firm. Hers is an impressive CV, but it was not an easy journey, just as it is not easy for most women like her who have breached the walls surrounding previously male-dominated workplaces.

Bert's and Iva's differing career paths also signal very different leadership styles. Bert is a problem-solver by nature, a practical person shaped by what Ed Schein calls the "operator culture" in which he grew up professionally.[3] Iva, by contrast, is a product of what Schein calls the "engineering culture." Because of this, by the time they became executives they brought with them very different mindsets. Bert tends to see a messy world of imperfect solutions achieved by committed people acting locally, often without much support from management. Iva tends to be "proactively optimistic," to use Schein's term, believing that complex problems can be understood and conceptual breakthroughs are possible.

The third member of the partnership is a gifted researcher, JoAnne Wyer. To her credit, rather than suppress the differences between Iva and Bert, as most would have done, JoAnne artfully accentuates them. The result is a fascinating tapestry of different perspectives facing the common challenges of transforming organizations. These are exactly the types of differing worldviews that characterize most management teams. When the differences are honored, synergies can develop. When they are suppressed, political gamesmanship tends to dominate, and the team as a whole is usually capable of little more than watered down compromises. So, in this way, Bert and Iva's conversations are a window into how real dialogue among truly different people can energize organizations. Lastly, Bert and Iva's differences not only highlight their views, but also make it easier to discover your own views. You will find yourself drawn in, taking sides, agreeing strongly with one and disagreeing equally strongly with the other. You will then discover that what you are really finding out about is yourself: their passions evoke your own. You are a party to the conversation. The circle of reflection is expanding.

Making the tapestry still richer are four exceptional executive leaders from other SoL companies, whose views are woven into the conversation. Bill O'Brien, former CEO of Hanover Insurance, helped a bankrupt company become one of the top performers in the U.S. property and liability industry over a 20-year period. Rich Teerlink was CEO during one of the most famous corporate revivals in recent history: the rebirth of Harley-Davidson. Phil Carroll was CEO of Shell Oil for five years, during which the company went from record losses to record profits (Phil is now CEO of Fluor Corporation). David Marsing, former VP of Assembly and Test Operations for Intel, has headed some of Intel's most successful manufacturing facilities, and is now COO of Intel's new Network Communications Group. Each also knows the difficulties of learning from history in today's crazy business environment. Together, this ensemble explores how one gauges the readiness of organizations for change, the "creative frustration" that often motivates change leaders, distinctions in organizational cultures that either enhance or inhibit learning, the art of finding the "right amount of tension" around change without triggering automatic responses from the "organizational immune system," and what it means to be ready personally to lead such change. In short, what develops is a fascinating conversation exploring both the inner and outer dimensions of deep change.

When Iva and Bert first told me of their intention to write a book based on their stories, I confess to having had some reservations. They had accomplished a lot in their careers, but I also knew that both left their organizations disappointed with not accomplishing all that they had intended. They had undertaken change efforts in exceedingly complex situations, with many forces outside their control. They made some mistakes, by their own assessment. Their stories are fascinating, and undoubtedly represent the great majority of change efforts. Still, I wondered how many would be drawn to such a book. I feared that many readers of management books are hooked on (often exaggerated) "great success stories," combined with three easy lessons for "how you too can succeed."

Then I read Bill O'Brien's comments. He too left his company disappointed, forced out after 20 years of dramatic improvements by a hostile takeover from a parent firm with majority ownership seeking greater control of Hanover's profit stream. "These are not isolated failures of strategy or execution," says O'Brien, "but inevitable setbacks on the road to transforming management." O'Brien observes that the large corporation supplanted traditional family businesses early in the 20th century, bringing with it a new style of governance. "I don't think there's any question that the basic governing theories that took us from 1920 to 1990 are being seriously renovated," says O'Brien. "We're going to have a new (governance) architecture, and this generation of management has the rare privilege of participating in the design of the architecture." O'Brien's comments helped clarify for me why this book is as important as it is fascinating—and why it will attract the serious readers it deserves. Those committed to the transformation O'Brien describes will know that the journey is perilous and that, over the long run, it is not individual successes and failures that matter but the cumulative learning we can accomplish.

Peter M. Senge
Massachusetts Institute of Technology
Society for Organizational Learning (SoL)
June 2000

Notes

1. For many other examples of successful management innovations that failed to spread, see A. Kleiner, *The Age of Heretics* (New York: Doubleday/Currency, 1995).

2. See, for example, G. Roth and A. Kleiner, *Car Launch* (New York: Oxford University Press, 2000), and A. Kleiner and G. Roth, *Oil Change* (New York: Oxford University Press, 2000).

3. E. Schein, "Three Cultures of Management: The Key to Organizational Learning," *Sloan Management Review,* 1996 (Fall): 9–20.

Preface

I am not a teacher, only a fellow traveler
of whom you asked the way.
I pointed ahead—ahead of myself as well as of you.

—George Bernard Shaw

Back in the fifteenth century, when the new world was beginning to be discovered, it was the Portuguese Prince Henry the Navigator who made the greatest contribution to modern exploration. Though he never ventured forth himself, he set about building an infrastructure for exploration. He encouraged and then required his navigators to keep accurate logbooks and charts and to keep careful notes about everything they encountered on their voyages. Before his efforts, the notes and charts were haphazard; now they were organized and kept in a single place. Sailors, travelers, and adventurers of all sorts gathered in that place and shared their experiences, adding their tales to the growing body of knowledge. Henry brought the sea captains, instrument-makers, shipbuilders, and mapmakers together to collaboratively plan expeditions and assess findings, creating a feedback loop. Under his sponsorship, cartography became a cumulative science and explorers were enabled to go farther and farther into the unknown.[1] We believe that organizational learning is also in a state of early exploration and in that spirit we've written this book.

Our book is written primarily as a conversation between two senior managers, Bert Frydman and Iva Wilson. It takes that form because we wanted to capture the spirit of exploration. The field of organizational learning is new, and the challenges to its proponents, especially to businesspeople, are many. We hope that the book will speak to businesspeople, especially those of you who are on the verge of committing yourselves to organizational learning but haven't yet done so. We hope that the conversation format will resonate with the kind of inner dialogue that you tend to have with yourselves as you go through a decision-making process, particularly prior to making a serious commitment.

We hope that the conversation will have a familiar ring—that you, the reader, will identify with some of our points of view. In this book Bert represents our pragmatic side, and Iva our visionary tendencies. Of course, everyone has aspects of both. We hope that by making the debate between these two poles explicit we can bring you into the conversation. We trust that we will say things you are also saying and ask questions you are also asking, and that you will have a sense of participating along with us. We need to explore ideas together, so the thoughts and ideas presented here are not definitive answers; they are open to challenge and question. As we share our experiences and reflections you are invited to shape your own arguments, your own change strategy.

The book is in the form of a conversation also because we wanted to capture the spirit of learning. Learning is a living process, and most businesspeople have little exposure to the process of reflection and only a superficial understanding of learning. This book will take you along on a learning journey with us. You will see learning emerge from reflection on experience.

These topical conversations are structured and woven together by commentary. The worlds of theory and practice seldom connect, so through that commentary I hope to provide some much-needed links between the practical experiences of two executives and the theories that support the concept we call organizational learning. In the commentary I pose questions and offer further reflections, hopefully leading us toward more discoveries and insights. This structure mirrors the process by which the book was conceived and written.

The book was created in a spirit of collaboration. Each of us brought our unique gifts to the process of writing this book. Along with her senior management experience in the field of consumer electronics, Iva brought energy, commitment, and, especially, the perspective of a visionary—one who sees possibilities and urges us toward the future with conviction and charisma. Iva set high standards and challenged us to meet them. Also a senior manager, Bert was a self-described pragmatist who earned his stripes in the telecommunications industry. Averse to discussing theory for its own sake and skeptical about the business world's inclination to change without proof, Bert kept us practical. He grounded our thinking, reminding us that there is still a wide chasm between the world we want to create and the world we have created. Both manifested courage. They were willing to let their guard down, to expose their missteps, to examine their mental models, and to probe deeper into many of the assumptions that drove their actions so that they and others might learn from their experiences. For my part, I brought a strong passion for building bridges between practice and theory and for helping change leaders to find the theory that would help illuminate their practice, as well as a desire to translate individual experiences into stories from which others could learn. I also had expertise in deep listening and a commitment to developing our capacity for reflection.

Through this collaboration—sometimes quite challenging to sustain—we created more than we would have been able to create separately. We came to realize firsthand the power of collaborative leadership, but this alchemy came about quite by accident.

Some three years prior to this book being published, I had played the role of catalyst, bringing Bert and Iva together to talk about their experiences with organizational learning. As they shared their stories about their struggle to create change and transformation within their respective organizations, they discovered common ground. This spark was enough to turn that first encounter into a series of telephone conversations. Together, the three of us began a more deliberate process of exploring what we might learn from Bert's and Iva's experiences with organizational learning. In time, we evolved a structure whereby we would come together to share insights and, hopefully, learn more together about the field of organizational learning. During these meetings I would fulfill the role of interviewer or facilitator, listening deeply to their stories and thoughts, catalyzing further reflection through the questions I asked. In this capacity I found the following questions to be continuously in my mind: What could Bert and Iva learn from each other's experiences? What could others learn from Bert's and Iva's experiences? What was the larger meaning behind their stories? How do their stories connect to the theory that supports organizational learning? I became the container for our process, both a witness to and synergist for their learning, focusing on drawing out the reflections, the insights, the deeper realizations.

In time we thought we had accumulated sufficient insight that we might be able help other early explorers of organizational learning, so our conversations became even more purposeful as we attempted to develop this practical wisdom into a book. Toward that end, I created a structure to guide our explorations, and then distilled some 150 hours of taped conversation into a manuscript. We then reviewed and edited that manuscript in continuous collaboration with each other.

Although quite different in many ways, all of us have a deep and abiding commitment to the field we call organizational learning. We believe that the path to organizational transformation is

still uncharted and therefore it is a *journey*—a journey to be traveled and spoken, argued and walked, told and debated. Just as
Henry the Navigator surmised, we need all of the aspects of the
journey. We need the ideas, concepts, and theories to spark interest, to get sponsorship and launch the ships. We need the empirical research to substantiate our ideas and confirm our sightings. We
also need the stories told by the early explorers. They especially
need to talk aloud about those outcomes that did not match their
expectations. They need the opportunity to reflect on, discover, and
value the learning that can be gained from those setbacks. They
need to do so in a collaborative setting that is sufficiently safe and
yet also adequately challenging so that learning can take place.
Through their commitment to reflect and learn together, those who
have gone before can help illuminate the path so that others can
find their way a bit easier. In time, we will understand the territory,
and, through learning, we will transform it.

In the beginning, we thought that this book came to be because
of chance. Later, we learned that what we thought was chance was
really an act of synchronicity. What are the odds that our lives
would cross and become intertwined in this way? Chance says the
odds are remote, but synchronicity says that it is no surprise.

JoAnne Wyer

Endnotes

1. For more on Henry the Navigator, please see Daniel J.
   Boorstin, *The Discoverers* (New York: Random House, 1983),
   pp. 156–164.

Acknowledgments

The authors wish to thank the following for their help and support:

- Arie de Geus, Peter Senge, and Dee Hock for encouraging us to start the project.
- C. K. Prahalad for giving us important critical feedback along the way.
- Phil Carroll, Phil Fazio, David Marsing, Dan Mlakar, Bill O'Brien, and Rich Teerlink for agreeing to be interviewed for the book.
- Richard Sachs and Ann Wilson for their help with illustrations, and also thanks to Ann for her help with our Web site.
- Nan Gill and Steven Gill for the care and understanding they exhibited when we asked them to read the manuscript and give us their critical remarks. Their reflections and honest comments allowed us to make significant changes that made this book better. We pay a tribute to them as exemplary practitioners of organizational learning.
- Vic Leo for reading the manuscript and sharing thoughts based on his own long professional experience in the field of organizational learning.
- Giovanna Morchio for her insights and guidance toward the literature that deals with complexity and organizational learning.
- Ken Murphy, Sarita Chawla, Peter Darbee, Tom Durel, and Cliff Havener for their reflections and insights.
- Don Seville for being a "thinking partner" on causal loop diagrams.
- Learning as Leadership in St. Raphael, California for the tools we used to develop our personal mastery. In particular, thanks to the late Claire Nuer and also to Lara Nuer for their personal support during the journey of writing this book.

Last, but far from least, we wish to thank our partners, Tom Wilson, Rosemarie Frydman, and Robert Levin, who provided support, understanding, love, and feedback throughout our learning process.

Introduction

Talking Revolution

The business world is in great need of change. If the recent burgeoning of trends and fads in management tells us anything, it's that the field is in flux. It seems that business is searching desperately for new ideas, quickly jumping from one to the other, hunting for the silver bullet. Yet, simultaneously, there is a sense that much in the world of business management is intransigent, staying the same despite a need for change and despite solid evidence that supports change. It is a contradictory image. To the same point, the cartoon *Dilbert* depicts the corporate environment as a place where people are frustrated, even defeated, by insidious and virulent nonsense, as if Alice's tea party were no longer the exception, but the rule. The popularity of *Dilbert* sends a frightening message, that a certain kind of madness is global.

In sum, the picture painted of many business organizations is that they are at a turning point—challenged by enormous change without, and enmeshed in inconsistencies and a good deal of personal pain within.

Can we recreate our business organizations, making them more effective and saner, transforming them through learning—or is this just a pipe dream? What will it *really* take to bring about this transformation? These are questions that an increasing number of people in the business world are beginning to ask, but where will the answers come from?

Most management books are written by well-informed and accomplished academics or consultants. These books advance a new theory or suggest a different approach to business issues. Generally, this new approach is based on research into a relatively small number of cases, and many of the assumptions that underlie the theory are not clearly in view. The next step is for the busi-

ness community to test the theory and see if it works. In this
model, the business community stands to benefit greatly from the
wisdom of these external experts, but businesses also bear the
lion's share of risk and consequences.

While such books stir hope, help create vision, and energize
passion, they often fail to discuss the enormity of the challenges
intrinsic to organizational transformation efforts. Because of their
theoretical nature, these books may chart new territory, but they
cannot address the very inadequacy of the untested navigational
tools they provide. And they generally do not address the very real
risks to both self-concept and career that practitioners who
embark on these journeys may experience.

For these reasons, we believe that the solutions cannot come
solely from the academics or the consultants. Ultimately, solutions
can come only from the people *within* the business environment,
businesspeople who are willing—and courageous enough—to
engage with the questions.

Where Are We Going?

In response to the needs of and the pressures on their respective
organizations, Iva Wilson and Bert Frydman were both looking for
solutions. They were experienced senior managers who had found
various management approaches to be lacking in one way or
another and were looking for a better way. Their searches led them
to a relatively new management concept called "organizational
learning." For us, organizational learning (OL) represents "the
process of forming and applying collective knowledge to problems and needs. It is learning that helps the organization continually improve, achieve goals, and attain new possibilities and
capacities. It is learning that taps into employee aspirations, fueling commitment and creating the energy to change."[1]

As our stories and reflections on those stories will show, there
is much to learn (and unlearn) about how to realize the potential
of OL. Primarily we had to learn that OL is a process. Because it is
a process, it can never be treated as program or a "thing" that, if
implemented, will lead automatically to the accomplishment of
results in the short term.

Early Hopes

Iva Wilson was a visionary engineer who was president of the U.S.
division of a global electronics manufacturing firm. A technologist
with a Ph.D. in electrical engineering as well as an MBA, Iva had
been involved in many facets of research, development, and man-

ufacturing of cathode ray tubes (CRTs) during her career. One of her most significant contributions was in the field of electron optics. She holds a major patent on the Extended Field Lens, which has been applied to a multitude of different electron gun designs for CRTs throughout the world.

When Iva first became acquainted with the concept of organizational learning she saw a new and possibly very powerful means for integrating the power of technological know-how with the aspirations of the people in her organization. Through organizational learning, Iva believed she could create an effective competitive strategy for her company.

Iva: What really spoke to me about organizational learning was the focus on systems, the idea that everything is connected. I had been familiar with systems dynamics from a technical perspective, but organizational learning provided the application of systems dynamics to human systems, to business systems. Now, suddenly, there was a way of applying what I thought was a strictly *technical* methodology to the understanding of all kinds of other systems: business systems and organizational systems and people systems. That was very exciting.

I saw a real opportunity for organizational learning to help us create results both for the business and for the individual. This was a completely new way of thinking for me. Before, my view was that people create their own circumstances and their lives are their responsibility. If people don't do things themselves—if they don't study and work hard—then so be it. But, among other things, organizational learning is about what's possible if we can create a shared vision. It's also about who we can be if we practice personal mastery. All of those things opened a door to a new world.

By contrast, Bert Frydman was a senior line manager in the field of telecommunications. Bert began his career on the ground and worked his way up—quite literally. He began by climbing telephone poles as a service technician. From there, motivated by a thirst to understand all aspects of the business, Bert moved on to hold management positions in various capacities within the telecommunications industry, including engineering, construction, operations, new products, procurement and staff methods, while also finding time to teach at the university level. Bert became involved in organizational learning in 1991 while serving as the Service Policy and Quality Vice President for Pacific Bell, responsible for the implementation of strategic initiatives regarding competitive service for all of Pacific Bell's core markets. Customer service had long been Bert's passion but, for a variety of reasons, it was not always easy for his company to keep the focus on the customer. Bert saw organizational learning as a natural complement to his work in Total Quality Management (TQM), and he believed that he could use the organizational learning approach, particularly systems thinking and simulations, as a way of generating a greater awareness of the relationships and interdependencies involved in customer service. If people understood these relationships, he believed, it would lead naturally to improvements in customer service.

Bert: After being exposed to organizational learning and listening to Peter Senge, it dawned on me that organizational learning would be a natural for us. We were already going down the Quality road, but I was concerned that with that approach we could be improving processes that have no business even existing. There was that lingering question: Is the process we're using really the best way of doing it? Organizational learning gave us tools for inquiring into the usefulness of our processes.

So I was really enthused about organizational learning. Also, I was very impressed with the potential of simulations, which is another aspect of OL work. Simulations allow for a business model to be represented in a computer model. In particular, I remember experimenting with one particular simulation. It was a powerful example because it showed very dramatically how you could get different results by making changes to the different variables. Depending on what decisions you made, the simulated company either succeeded or failed. You could see the relationship of your decisions to that failure because it showed how you could get dramatically different results by making small changes to certain variables. This was particularly salient because the company actually failed in real life just as the simulation predicted it would, given these same decisions. From that example I saw clearly how we could use simulations to help us make better business decisions. A simulation could help us see those connections and understand the consequences of our actions.

Excited about the potential they saw in organizational learning, both Bert and Iva set out to apply what they had learned. They began what they hoped would be successful organizational transformation efforts, introducing organizational learning concepts into their respective companies. Despite the differences in industry, focus, and strategy, they both discovered that they faced a myriad of unanticipated obstacles, some common and others unique.

Implementation Blues

Bert: You could say that a funny thing happened on my way to building a learning organization. In fact, a lot of funny things happened—things I didn't expect or anticipate.

Iva: My journey was also full of surprises and, as a result, new questions. I wonder, did either of us fully comprehend what we were getting into when we started? Books are helpful, of course. You can learn a lot from them—but true learning can only occur when you practice organizational learning in a real organization with real people under real pressures.

Bert: That's when you begin to realize how much needs to change—and conversely, how little we understand about how to change it.

Iva: You realize how many dilemmas you can get into by thinking about things in the same old way—

Bert: And how fiercely the organization itself will resist all your good ideas and intentions. That's when you come to terms with a fundamental question: How deep is your commitment to this work? Are you willing to work through those dilemmas and learn from them?

The task of bringing about organizational change has never been for the faint-hearted, and Bert and Iva were no exceptions. They encountered many of the typical responses to change efforts. For example, many times people in an organization adopt a "this too shall pass" attitude. Having seen leaders go off to classes and then return "talking funny" for a few weeks, people don't expect new behaviors to be sustained over time. If the leader does sustain commitment to OL work, people within organizations that are on a learning journey will most likely feel "at sea" because their leader's actions will now be harder to decipher. Those who have grown used to a command-and-control environment will be bewildered when the newly energized leader suddenly starts asking their opinions. Most likely, they will tend to distrust this sudden shift and hold back. They may even resent being asked to become more involved in decision making, for command-and-control has its comforts. As organization members begin to engage with organizational learning they may experience a disorienting alteration in perspective. Transitions—even those that may be profoundly beneficial—confuse because they confound expectations.

These are some of the issues that leaders of organizational learning efforts will face and some of the experiences they can expect. Furthermore, the idea of transforming a business into a learning organization presents its own unique set of challenges because the journey to the learning organization requires passage through unknown and uncharted territory.

Heroes, Heretics, or Prophets?

Why did Bert and Iva encounter these dilemmas? One reason lies in the very nature of organizational learning itself. Both Bert and Iva discovered organizational learning as expressed by MIT's Peter Senge in his now classic work, *The Fifth Discipline: The Art and Practice of the Learning Organization* (1990). *The Fifth Discipline* is a powerful synthesis of theory, philosophy, and good business sense, and describes an array of tools and methods that can be applied in organizations to bring about increased learning. But before we can realize the promise of OL, Senge cautions, we may need to give up our illusions. "The tools and ideas presented in this book are for destroying the illusion that the world is created of separate, unrelated forces," writes Senge on page one of *The Fifth Discipline*. "When we give up this illusion, we can then build learning organizations."

Business leaders and would-be change agents who embrace the learning organization as a logical, practical goal may not initially see themselves as "destroyers of illusion" or corporate "heretics," but that is, in fact, how they will be viewed by many. They must anticipate and be prepared for this eventuality—and for many other surprises.

The reality—and the irony—is that these people of vision will be at risk because, unfortunately, the illusion Senge alludes to is the very linchpin of the worldview that dominates the business arena. We live in a world defined by reductionistic thinking, more driven to break things down into component parts than to see the whole. We tend toward the compartmentalization of thought and feeling, often valuing one over the other as if they were actually in competition with one another. We have a strong tendency to dichotomize, to set both ideas and peoples in opposition to one another rather than seeking to understand how they relate both to ourselves and to each other. Rather than bearing witness to complexity, we tend to hold the perception that there is a simple, easily discernable relationship between cause and effect.

As we are beginning to learn through pioneering work in the field of physics and other disciplines, these aspects of the current Western worldview are inadequate for representing all of reality. Furthermore, we are beginning to see that by relying solely upon these concepts we have created an illusory sense of reality that, in turn, produces beliefs and actions that can be faulty or even harmful. The word "paradigm" is so frequently used as to be overused, but that doesn't make it any less real. The business world is immersed within a paradigm of its own creation. In many respects, it is a system based upon this outdated worldview and, for that reason, it does some things well and others quite poorly.

Ways of thinking and acting—and the illusory reality they create—are deeply entrenched and hard to dislodge. At its best, organizational learning enables us to explore how these ways of thinking and acting may be limiting our ability to get results in the traditional business sense and to create the results we truly want in the larger sense. Through practice in organizational learning we can begin to dislodge these inappropriate beliefs, ideas, assumptions, and actions, and we can begin to replace them, not with other fixed and rigid ideas, but with the dynamic process of learning.

When we say that we need to transform our organizations in significant ways, we mean that we need to bring them in alignment with the significant shifts that are taking place in our understanding of the world and the way it works. Breakthroughs in physics, in our awareness of the complex interrelationships of large systems, as well as the unprecedented globalization of the economy, all have implications for our institutions and our organizations. Business organizations are also being asked to reexamine their ethics and reconsider their responsibilities to the health and well-being of individuals, the community, and the natural environment. We are just beginning to understand what those implications might be and how to come to terms with them. We suspect, increasingly strongly, that we must respond.

To creatively address the present and the future, we need to understand what that task involves and why it is an order of magnitude different from any other task we have encountered in our lives. This presents another reason for why our learning projects may not meet our expectations. Chris Argyris, consultant, author, and the James B. Conant Professor at the Harvard Business School, has observed a pattern that he sees as characteristic of the way businesspeople have approached organizational changes such as TQM, flat organization, reengineering, and management empowerment.

The pattern begins when we see a prescription for organizational reform (such as "empowerment" or reengineering) appear on the horizon. More often than not the new idea even contains a genuine insight and is supported by theory as well as stories of successful implementation. All of this gives us hope and we reach out. Almost inevitably, however, we turn the idea into a "fix"—we

condense it down into what we think is an understandable package of procedures. Too often we accompany the package with an
ideology that has quasi-religious overtones. Managers latch onto
the package because they're hungry for solutions to persistent
issues and tired of gurus advising them to "wrestle with complexity" (or suggesting that they're colluding in creating problems). As
the managers sign on, a bandwagon effect ensues. Then the resistance and the defensiveness show up. The top level becomes frustrated at the resistance of the lower levels. In time, disillusionment
begins to appear and, along with it, cynicism. People begin to say,
"We tried that!" The change effort ceases, only to start all over
again when the next reform appears on the horizon.[2]

In sum, we are primed to turn good ideas into organizational
"fixes" because our ways of being, acting, and thinking are deeply
rooted in mechanistic, reductionistic worldviews. Because of this
automatic response, we may tend to see organizational learning as
a "thing" to be implemented rather than a process to be lived.
Even the word "tool" (as applied to OL tools and methods) is dangerous because it supports our tendency to tinker with parts, to
repair the machine, rather than to conceptualize living wholeness.

This idea gives rise to a third reason that change may be difficult: as leaders of change in organizations, we may have underestimated the need for our own personal learning. In order to come
to terms with how to bring about organizational learning, we
must each engage in a process of deep and complex learning.
Because so much has changed and is changing—and we are not
fully aware of the extent nor the implications of those changes—
we must be willing to acknowledge that we do not, perhaps cannot *know*. We must surrender the sense of security that our knowing provides and learn to inquire, asking and holding questions
when the answers do not immediately come. We must encourage
diversity in order to become unstuck, to provoke new ideas and
challenge old ones. We must make ourselves vulnerable to a deep
and apparently threatening form of learning. We must allow our
most tacit and closely-held assumptions to be open to question.
Rather than deploying our well-oiled defenses, we must allow ourselves to show vulnerability. Each of us must learn again what it is
to learn, not superficially, but deeply. And we must learn to
unlearn as well. Moreover, we must do this not as heroic individuals, but in community with others who are also engaged in learning. In collaboration lies the greatest power, and this is the journey. The process of organizational learning is about actualizing
the power of collaborative leadership.

Is there another reason why we may not succeed with organizational learning? Perhaps we may discount the gift of failure for,

in times of uncertainty, it is exceedingly instructive. At its best, organizational learning is not business-as-usual. It cannot be nor should it be—and that is problematic for leaders of learning efforts. The potential rewards of organizational learning—and of more collaborative leadership—are great, but getting there is no walk in the park. It is a journey, and we will have apparent failures.

Therefore, to be effective as leaders of learning efforts, we must accept that a mere incremental shift in business-as-usual will not be sufficient. The shift to an organization steeped in and shaped by learning requires a significant transformation of an organization's ways of being and the development of new ways of taking in information and transforming it into knowledge and wisdom. In addition, this organizational transformation must proceed from the personal, inward transformation of its members. There will not be one without the other. And so, there are significant implications for leadership as we begin to confront the realization that sharing power is actually more effective than hoarding power. If we sustain our commitment to organizational learning we will both stimulate and help bring about a sea change. Of course, we can try to subvert learning. We can try to implement it in such a way that it turns into yet another short-lived management fad, but we will be doing ourselves a disfavor. Furthermore, personal transformation requires deep, complex learning—a kind of learning that occurs most effectively in community with others who are also learning. This is a new practice for most of those in business organizations.

Bert: As Iva and I compared stories we learned that we shared many of the same experiences. Things did not happen exactly as either of us had planned or expected.

Iva: Although we began by expecting that we would be changing others, the most surprising outcome was that *we* had to change. *We* had to learn. I have come to understand why we need to do more of this kind of learning, even though it may sometimes be painful.

The experience of deep learning shifts expectations—particularly those expectations that have been shaped by the current business environment. When one allows oneself to live in learning, one's basic assumptions are up for grabs. For example, Bert and Iva began by expecting that they would be changing others—after all, they thought, this is the role of a leader, isn't it? But, in time, they realized that the most significant outcome of their endeavors was that they began to learn what it is to truly learn. In the course of their change efforts, Bert and Iva also learned a great deal about organizations, about organizational culture, about the nature of change and resistance, and about themselves. They learned the value of reflection, a practice that is almost nonexistent among businesspeople. Moreover, they learned the value of reflecting together within a space that was both dedicated to learning and safe.

Learning As We Go

After the visions have been articulated and the theory formulated, the job of bringing about organizational learning ultimately falls to the businesspeople who see the genuine potential in this field for remaking their corporations. Those who accept the challenge of the learning organization journey will encounter multiple paradoxes. As they get deeper into OL work they will find that the tried-and-true methods that led them to so much success in the past might now fail them.

Therefore, businesspeople need to be supported in taking up this challenge. There may be a vision, but a clear pathway to that vision is uncharted. Organizational learning is a field in the process of becoming. In other words, we are still learning what it means to learn together and how to bring about significant learning within an organizational context. There is a rich body of thought on organizational learning, some empirical research and anecdotal evidence, and much incisive philosophy, but the bridge from the present-day business world to that vision has not yet been built. Although some of the elements have been defined— such as the five disciplines put forth by Peter Senge—there is not yet a blueprint for that bridge. There is no proven architecture of engagement and no guaranteed method for successfully including the doubtful, the indifferent, and the adverse.

If the organizational learning is to thrive, we must bring about more collaboration. We must have more true partnerships. There must be a more equal sharing of accountability and trust between the theory-makers and the theory-testers, more opportunities for genuine dialogue. To start that dialogue, we must begin to hear more voices from the trenches. Businesspeople need to share their stories because too little has been written about organizational change from the viewpoint of those involved. Those stories then need to be placed within a larger context so that others might learn from them. To that end, Bert, Iva, and I collaborated to write this book, joining our voices and weaving together the perspectives of the visionary, the pragmatist, and the witness as learning analyst. Hopefully, this is a step toward realizing the power of collaborative leadership.

The organization of this book is as follows:

In Part 1, The Vision:

- Bert and Iva describe how Peter Senge's work in organizational learning engaged them and why they, two senior executives, became deeply committed to this work.

- They describe why they see organizational learning as the next evolutionary step for business organizations, framing that argument within the context of their experiences with restructuring, TQM, reengineering, and downsizing.

- They present a range of additional arguments for the widespread adoption of organizational learning. They acknowledge the barriers and discuss why there is still more work to be done so it can be widely embraced.

- We close Part 1 by encouraging readers to hold the tension between current reality and the vision of a future in which learning holds a prominent place in organizations.

In Part 2, The Journey:

- We provide a framework for interpreting Bert's and Iva's journeys. We describe organizational learning as put forth by some key thinkers in the field. We introduce Chris Argyris's thinking because we feel that double-loop learning is very important (and very difficult) for individuals as well as organizations.

- Bert and Iva share their learning journeys as case stories told by the protagonist. You, the reader, will experience the gaps, the subtleties, and the struggles both pragmatists and visionaries encounter on their respective journeys.

- We debrief Bert's and Iva's journeys.

- In the spirit of Chris Argyris's double-loop learning, Bert and Iva share what they subsequently learned from their journeys. It is our intent to model double-loop learning. We hope that our collective reflections will inform yours.

In Part 3, Leadership:

- We share what they have learned about leading a learning effort from four leaders (Phil Carroll of Shell, Bill O'Brien of Hanover Insurance, Rich Teerlink of Harley Davidson, and David Marsing of Intel) who were early pioneers and are still involved in applying OL thinking in their work.

- Bert and Iva then reflect on their collective experience of leadership and provide a possible framework for thinking about the transition from traditional command-and-control leadership to a form of leadership that develops through a process of learning.

In Part 4, Mapping:

- We offer some reflections on how you might map your own journey. Based on the collective experience of the authors and the other OL leaders interviewed, we describe an approach to mapping the journey.
- Bert and Iva share their reasoning and suggest questions to ask, the questions they discovered as being important while they were travelling on this road that is full of surprises, difficulties, and exciting experiences that hold great promise for the future.

We end, as you might expect, with a call to action. We call to pragmatist and visionary alike. Whether you arrive by way of self-interest or awakening, science or philosophy, all paths seem to converge on learning as the primary mode of transport to a viable future. Learning is the means and, for reasons still unfolding, the business organization is the crucible. Please join us.

Endnotes

1. Steve J. Gill, *The Manager's Pocket Guide to Organizational Learning* (Amherst, MA: HRD Press, 2000) p. x.

2. Chris Argyris, *On Organizational Learning, Second Edition* (Oxford, UK: Blackwell Publishers, Inc., 1999) p. 51.

Part 1
The Vision

When you engage with the promise of organizational learning you are being asked to open yourselves to the following ideas:

1. It is not only rational and desirable but also necessary for us to pursue the goal of organizational transformation;
2. The field of knowledge known as organizational learning holds great promise for the positive transformation of our organizations.

The learning organization is a compelling vision because it holds out a two-fold promise. It promises greater competitive effectiveness through improved learning on a collective scale, and it promises a more honest, life-affirming, energizing workplace.

Underlying the promise of organizational learning is another premise: that, ultimately, greater competitiveness and workplace transformation go hand-in-hand. They are inseparable. The one is not sustainable without the other.

And there is a further implication that has to do with the *way* in which the promise of organizational learning is to be realized. It seems that organizational learning requires that many of the old rulebooks be set aside. Specifically, we do not change our organizations as we ordinarily do: by tinkering with or manipulating them. We do not create learning organizations by restructuring, reorganizing, reengineering, or downsizing them. These options are not precluded; rather, they are transcended. Manipulation and control are superseded, replaced by a deceptively simple notion. *We transform our organizations by doing the hard work of trying to transform ourselves and the teams we are part of.*

This idea is quite profound. It is also fraught with difficulty because we do not yet know exactly *how* to transform ourselves. We are still finding our way. The road is only partly illuminated. Furthermore, there is no one path that everyone can follow. It is a highly individual journey, yet it is also a collective journey—we are on the road, exploring, finding our way together. In a sense, we *are* the journey.

Chapter 1

The Premise and the Promise

Bert: The term "organizational learning" may seem too theoretical or conceptual or visionary. There's nothing wrong with theories or concepts or visions, but I want to give people a sense of what it would be like if it were real and alive.

I think it was Guaspari who said about Total Quality Management (TQM), "I'll know it when I see it." I have the same feeling about organizational learning. People need to know what it would feel like if their organizations were learning organizations. If they walked around the halls where people were truly living organizational learning out, what would it look like? Would it be dramatically different? Are we all talking about the same thing? Here's my vision:

A Learning Organization: A Practitioner's Vision

- People speak in terms of continuous improvement:
    e.g., "Leave it better than you found it."

- People are more involved in rapid decision making without being sure:
    e.g., "Seven out of ten is better than three out of three."

- People openly speak of failures in a reflective tone and without fear of reprisal:
    e.g., "If you haven't failed recently, you are not trying hard enough."

- People openly share what they are doing, without ego and in the spirit of teaming and collective discovery:
    e.g., "The whole is greater than the sum of the parts."

- People are not limited to vertical thinking and are ready to revisit the old ways and reconnect or rebuild past practice:
  - e.g., "You have to break an egg to make an omelet."

- People view training as an investment, not a cost:
  - e.g., "People are our only sustainable competitive advantage."

- People value diverse opinions and actively seek them out:
  - e.g., "The successful companies will be the ones that see the future and its opportunities faster than the competition and act on them."

- People share openly and willingly and, at the same time, steal good ideas shamelessly, replicate, and give credit and honor to innovators:
  - e.g., "The popularizers will inherit the earth."

- People build on each other's ideas using phrases like "yes, and . . ." instead of "no" and "but":
  - e.g., "Great oaks grow from small acorns."

Iva: We also need to tell people how we first became engaged with organizational learning through the work of Peter Senge. Senge's work started the shift in our thinking. In particular, his five disciplines influenced the way we introduced OL into our organizations.

The Five Disciplines of Organizational Learning

In *The Fifth Discipline*, Senge defined five "component technologies" that can help organizations learn, that is, develop the capacity to realize the highest aspirations. These are the primary tools of organizational learning. They are described below.

- Personal mastery—learning to expand our personal capacity to create the results we most desire, and creating an organizational environment which encourages all its members to develop themselves toward the goals and purposes they choose.

- Mental models—reflecting upon, continually clarifying, and improving our internal pictures of the world, and seeing how they shape our actions and decisions.

- Shared vision—building a sense of commitment in a group, by developing shared images of the future we seek to create as well as the principles and guiding practices by which we hope to get there.

- Team learning—transforming conversational and collective thinking skills so that groups of people can reliably develop intelligence and ability greater than the sum of individual members' talents.
- Systems thinking—utilizing a way of thinking about and a language for describing and understanding the forces and interrelationships that shape the behavior of systems. This discipline helps us to see how to change systems more effectively and to act more in tune with the larger process of the natural and economic world.[1]

The premise of Senge's book was that these five disciplines, or areas of practice, if introduced and cultivated within an organization, could help to enhance the learning capacities of that organization. Organizational learning is the means by which an organization might transform itself and its members.

Iva: As I've reflected upon my experience I see now that the five disciplines are just one way of thinking about OL.

Bert: It could be that each company's definition of organizational learning will be slightly different, depending upon what learning means to them.

Iva: If there is one thing I have learned through my engagement with organizational learning, it is that there is no "one size fits all" in this work. These ideas should serve only as starting points.

Bert: It's also true that for some people even these definitions will not be sufficient to convey why these ideas are so compelling. After I read Senge's book, it was still abstract for me. I didn't have a real, gut sense about what it was until much, much later—when I had a realization that related directly to my personal experience.

Iva: That is one way in which we are different. I was very stirred by the ideas even just reading the book, but for you it took the experience. My sense is that that is true for our readers as well. There will be differences in what draws them to organizational learning and how they come to learn about it.

Awakening

David Whyte, the poet, in his book about the corporate workplace called *The Heart Aroused,* quotes a poem written by a woman who worked at AT&T. She wrote:

> Ten years ago . . .
> I turned my head for a moment
> and it became my life.[2]

Perhaps for every person who decides to explore organizational learning there comes another turning point . . . a moment when they turn their heads away from many of the accepted ways of doing things in organizations and begin to consider that there may be another way. And in that moment, however fleeting, they may catch a glimpse of another possibility.

Iva: Bert, do you remember what it was that first captivated you about the concept of organizational learning—the moment when you first said, "Aha! Now I understand. This is the direction we should go in"?

Bert: Yes, I do. It was right after I finished playing the "Beer Game." I remember the day vividly. We were in the middle of a five-day course on organizational learning being taught by Peter Senge. A whole group of us had just finished playing the Beer Game, and it had been a total disaster for our team! We'd been doing all the things we thought were right to manage the beer business, and what did we have as a result? We had crisis after crisis. First, we didn't have enough beer to match the orders. Then we had a whole warehouse full of beer and very few orders. So we felt ridiculous. And then we learned that all the other teams had had the same experience. Nobody could prevent the crises. And then we heard that thousands of people have played the game and *it always comes out the same.* And I thought to myself, "Oh, is there a message in this!" The Beer Game showed me the power of thinking in terms of systems.

Systems Thinking and the Beer Game

The Beer Game is a particularly powerful illustration of the power of systems—and the illusions that trip us up because we do not think in systemic terms. As Senge explains in *The Fifth Discipline,* the Beer Game was first developed in the 1960s at MIT's Sloan School of Management. It immerses the participants in a management game simulating the production and distribution of a single brand of beer. There are three main roles in the simulation game: a retailer, a wholesaler, and a marketing director of a brewery. As the participants take on each of these roles, they are completely free to make any decision that seems sensible. Their only goal is to manage their position as best they can to maximize their profits. The primary rule is that the players in the various positions refrain from communicating with each other.

The game has been played thousands of times in classes and management training seminars over the last 30 years by people of all different ages, cultures, nationalities, and business backgrounds. *Every time the game is played, the same crises ensue.* First, there is growing demand that can't be met. Orders build throughout the system, inventories are depleted, and backlogs grow. Then the beer arrives en masse, but incoming orders suddenly decline. By the end of the game, almost all players are sitting with large inventories that they cannot unload.

What does the Beer Game tell us? If the same qualitative behavior patterns are generated by literally thousands of players from enormously diverse backgrounds, then the causes of the behavior must lie beyond the individuals. The "Aha!" is that the causes of the behavior must lie *in the structure of the game itself.* Another "Aha!" is that this same explanation can be applied to production-distribution systems in real business life. Structure often determines how events play out in business life.

When people play the Beer Game, they take on a role, either a beer retailer, a wholesaler, or the marketing director of a brewery. If they "manage their position"—which is typically what people do—they don't see how their actions affect the other positions. The players are actually part of a larger system, but most perceive that only dimly at best. The game is also designed to limit communication between the roles so that people can see clearly how the lack of effective communication contributes to a system spiraling out of control. That parallels what tends to happen in real life: effective communication across functions is limited, partly by the "silos" created by organizational department structures and partly by our lack of competence in the art and practice of generative conversation.

Senge describes three lessons to be learned from playing the Beer Game:

1. **Structure influences behavior.** When placed in the same system, people, however different, tend to produce similar results. When there are problems or performance fails to live up to what was intended, it is easy to find someone or something to blame. *But more often than we realize, systems cause their own crises, not external forces or individuals' mistakes.*

2. **Structure in human systems is subtle.** We tend to think of structure as external constraints on an individual. But structure in complex living systems, such as the "structure" of the multiple "systems" in a human body, *means the basic interrelationships that control behavior.* In human systems, structure includes how people make decisions, i.e., the "operating policies" whereby we translate perceptions, goals, rules, and norms into actions.

3. **Leverage often comes from new ways of thinking.** In human systems, people often have potential leverage that they do not exercise because they focus only on their own decisions and ignore how their decisions affect others. In the Beer Game, players have it in their power to eliminate

the extreme instabilities that invariably occur, but they fail to do so because they do not understand how they are creating the instability in the first place.[3]

Players can improve their performance in the Beer Game if they learn how to work with these lessons. The lessons of the Beer Game also apply to real life. The deepest insight, Senge says, usually comes when people see how both their hopes and their problems connect to the way they think. We tend to find ourselves caught between reacting to events and trying to create our future—without necessarily having the tools to make that shift. If we can stop thinking in terms of "events" that we must react to and begin to acquire "systems thinking," then we can see the structure of the system and discern the structural causes of behavior. With that insight, we can begin to create the outcomes we desire rather than react to things that happen to us. Another key lesson is that each player in the system must share this systems viewpoint. If any one player in the Beer Game panics and places a large order, panic tends to spread throughout the system and instability ensues. So, too, in real life. Another important aspect of systemic thinking is that players must learn to anticipate that there will be a delay between actions and consequences, and acquire the patience to cope with the delay. Interestingly, in the Beer Game—and in many other real-life systems—in order for one to succeed others must succeed as well.[4]

The Beer Game is a very rich wellspring of learning; participants respond to the insights that are most compelling for them, the insights that shift their thinking.

Bert: The Beer Game proved to me that when you're in a system like that, it doesn't make any difference who you are or what your qualifications are, you are destined to fail. Yet, in the business world we actually fire people on the basis of performance when, in fact, an individual's performance doesn't make any difference. The effectiveness of any individual performance is very much determined by the system the individual is in. Of course, there are a few cases where the person in question is, in fact, incompetent, but in most cases it wouldn't make a difference who you put into the job. Given a dysfunctional system, he or she is going to fail. That's what the Beer Game taught me.

Iva: For me, the turning point came during the systems dynamics part of the training on organizational learning given by Peter Senge, but it was during a different part of that discussion. On the third day or so, we were asked to divide into groups of five and practice creating causal loop diagrams to represent some of the major problems we had in our businesses.

Systems thinking is "a discipline for seeing wholes, a frame-work for seeing interrelationships rather than things and patterns of change rather than static 'snapshots.'"[5] One way to begin to see the world systemically is to begin to tell stories differently. We can break our tendency toward linear, reactive thinking when we express those interrelationships by actually drawing them as "cir-cles of influence." These circles, or causal loop diagrams, enable us to see that what we think of as random events are actually patterns that repeat themselves.[6]

Iva: There were approximately one hundred people in the training so there were a great many groups drawing these diagrams. When we were all done, I looked around the ballroom. Each group had drawn its causal loop diagram on an easel, and as I looked I realized that *every one of the easels depicted one of my problems.* Oh, sure, the specifics were different. The problems might concern circuits or automobile parts or oil rigs instead of picture tubes, but you just had to change one or two words and their diagrams described one of my problems. For example, there were problems with supply chain, problems coordinating marketing and engineering, et cetera.

The issues looked exactly the same! It was uncanny. When I saw that similarity I began to be convinced that there was something here worth paying attention to.

Bert: So we both were struck by the common patterns we saw in those experiences. You saw a pattern in the kinds of business problems that people drew and I saw a pattern in the way people were reacting to the system they found themselves in during the game—a system that was very much like a real work environment.

Iva: Right. I began to see that many of the problems that we expe-rience in business are shared; they seem to cut across all industries. Furthermore, these problems appear to be the result of patterns that we ourselves continuously create and repeat—even though they lead to undesirable results!

Once I saw that, I wanted to find the way out. Organizational learn-ing, I thought, just might be able to teach me something.

Patterns and Systems of Our Own Making

When you first begin to comprehend the power of systems, the feeling can be overwhelming. As you begin to see how interrelated and interconnected all the aspects of a system are, you can begin to feel powerless to make improvements, especially if you perceive the system to be dysfunctional. However, this initial realization can be tempered by a further realization. Gradually, you begin to see how your individual thoughts and actions help to create the systems in which you find yourself. Once you understand and accept that you are also creating the system, your creative energy is freed to create something new and better. You must then learn how to use that freed energy to create what you really aspire to.

Iva: There is a way to escape the system that you talked about, Bert. But before you can escape, you need to understand the system you're in. You need to realize how the structure of the system influences your behavior and how your own decisions contribute to the crises you experience. If our readers come to understand this, then they will be able to relate to organizational learning and perhaps see its value as well.

Bert: We need to share those insights. But even more importantly, we need to share how we came to those insights because people can't get them from reading a book. They're all there in *The Fifth Discipline*, but reading about them will only take people so far. I had to get there by following my own path, making my own discoveries and mistakes, and relating my own experience to the things I was learning. Our readers will want to do that also.

Iva: You're saying that there is something qualitatively different about the way we learned about organizational learning that distinguishes it from how we have learned about other things in our careers. It really has been a journey for me. And it continues to be a journey.

Bert: Yes, for me also. And so perhaps the best way to share what we have learned is to tell others about the journey we have been on, what we have discovered, and the questions that arose along the way.

Iva: First, we need to set the context of our journey.

Bert: And tell the story from the beginning. Because in a way our stories are every manager's story.

The Well-Traveled Road

To understand both the appeal and the logic of organizational learning, we must begin further back, tracing the progression of ideas that led Bert and Iva to believe that organizational learning is the next evolutionary step for organizations.

To accomplish this, we will take a critical look at several approaches that are widely used to improve organizations: restructuring or reorganizing, downsizing, reengineering, and TQM. While these methods often prove valuable, we believe that they are essentially incomplete and therefore inadequate to the task of truly transforming organizations. We will discuss why organizational learning holds more promise.

Iva: As senior line managers in two old, established companies, we have been through the waves of so-called organizational transformation and many of the management programs that some consider fads. We are veterans of TQM programs, reengineering, and downsizing. And before that, we often tried to solve problems by reorganizing or restructuring—usually with very mixed results.

First Stop: Reorganizing

Bert: We've been using reorganizing and restructuring as strategies for solving problems for ages. Of course, there are times when restructuring or reorganizing makes all the sense in the world. Sometimes changing the external structure can drive us to be more efficient or creative—but there are also times when reorganizing is a mistake.

It can be a mistake when restructuring is an automatic response to a problem. It can be a mistake when we don't search for the underlying cause of the problem—which can be systemic—and instead try to change or improve things by rearranging the organizational structure or by putting different people in the same slots. Generally, that doesn't accomplish anything; it just shifts the problem someplace else and creates a mess in the meantime because we disrupt all the relationships that had been developed in the old organization.

Iva: Let me give a specific example. In my manufacturing firm, we had a perennial discussion about whether equipment maintenance should be part of the equipment group or the production group. Now you might think the best people to lead that effort would be the equipment group. But when that was the case, whenever there was downtime and more scrap, the people in the equipment group pointed their fingers at the production people, saying that the problem wasn't the equipment but that the production people didn't know how to use the equipment properly. So then we put equipment maintenance under the production group.

Bert: On the theory that they're the ones who are going to suffer if it's not properly maintained.

Iva: So we moved the boxes around and, lo and behold, when we had a problem the finger pointing went in the other direction. That was when we realized that we had a larger issue. We needed to figure out how to get these people to work together and stop the finger pointing. It doesn't matter whether you are part of maintenance or production or whatever, if you are part of a process, the most important link you have to establish is with your internal customer, the guy down the line whose job is dependent upon your job.

Bert: My experience with reorganizing revolves around the question: What is the core competency that the organization will structure itself around? For example, our original structure went back to the days when we were part of AT&T. We structured ourselves around different technologies. The impact on us employees was that we spent our careers becoming experts in one aspect of the business, climbing the corporate ladder in one "silo" until we reached a certain level. Then we were shifted around to other groups to give us a broader perspective of the business.

Some years later we reorganized based on geography. The impact was that now we had to be technically competent in everything—all forms of engineering, operations, marketing, etc.—in order to be in senior management. I remember my boss saying that any person who gets a top job needs to get a big "S" on his or her shirt because he or she is going to have to be Superman.

The unintended consequence of this structure was that fiefdoms were created. There was very little collaboration between the geographic regions and the focus was all on the internal metrics. Which geographic region was better than the other? As a consequence, the customer was forgotten. This was most evident during natural disasters, when we needed to loan people from one group to another. The different regions were reluctant to do that because it might impact their results.

Sometime later we reduced the seven geographic regions to four, but that didn't change anything. The competition just got more intense.

Iva: I've had a similar experience with reorganization. Philips has been organized in a matrix (product/geography) for a long time. We flip-flopped many times between having more focus on products than geography and vice versa, but neither focus seemed to create the results we expected. That was because of the way we thought about the question. The question was always framed as, Should we focus more on A or B? What was missing was a way of understanding the relationships between geography and products and working with those relationships such that we could improve the results.

Bert: Most recently, partially as the result of a major downsizing, the company decided that customer-facing functions were the most important, so they structured the company into customer-facing units driven by marketing. The advantage of this arrangement was that the customer voice got much louder, but there was still poor cross-functional communication. For example, the marketing department would launch a promotion for a product that the operations department did not have sufficient manpower to support. Also, non-customer-facing employees felt demoralized.

Iva: So we reorganize hoping to get a certain result, but most frequently we don't get the results we intend. Nevertheless, we continue to look for how to arrange the boxes, convinced that *this time* it will work.

Bert: Well, the Beer Game teaches us that structure influences behavior. It's almost as if we sense that people placed in the same structure tend to produce the same results, so we keep trying to produce different results by changing the structure. . . . But I'm not sure that we know how to go about defining the right structure because we generally don't understand the root cause of the problem we're trying to solve.

Iva: Maybe there's no such thing as the "right" or "wrong" structure. Yes, the Beer Game teaches us the power of structure to affect behavior, but we shouldn't take that as affirming that all we managers need do is change the structure until we find the structure that reinforces the behavior we want. A structure that tends to enable one behavior will disable another, yet both may be important to the business. So we need to look beyond the structure and think about how we are connected. As the Beer Game also taught us, how we act and behave *within* the structure is just as important as structure itself.

Bert: I don't think business has learned that yet.

A Fork in the Road: The Total Quality Movement

Iva: No, so we keep searching. The TQM movement presented us with an alternative to restructuring. In fact, to your point, one essential element of TQM work is the search for the root causes of problems. Of course, American businesses rejected TQM in the beginning. We only began to embrace the TQM movement after we saw that the Japanese essentially eliminated the American electronics industry and were threatening the American auto industry. The Japanese auto manufacturers had been successfully experimenting with TQM for some ten years, so now we thought we'd better pay attention.

Bert: First there was the fundamental Quality approach with the basic seven tools of Quality. Then there were the *enhanced* seven tools of Quality. Nobody's against TQM in principle. It's Motherhood and Apple Pie. But some of the ways in which we tried to implement TQM limited its effectiveness. Let me give you an example. We got into TQM rather late—about 1989. We trained thousands of people in TQM using stand-and-deliver training. That was the first turnoff. People resented going to TQM meetings because they perceived it as time taken away from "real work." We didn't involve the union up front so the union saw TQM as a ploy to get rid of workers. The TQM teams took forever to get something done. As a result, there was a lot of disillusionment and very little return on our investment (ROI).

Iva: Again, there are similarities to my experience. We started our TQM efforts in the early 1980s. We had to restart our program several times because we didn't really understand how to do it. We learned you can't copy what other people have done; you have to figure it out for yourselves in your own workplace. Eventually we were able to involve everybody—manufacturing, engineering, finance, marketing—but again our results were not always what we expected. In one sense we were successful because the improvements that we made to our product increased our market share—but then we didn't have the capacity in our factory to meet the demand so we weren't able to achieve a return in our investment in Quality.

Bert: Our TQM efforts were focused on our internal issues rather than on customers and, for me, *TQM has to include customers.* Yet, very often when I heard people refer to "Quality" they were actually referring to production quality using statistical process control. In my view, that's quite a limited view of Quality.

As a result of this limited view, being rated number one in "Quality" did not necessarily mean that you had business success. The fact that it is necessary, but not sufficient, to have Quality was not understood by a lot of people. I believe that ISO 9000 is in the same boat.

Iva: It's worse.

Bert: It's worse because it doesn't involve the customer. ISO 9000 is a "say-do" verification. Basically, with ISO 9000 you go through a process of saying, "This is what I *say* I do. This is what I do. Here's the documentation to prove it. You can come and audit me." It says nothing about whether or not what you're doing is appreciated, valued—

Iva: Or useful.

Bert: Or useful. Or whether there's a market for it, or whether it's customer-focused, or anything. So you could be making buggy whips—things that customers have no use for—and still be ISO 9000 certified.

Iva: ISO 9000 is, I would say, only an entry point into TQM.

Bert: Right. ISO 9000 essentially documents the processes and guarantees that you do what you say. It doesn't say anything about whether or not you're meeting market needs. So, for reasons like that, I was one of the TQM people in my company who felt that Quality didn't do enough. I began to feel that there was something missing from the TQM movement.

Iva: I shared that perception. I, too, was looking for something more. I felt that people were not able to truly engage with the TQM effort. There was something missing.

A New Vehicle: Reengineering as Strategy

Iva: I want to expand on what you said, Bert, about how ISO 9000 did not include the customer by talking about the next important trend, reengineering, because there's a connection. Reengineering promised improved efficiency that would quickly show itself in improved business results.[7] I never really took this path because we understood that reengineering was just a camouflage for cost reduction via elimination of people.

Bert: We got into reengineering via activity-based costing (ABC).[8] We hired a consultant group to translate our processes into ABC, but then they said that we didn't really have our processes identified and that we had about 40 percent rework. So we adopted reengineering as the way to deal with that. The consulting firm convinced upper management that they could reduce some of our costs within the year. In fact, they promised three times the ROI so, of course, we went ahead.

The problem was that everybody understood that we were using reengineering to drive our costs down, but the official position was that we were using it to improve our customer positioning. As a result a lot of people became disenchanted with what they called "the big lie." People viewed it as a program that was driven from on high and they didn't feel that there was much attention being paid to the employees. Projects were stopped in the middle of their tracks and people didn't know what they were going to be doing next. Also, people suspected that it would lead to downsizing. And sure enough, that was the outcome. It led to downsizing big-time.

Iva: We learned some things from the reengineering experience. The reengineering premise—which is now commonly accepted—was that in order to create value for the customer, we need to refine our business processes to ensure that the customer receives what he or she desires. So we believe that a business's processes must be aligned with the external demands of the market, i.e., customer demands. It is equally important that the internal processes of the company be aligned with each other. The field of process management deals with creating such processes, modifying them in accordance with agreed-upon expectations and making them efficient. This is where reengineering enters in, because existing business processes often have to be "reengineered" in order to make them more efficient and effective.

Now here's where there are some parallels between ISO 9000 and reengineering. While ISO 9000 failed to take into account the customer, *reengineering failed to fully appreciate the role of people as human beings in relation to the processes that were to be reengineered.* Often reengineering led only to downsizing, with its positive effects on business results and negative effects on people. Let me be more specific. When processes were found to be inefficient we would reengineer them to make them more efficient. This often led to downsizing because some of the people who worked on those old, inefficient processes were displaced. It was the downsizing that often resulted in quick, short-term improvements to business results, so we in management tended to focus on finding those opportunities to downsize.

Now a problem arose because in order to understand those processes we needed to interview the people who were involved, but many times people were afraid to tell the truth because they knew that they might lose their jobs if their part of the process was redundant. So, often with the best intentions, we in management set up a situation where we would actually punish people for their honesty.

Consequences: Downsizing as Strategy

Bert: Yes, and that's how downsizing started to become the strategy of choice for a lot of companies. In most cases, you couldn't get the cost reductions that reengineering promised without doing workforce reduction because that's where most of your expenses were. Essentially, you couldn't get there from here *without* downsizing.

Let's talk about downsizing as a strategy. Whereas the image left by TQM was that progress takes forever, downsizing got financial results fast. That was very attractive given where we were in the evolution of the "Big Squeeze." It's ironic because other countries were doing better, including Japan, which had embraced TQM, and they were putting squeezes on us.

Iva: Downsizing was the tragedy of our business as well. I have had to do a lot of downsizing in my career because traditional cost reduction programs in manufacturing tend to involve workforce reduction, almost without exception. The thinking is straightforward. When our labor cost as a percentage of total cost was higher then our competitors, we had to act on it. That often meant reducing the number of jobs.

The reason for that is quite simple: If we have fewer people on our payroll, our payroll cost is less. Unfortunately, it is not as simple as it seems. The cost of labor (both fixed and variable) depends not only on what we pay for the labor per se (i.e., your labor cost); it depends even more on how good a job labor does.

This is where our traditional ways of measuring things breakdown. Assessing how good a job labor does requires an entirely different way of accounting for labor. We are beginning to evolve some more sophisticated ways of looking at labor cost. For example, Activity-Based Costing provides a methodology to make those assessments, but that methodology requires that we first understand the business processes and improve upon them, so we can achieve the best efficiency through reengineering.

In the past, however, the only thinking management knew how to do was to give directives to reduce the percentage of labor costs—which essentially meant the percentage of people employed. Then, of course, Hammer and Champy made their contribution: Reengineering told us how to select the jobs to be eliminated.

Bert: Companies that did reengineering became too focused on downsizing. Reengineering was supposed to be about cost reduction. The theory behind reengineering was that we could do many of our processes more cost effectively, but many of us in management equated that with reducing the workforce. As a consequence *reengineering often became a cost reduction strategy that was put in process terms.* Many times we really weren't looking for the best processes. . .

Iva: Right, the focus on process in reengineering provided a kind of camouflage for cost reduction.

Bert: We reinforced that when the success factors we defined for reengineering were all geared to cost cutting. So, if a process was better but cost more, it probably wouldn't have seen the light of day.

Iva: Exactly. And the thing that is so striking is that we were in two different companies in two different industries—telecommunications and electronics—yet the experience was essentially the same. That tells me that our management practices have created a systemic structure that makes certain types of things happen.

How We Create Results We Don't Want

Iva: For example, when we embark on a program like reengineering, our goal is to improve processes. We also have an underlying goal, which is to reduce costs, but when we announce the program to our people we tend to paint it in the best possible light. We tell them it's about customer service. Now, of course, they've already jumped ahead and anticipated the impact, so when it comes to describing processes they're afraid to be completely honest because they know it could mean their jobs.

So now we have all created a situation in which there is a good deal of distrust—and *the results that we create are not the results we want*. Why is it that we in management act in these ways?

Bert: We tell people we need to do these things in order to remain competitive and for the good of the business because we believe it and we see it as our only alternative. We really believe that the competitive realities and customer requirements are such that we need to do this for the enterprise to survive and for most people to preserve their jobs. We also believe that if our costs are reduced customer demands will be enhanced.

The reality is, however, that certain functions *are* targeted and the people who perform those processes are at risk. But we tend to smooth over that information. Why do we do that? It's because we don't want to confront the inevitable questions: Which people will be affected? When? How many? We don't want to confront those questions because we don't know the answers yet. So we don't say anything. But since nobody's talking, imagination takes over and people get very defensive. Yet, as managers, we truly believe what we're saying and we feel that we are acting in the best interest of the whole.

Iva: So, we create a system that compels us to act in certain ways. We contribute to creating outcomes we don't want because we can't admit that we don't know something. We have been trained to create these structures without questioning the value of them.

Bert: This happens because we have a limited ability to envision alternatives. And this is where organizational learning can help—we can learn to seek other alternatives.

Iva: But until businesspeople come to that essential realization, there's not much that will change.

Bert: Perhaps the business community is starting to get a sense of this. Take what happened with reengineering. Many organizations that had gone through reengineering started having problems. Then came the criticisms. The big criticism of the reengineering process was that it left out the needs of people.

Even the purported guru of the reengineering movement, Michael Hammer, seemed to acknowledge this when he came out with a new book, *Beyond Reengineering*.[9] Even he recognized that something was awry.

Iva: If you look back and reflect upon what we have been seeing, you come to the conclusion that the problem is that we in business are always looking for the silver bullet. That's often why we seem to be following fads and implementing "another fine program," only to drop it several months later.

Bert: That's how we get ourselves in trouble.

Iva: Not only do we keep looking for a silver bullet, but when we think we find one we implement it in a way that actually diminishes its likelihood of success. For example, let's look at reengineering again. I've read that 80 percent of all companies that tried reengineering *didn't* make lasting improvements. Now people say that's because reengineering doesn't work.

I have a theory about that. When a company says, "Let's reengineer our practices," or "Let's do team building," they're acting as if they *know* that those strategies or tactics are going to do something positive. But they are not really speaking from knowledge. They're talking from opinion or conviction. In our American culture, strong belief in an idea is often confused with knowledge.

When you look at the actual documented evidence about this question, the results are all over the map. So what we really *know* about business management is actually very equivocal. We advocate many of these management tools and practices because of our conviction about their value, but we don't really know. We don't have a research base that tells us whether some tools are better able to solve problems than some other tools.

Bert: We also don't accumulate knowledge very effectively, so when we find that our silver bullet of the month didn't yield the results we expected, we have a tendency to throw the baby out with the bath water rather than investigate further.

Iva: And then we're on to the next thing. I believe that in each of these cases we failed largely because of the way we went about implementing the programs.

Bert: Oh, absolutely. We forgot about the needs of people.

Iva: Worse, we didn't know how to engage them. Look at process reengineering. The precursor to reengineering was industrial engineering (IE). IE helped us refine processes, but it looked at the people involved in processes as just a set of hands. In fact, when we mapped the process we'd use the icon of a hand to show that a person was involved. IE only looked at discrete processes. Then reengineering came along and helped us look at an entire set of processes across our organizations, but we didn't get much better at taking human beings into account. Reengineering, for example, has to be done collaboratively with the people who are part of the process. If we took an organizational learning approach to reengineering we might learn how to improve processes while also including the needs of people.

Is There a Different Path?

To this point, we have been following a logical trail. The argument for organizational learning largely rests on the idea that, when analyzed rationally, many of the alternative management approaches to change and improvement have been deficient in one way or another.

There is another argument, however, and it is more personal. It lies in the personal experiences of managers who have had to make sense of the human aspect of organizational management.

Bert: So there we were. As we participated in all these waves of management theory we apparently both began to sense that something important was missing. Both of us were experienced managers, very practical, and a little cynical, perhaps . . .

Iva: Maybe you were cynical, Bert, but I was neither cynical nor doubtful. When the doubts came, I always found a way out of them. I always found a way to go over barriers or around them. That's what made me successful in my career. I was seen as tough and decisive. But about the time I became the president of my firm I was beginning to see things a little differently. As I began to assess the situation I saw that a lot of tough decisions were going to have to be made. I didn't know how to avoid them.

For example, the company that I was heading needed a major overhaul. It had been neglected by its previous parent company for a long time and as a result it was woefully behind the times competitively. When we acquired it, the company was riddled with inefficiencies and it lacked both modern technology and people with technical competence. We were a badly outdated American manufacturing company that was suddenly acquired by a European conglomerate and expected to compete effectively in an increasingly global economy.

When I was put into the job as president I was expected to turn the company around. I had always been a high performer, so I *knew* I was going to succeed in accomplishing this. But I could not figure out how to deal with these problems and at the same time preserve the jobs, preserve the people in the jobs. My excuse was that in order to save the most jobs, something's got to give. This is a typical and normal reaction of all executives. We rationalize our actions by saying that we're going to save the majority of employees, but we're going to get rid of some.

I was a new president and I had never done this kind of thing before. I saw the logic of it, but what was difficult for me was that I began to make certain connections in my mind. I began to see connections between downsizing in this plant and how it would affect the community, the larger company, the whole country, and even the entire world.

You know how in chaos theory we say that a butterfly flaps its wings in the Amazon and there's a storm in China? Well, I was making these connections in my mind, but they were not obvious to many people, so I was struggling for a way to make them clear to others.

I could not come up with any other solution. Finally I said, "This is how it has to be. Some people are going to have to go." Once I came to that conclusion, I wanted to make sure that when we did reduce the workforce we were as clear as possible about the criteria for who stays and who goes.

Bert: We had a similar experience. We were under extreme pressure to reduce our costs dramatically. Our labor costs were 70 percent of expenses and our reengineering efforts pointed to downsizing. The president announced that we were entering into a four-year program with the goal of downsizing 10,000 people. We had downsized before but never had there been a corporate objective with a specific number attached.

That experience with downsizing was something I was never able to rationalize to myself—for a variety of reasons. I remember that we felt that the downsizing was not going well. We tried to do it humanely, via the early-out process, but this quickly degenerated as the best people started leaving. We then had to create some work-arounds to keep good people in some key positions. Everyone knew about these "secret" arrangements, so there was a lot of resentment. Productivity declined and the whole culture began to change. For example, line people were seen as valuable because they interacted with customers, whereas staff people were not valued.

More than that, we were sacrificing service at the expense of cost. I stood for the idea that you could do both—but you have to bring service and cost together in a way that makes sense. Yet, we kept reducing costs so much that we were "cutting into the bone." That's the phrase people used to describe what was happening. So we were in the process of downsizing 10,000 people and cutting costs and we were having cash flow problems. We eventually got bought out. Then, the new management hired 2,000 people.

Iva: That is a typical story of a typical enterprise.

Bert: Your ability to build the competence of your organization also suffers whenever there's downsizing. You may actually downsize only 10 percent of the organization, but you absolutely jeopardize the 100 percent because then everybody is fearful. You can't get quantum positive changes when everybody's acting out of fear. Most businesspeople believe that growth is fundamental to business, but downsizing is a recipe for retraction rather than growth.

Iva: Organizations are not machines, they are living things. That's the premise that Arie de Geus[10] is promoting, the idea that a company is a living organism and that we should be interested in actions that are life-giving, that enhance the life of the organization. I can see how you'd say that downsizing is not life-enhancing, but you could also say that downsizing is like pruning the tree—that cutting back now will help the business to grow later.

Bert: Yes, you can make that argument. But that argument only works in the abstract. When you're actually making decisions that affect people's lives you feel differently. I mean, hopefully, you feel differently.

What happened in my company when we were downsizing was really, I think, wrong. I believe that the leadership team ought to show more sensitivity and share the pain. For example, the CEO of Netscape decided to forgo his salary for a year when profits went down. There needs to be more of that in business. I say we forgo our bonuses, we forgo our perqs if we're downsizing.

It's not that we're going to fall on our swords because we have to downsize, because we still have a job to do. But we should make the point of solidarity with this whole process.

Iva: I would agree. I would say that was the guiding light for me. I hated to downsize, but I believed that I had no choice. I had lack of competence. I had swollen budgets. We were losing money. I had to move the company. All of these things are not pleasant to people and their families. But when it was all said and done, I did not hear a lot of criticism about *how* it was done. And then, with time, people realized my intention. I did not have to say we're not going to have layoffs any more. It was expected that I would work toward creating conditions so that we didn't have to lay off people. And we didn't.

Bert: I always thought there's got to be a better way than downsizing. *There's got to be a better way.* And that was the ethic that drove my interest in Quality. I thought there had to be a way to connect our personal values with our business goals.

Then I encountered a new concept: organizational learning.

Endnotes

1. Peter Senge et al., *The Fifth Discipline Field Book* (New York: Doubleday, 1994), pp. 6–7.

2. David Whyte, *The Heart Aroused: Poetry and the Preservation of the Soul in Corporate America* (New York: Currency/Doubleday, 1994), p. 231.

3. For more information on "The Beer Game" see Peter Senge, *The Fifth Discipline: The Art and Practice of the Learning Organization* (New York: Doubleday, 1990), p. 40.

4. Senge, 1990, op. cit., "More on the Beer Game," pp. 27–54.

5. Senge, 1990, op. cit., p. 68.

6. Senge, 1990, op. cit. In Chapter 5 "Shifting the Mind," Senge introduces systems diagrams (or causal loop diagrams). To learn more about practical application see: Anderson, Virginia, and Lauren Johnson, *Systems Thinking Basics* (Cambridge, MA: Pegasus Communications, 1997).

7. For more information on reengineering see Michael Hammer and James Champy, *Reengineering the Corporation—A Manifesto for Business Revolution* (New York: HarperCollins, 1993).

8. For more information on activity-based costing see Gary Cokins, *Activity Based Cost Management, Making It Work: A Manager's Guide to Implementing and Sustaining an Effective ABC System* (New York: McGraw-Hill, 1996).

9. Michael Hammer, *Beyond Reengineering: How the Process-Centered Organization Is Changing Our Work and Lives* (New York: HarperCollins, 1997).

10. Arie de Geus, *The Living Company* (Boston: Harvard Business School Press, 1997).

Chapter 2

The Dilemma

Iva: Through systems thinking I learned to see things differently. For example, our lenses, the mental models through which we view the world, tell us that the cost of labor is simply a function of the size of the labor force. So, if we lay off some workers, we have a resulting cost savings. What could be simpler?

This is what virtually everyone in my company seemed to believe. However, I had a very different picture in my mind. I knew that our labor costs were primarily caused by the problems we inherited when we bought the business, including legacy machines, substandard technology, and poor labor relations. All of these things contributed to high labor costs and none of them were going to change if we merely reduced the number of people we employed. I knew these things intuitively, but I lacked a method for more deeply understanding and expressing these relationships.

A Light in the Tunnel

Iva: Then I learned how to look at the world through the lens of systems dynamics. When I looked at our situation through that lens, I began to get a more profound understanding of the various relationships. For example, I saw that there was a relationship between labor costs and the efficiency of the labor practices mandated by the union. That led to an "Aha!" I saw that if we laid people off we actually ran the risk of *increasing our long-term labor costs.*

Here's what really happens: If I lay off workers, the union's trust of management is affected. This distrust creates an antagonistic relationship between union and management which, in turn, makes it harder for us to reach agreement next time. Without the ability to reach agreements with the union on labor practices, these labor practices can become less and less efficient. Eventually those inefficiencies can outweigh any cost saved by decreasing the size of the labor force. So my action actually exacerbates the problem rather than relieving it. That was a very powerful revelation.

Bert: I had a very powerful realization about systemic thinking also, but it was a little more prosaic. Ever since I was a kid, I've been a fan of *The Three Stooges.* There's a sequence where the stooges are trying to close all the drawers in a bureau. They push in one drawer, and another pops out. They push in two drawers and the third pops out. That scene popped into my head and suddenly I realized that that's a perfect metaphor for systems thinking.

We try to fix something in the system, but we fix it here and it pops out there. We improve the cost structure of one department, but then we find that another department downstream has absorbed the impact of that cost savings. For example, we try to save costs by not using certain forms, but then people do extra manual work in another department because we don't give the forms to them anymore. Then it dawned on me—there's the system! We should all ask ourselves: What do *our* three drawers look like?

I kept that analogy in mind when I tried to explain to others why I thought that TQM was insufficient. I talked about how TQM deals with improving processes whereas systems thinking gives you tools for looking at the whole and all of the interrelationships. Systems thinking can help you examine whether or not the process you're trying to improve should exist in the first place.

Iva: I thought I saw the light with Senge's work. I thought that I could find a different path. There came a time when cost reduction wasn't working, you see. We reduced the cost, but then suddenly we couldn't go any further. We were in a commodity business, and the prices that our customers were willing to pay for our products kept going down. The most we could do was just keep up with that. We began to believe that we could never make more money. In short, we were desperate . . . and maybe that's why we were able to consider a new perspective.

Having traveled down this road for so long with TQM, ISO 9000, and reengineering, I felt I knew what was missing. I began to feel strongly that if you align your business processes with the vision you have for the company and really understand how this alignment works, you will find where the added value is and where it isn't. That was something that reengineering couldn't give me. So I began to think that if I brought organizational learning tools together with reengineering then maybe I could create a new strategy that would improve business results. I called that strategy "process recreation."

Bert: What resonated with me about the organizational learning approach was that learning brought people back into the equation. From all accounts, learning is going to be the competitive advantage of the future. That only makes sense. If you can learn faster than your competitor you will survive and prevail. And because people are the only rational animals, learning must involve people. You put those two thoughts together and you say, "Oh!" You get to the natural conclusion that we ought to move toward organizational learning. That's the path that my thinking followed.

Then I thought, organizational learning can accomplish the same thing as downsizing, but it keeps the people in the equation. Let me explain.

The assumption behind downsizing is that the function under inspection can be done more efficiently. If you apply systems thinking to the same problem, you might come to that same conclusion. But systems thinking can also help you see where you have the potential to expand as well as downsize. With a systems thinking approach we can stream-line a process, and then actually help people move to other places where there is potential for growth. So, while you are downsizing a specific function, you can also grow the enterprise.

If we were able to demonstrate how organizational learning can cir-cumvent the downsizing strategy, it would be considered a very valuable tool—because downsizing is the tool of choice these days. But downsiz-ing has a very debilitating effect on the organization that does it, and that effect is not well understood.

Iva: Downsizing is the result of inappropriate planning for the future, or put another way, downsizing is the result of an inappropriate way of creating the future. Specifically, I mean that we resort to downsizing because we want to rebuild for growth. We want to create something new. We want to take advantage of new ideas and new technology. Organizational learning has the promise of helping us to create a future in which there would be much less need for downsizing.

Bert: That's true. That's true. With systems thinking in particular you take into account more of the various forces that are influencing the sys-tem. The more you understand about the system that effects what you are dealing with, the better you're able to anticipate results and changes. If all of the forces are respected, you have a better chance of selecting the most advantageous leverage points and, thus, making decisions that will have the most positive impact on the organization.

Royal Dutch Shell is a very good example. They engaged in a prac-tice known as scenario planning which enabled them to consider a vari-ety of different possible futures for their company.[1] As a result, they were quite well prepared when the oil crisis occurred. So, the more you are able to look into and understand the system that you are a part of, the more you will be able to move in accordance with the forces at work in the system.

In short, we are suggesting that there is another way to look at how to create the future. It would be too utopian to suggest that we will be able to create the future without ever needing to downsize. But, by using systems thinking to expand your understanding of the context in which you are operating, you may arrive at a different future—a future where you might not need downsizing.

Iva: It's more than that. Through learning we may come to better understand how to manage in difficult times so that we are no longer jumping from solution to solution, looking for the next silver bullet. Instead, we understand what is most likely to work when and why.

Organizational learning increases the possibility of our creating more effective companies. Organizational learning is a way of thinking about how to create the future.

Bert: When you look at it that way you see that each of the management programs from restructuring to quality to reengineering to downsizing was not really a fad, but rather an incremental step on the path. Each step accomplished some things, but left out others—particularly people.

Iva: Let's summarize our thinking. (See Table 2.1.)

Table 2.1
Potential Benefits and Pitfalls of Management Methods

Methodology	Potential Benefits	Potential Pitfalls
Reorganizing, restructuring	Can stimulate creativity Focuses on core competency(ies) Enhances control and communication in some areas	Can be a "quick fix" that does not address the real problem Destroys existing communication paths Can make it harder to get commitment next time
Quality	Finds root cause of problems Reduces cost of processes Free (over time)	Takes a long time Does not identify unnecessary processes Does not reveal systemic structure Does not explore all relevant interrelatedness
Reengineering	Streamlines processes Cost savings Fast ROI	Does not engage people in the organization or take into account the effect on people May not lead to lasting improvements Generally leads to downsizing

Downsizing	Reduces labor cost	Unintended consequences to organization (demoralization, paralysis, etc.)
Organizational Learning	Can involve people in the organization in creating the results they truly want	Delays in obtaining results
	Results can be sustainable	Difficulty in measuring effectiveness
	Can facilitate restructuring, reengineering, and Quality—perhaps avoid downsizing	Requires multiple change agents (executives, networkers, line management)

Bert: If you look at it this way, organizational learning is the next logical step. Organizational learning can help shift our sensibilities and provide tools and methods, such as the five disciplines identified by Senge, that can help us bring people back into the equation—not just in a humanistic way but in a very practical and effective way.

Iva: If we take an organizational learning approach I believe we can avoid the mistakes and the unintended consequences that we both experienced when we tried to implement the other programs.

Bert: The reason that we were drawn to organizational learning is that we both subscribe to the same value proposition—that people make a difference. And in a business context, people are our only sustainable advantage. Our career paths may have taken some different turns, but the unifying thing is that we both fundamentally believe in the capability of people in the business environment.

Iva: Organizational learning spoke to that essential belief.

Three Additional Arguments

Iva: There are a number of additional very solid arguments for why organizational learning is the next logical evolutionary step for businesses to take. Let's develop that value proposition.

Argument #1: The World Is Changing

Bert: We are beginning to realize that the ability to learn and act quickly in the right direction is an important advantage, especially if you can do it better than your competition. The ability to meet changing circumstances and conditions that happen around the world is a function of being able to learn quickly and to act based on that new learning. If you act irresponsibly or unintelligently, you pay the supreme price. You lose your company or you lose your job.

Furthermore, Arie de Geus has argued, rather eloquently, that learning may be the critical economic factor in the future.[2] He bases his argument on a historical analysis of economics. Economics is based on three factors: land, capital, and labor. Land was the dominant factor centuries ago as we saw in the establishment of empires and feudal systems. Then, with the Industrial Revolution, came the dominance of capital.

Now we are seeing the rise of labor in the form of the knowledge worker. If we view labor as the knowledge worker, and the creation of greater knowledge as the way of the future, then the winners will be those who master the application of competitive knowledge and apply it quickly and skillfully. In other words, learning faster and applying that learning faster is the key to competitive advantage. It follows that the competitive advantage for the foreseeable future is going to be obtained through people. That view can't be given simply lip service anymore, for the reason I just stated. We have to realize that people have options and choices, and that changes in their value systems can make a company fantastically successful—or sink it.

There is a further implication to this argument: that the future success of business demands a greater integration of individual goals and business goals. At present these sets of goals are actually interdependent, but they exist in a kind of tension with one another. That tension is relatively stable, at least in most situations most of the time. But as we continue to globalize, two things will happen. Globalization will intensify the interdependency of those goals, and the rapid change that accompanies globalization will exacerbate any apparent dissonance between individual and business goals.

Consider the increasing evidence that the work ethic is changing. It used to be that your job and your company were your life. That's disappearing. Gary Heil, a management consultant, says that people are refusing to work overtime, refusing to move, and refusing to do the things we used to think companies had the right to demand. Now the integration of personal goals, free time, and family things with work is a priority. Many people are no longer willing to accept the company doctrine of "we need you to be here and to do what we say."

Today, many workers—certainly not all, but many—have more options. Many seem to have a relatively high disposable income. They're willing to job-hop like crazy. Downsizing has done a lot to erode loyalty to impersonal corporations. There's a whole demographic change. And there's a lot of entrepreneurship, which means that people are willing to take more risks because they recognize that if they have a better idea or if they can do something faster, they can go in a garage and create a company.

This tension between personal and organizational goals will have to be resolved because the system can only hold so much tension for so long. The question is will we be able to resolve it in the direction of greater harmony, synthesizing into something powerful and mutually rewarding, or will we create some sort of catastrophic separation?

Iva: We live in a democracy, but that applies *only* to our form of government. Businesses are neither democratic in their structure, nor democratic in their behavior. Our economic system is capitalism with a free market economy. Business behavior is governed by competition, not collaboration; we think in a win/lose context, though we advocate win/win. Win/win is easy when there is enough to go around for everybody to get what he or she wants, but that happens very infrequently. Our mental models tell us that our resources are limited, and we in business are driven by the demands of capital and other markets. This is why it will take much more work to change what you are describing, Bert.

Let me give you an example. Because we live in capitalism and because we have Wall Street determining the value of our work, we cannot ignore the processes that exist on Wall Street which assess what is good and what is bad. In my judgement those processes and tools need updating. For example, we talk about people as being assets, but we treat them on the balance sheet as if they are liabilities. To make the assets capable of continuing to produce value, we need to make investments in those assets. If people are considered assets, why is training not considered an investment, but a cost?

Wall Street uses primarily financial measurements to assess the value of the business, while businesses are already expanding those measures by adding other nonfinancial measures. Many of them came about through the TQM efforts. The next thing that needs to happen is the development of tools and measurements that would more effectively assess the contribution that people make in value creation beyond that which is measurable today.

I suggest that we devote focused time to reflecting on this subject. But before we do that, there are a lot of other things we need to clarify. I am suggesting at this point only that practicing, researching, and increasing the capacities of organizations to learn will create the answers we are searching for today.

Many of these things are in the process of changing, and the question is not *will* it happen, but *when* will it happen. So the questions for me—and perhaps for all of us—are: How much risk do I want to take? Do I want to be a pioneer who gets the first mover advantage, or a settler waiting for others to take the first hit?

Bert: What you just said, Iva, provides a compelling reason, a burning platform, for organizational learning.

Argument # 2: Igniting the Resource Within

Iva: Gary Hamel authored the lead article in an issue of the *Sloan Management Review.*[3] The topic was strategy. The theory Hamel puts forth is that business strategy is best developed by integrating the technology of the business with the capability of all the people within the company. You won't create an effective strategy by bringing in some consultant company from the outside to develop it, he says. Your own people should be engaged in developing it. I see this as another signal of something that is happening. Here is where learning and tacit knowledge become a core competency—a competency that will be difficult to beat because it's embedded in the organization.

Bert: That's an important point that you made. It's going to require someone on the *inside* to develop the potential that is already there. It isn't going to happen by hiring a bunch of consultants.

Iva: Because the resources you need are already in your organization. You just have to figure out how you are going to get those resources to surface. You have to find a way to engage your people so that they are willing and happy to participate—and that can only happen when they are committed to a vision that they care about. Because it's all connected.

That's where the tools and methods of organizational learning become a vehicle to make that happen. Organizational learning can help you develop a shared vision and can help you to surface the potential that's already within your organization.

Argument # 3: The Value of Simulations as Infrastructure for Collective Learning

Bert: Organizational learning says that business organizations ought to be able to learn just as children learn. After all, businesses are collections of people. But first we've got to put the infrastructure in place to help us do that collective learning. Simulations could provide some of that infrastructure. I'm very optimistic about the potential of computer-generated simulations in the business world, because you can play with variables in a safe environment and learn the consequences of your actions without running the risk of losing your job or your company. The way we're doing things now in the business world is too costly. That's why it's so important that we take these tools seriously.

Iva: We know that Boeing can test an airplane today without ever flying it, because everything is tested on the computer. They can simulate the plane taking off, flying, and landing without ever actually leaving the ground. With a simulation, you can practice without pressure because if the results are negative, they're only on paper.

Bert: You wouldn't think of building an airplane without simulating the performance of your simulator design. You wouldn't think of putting a pilot into an airplane without running him through a flight simulator. Yet we don't use simulations to help us make better business decisions. That robs us of a chance to learn about the dynamic relationships that affect our business and it robs us of the chance to test out the thinking behind our strategies. So we have a hard time learning because by the time we find out that we made mistakes in a major strategy decision, it's too late.

The disciplined thinking that goes into designing a simulation is an excellent way to learn about your business. It forces you to define a set of parameters—or assumptions—and then you must define what the inputs are and what the outputs should be. If you haven't got all of that defined, then you don't know what to do when the output is different from what you expected. And, therefore, you don't learn because you can't correlate your input with the output you saw. You can't see that a certain delta in input yields that delta in output.

We ought to be building more simulations based on systems thinking principles. We ought to be incorporating that learning into the way we run the business.

In the arguments that Bert and Iva have put forth, organizational learning can be seen as the next logical, evolutionary step in management practice. Theoretically, organizational learning tools and disciplines can greatly facilitate current management practices, such as restructuring, reengineering, and TQM by enabling people to understand the systemic nature of their business and providing tools and methods for working more effectively with those relationships. In so doing we may be able to improve profitability without harming people. Moreover, organizational learning can support organizational goals by involving people in the organization in creating the results they truly want—results that are sustainable.

Organizational learning holds great promise for greater competitive effectiveness through improved learning on a collective scale and for a more honest, life-affirming, energizing workplace. Yet, organizational learning concepts and practices have not been widely embraced. There appear to be significant barriers to its proliferation.

Reaping the Promise

Iva: So why are we in business not doing more with organizational learning? Why are we not taking advantage of all the work that's been done in simulations? Why are we not taking advantage of all the work that's been done in organizational learning in general?

Bert: Well, now comes the more difficult task. Now we have to take a hard look at our current reality.

Iva: Ah, but we have come upon another of the tenets of organizational learning—that it is not enough to have a vision of the future, no matter how wonderful that vision might be. We must also do an unblinking assessment of current reality. Our minds tell us that will automatically kill the vision, but what it will actually do is set free the creative energy so that we can create the future.

Bert: That's the theory, anyway.

Iva: What better way to test the theory?

Current Reality

Bert: Despite the commitment of a few companies, if we look closely we arrive at the conclusion that this transition from traditional organizations to learning organizations is not yet working. The body of knowledge around organizational learning—which is deemed to be valuable and important—is not translating into mass adoption.

We have to understand the reasons why so that we can be as successful with organizational learning as we were with the quality movement—but also so we can avoid the pitfalls that we encountered with quality. We don't want to have to lose an entire industry to another country before we figure out that learning is important.

Compatibility Between OL and Current Business Thinking

Bert: One possible barrier is that the approach, sensibilities, and methods associated with organizational learning—for example, systems thinking, shared vision, mental models, personal mastery, or dialogue—can seem somewhat exotic or inaccessible. They don't always fit easily within the context of most business environments. Is it possible to demystify these ideas so that they are more easily accessible to everyone in the business environment?

The Change Agent's Challenge

Iva: Another dilemma, ironically, is the sheer appeal of these ideas. Businesspeople who are stirred by the elegance of the arguments for organizational learning may become swept up in the exuberance of possibility. As the work and the learning engage them more fully—and, as we both know, the learning is compelling—people involved in organizational learning may find themselves separating from others in their organizations. They may feel that they have answers and knowledge that others do not have. They may become converts or advocates. In time they may eventually find themselves in difficult, if not untenable, situations. They may find themselves pushing their newfound idealism on a resistant organization.

Bert: They also might find themselves feeling very uncomfortable, caught between the world of vision and the practical world of current reality. In their excitement, leaders may be pushing for change. Then they meet up with some unanticipated obstacle and what do they do? They have to keep their new aspirations under wraps. Most aspiring leaders of change will not be prepared for these new experiences and emotions.

Iva: Also, the nature of resistance to organizational learning is not yet sufficiently understood by businesspeople. Why is the organization resisting? If we detect resistance, what can we do about it? Can we develop a productive relationship with resistance? What insights—or possibly answers—lie in a greater understanding of the nature of the resistance?

Unlearning

Iva: Organizational learning is a very complex idea and we don't know enough about how to implement it yet. For example, new learning often requires that we "unlearn" old ways of thinking and being. But unlearning is profoundly difficult, perhaps more difficult than learning itself. How well do we understand the nature of unlearning and what it takes to unfreeze our most damaging beliefs and actions?

Delays

Bert: The time frame for organizational learning is another barrier. The business world has grown accustomed to seeking immediate gratification. In this way, OL is similar to TQM. Despite the many wonderful attributes of the TQM approach, it was not widely accepted in the beginning. The criticism aimed at TQM was that it took too long. Oh, sure, we said, TQM works in Japan, but the Japanese have the patience of Job and therefore they can spend ten years doing it. But Americans? No! We want results yesterday. TQM work takes a long time to produce results, so it didn't seem compelling for a lot of businesspeople. TQM is *still* not widely accepted, whereas reengineering efforts appeared to provide just that sort of gratification, at least initially.

Organizational learning work has an inherent incubation period. It is different in kind from a reengineering project, and the result can be a quantum increase in the sustainability of the organization.

The Value Proposition

Iva: Your references to TQM and reengineering spur me to ask this question: Why do some management theories create a bandwagon effect where we all climb on, while others do not? What makes the difference? Why, for example, did Hammer's theory of reengineering create such a movement toward reengineering in corporations, but organizational learning has not been as widely adopted? In the end, the results of reengineering are not that fantastic.

Bert: Well, I have a theory. Let me try it out on you. There's no question that the idea of organizational learning strikes a responsive chord in many people. It has great "grab appeal." In fact, the idea is even rather seductive. In some ways, it's like the utopian ideals that have been beguiling people for centuries. Who could argue with the idea of a saner, more effective, perhaps more fulfilling workplace? It's only later—when you get into the practicality of implementation—that you see the problems with actually making it work in the real world.

Yet, organizational learning has enough substance behind it that a series of companies have invested in it over a period of years. Those companies have been able to make that investment, despite the lack of quantifiable business results that can be directly attributed to organizational learning. That's almost the Japanese way of doing things. The way we've been approaching organizational learning says that its success doesn't depend upon the next quarter's financial statement. Rather, we're investing in organizational learning because of its long-term potential.

But there's a problem because very few companies—particularly in the U.S.—are going to invest in something like organizational learning because of long-term potential. We're talking about learning, we're talking about knowledge, even training. All of these are considered to be costs. *Currently, there is no value proposition about knowledge that is broadly accepted in business.* And until you have that, it's going to be like the Deming story.[4]

The Deming story is a great example of our unwillingness to learn for knowledge's sake, of our inability to see the intrinsic value of an idea. The TQM movement was first offered in the United States in the 1950s. We turned it down because it did not pass the "CFO test." By that I mean that we couldn't immediately relate Deming's TQM to bottom-line results.

Americans couldn't learn from Deming, but the Japanese could, and over time they honed TQM to the point where it became a powerful methodology. The Japanese changed the global definition of "made in Japan" from cheap and unreliable to cost-effective with high standards of excellence and conformity to requirements. Deming's TQM approach had a lot to do with that.

Iva: But the parallel between TQM and organizational learning isn't exact. Deming's work in TQM received very little attention in the U.S. in the 1950s. I mean, *nobody* listened to Deming. But Senge and others who are writing about organizational learning have gotten their work publicized—which is a hopeful sign. Yet, it's still moving slowly. This troubles me because there is an opportunity to really gain competitive advantage by taking organizational learning seriously.

Organizational learning could help us to both tap individual creative potential and find ways out of the repetitive patterns that limit us. But we're still not taking the organizational learning tools and methods and applying them to make that happen. That's the big question we need to ask ourselves: Why are we not applying organizational learning and what can we do about it?

If you look at the research, you see that companies that made a serious commitment to TQM are more profitable and have higher share
prices than their competitors. But that same research shows, as you say,
that TQM has not been widely adopted. Fewer than 100 companies in the
Fortune 1000 have well-developed TQM infrastructure. In fact, the
majority of U.S. managers think that TQM is "deader than a pet rock."[5]
So what does that say?

Bert: It says several things. One of the things it says is that even if
we can prove that something is good for us, *we won't engage with it if
it's incompatible with our culture*. TQM just doesn't fit with the culture
of most American businesses, which want a fast return on investment.
Engaging an organization in TQM and getting results takes time, which
may not be in line with the speed expected for returns on investment.
Therefore, the majority has rejected it. Similarly, top management has
not accepted the value of organizational learning as eagerly as it has
other management trends.

Iva: I wonder about a culture that rejects things that are good for it.
That seems nonsensical, illogical, and maybe even suicidal.

Bert: No, it is very logical. The business environment is demanding
more rigor and more hard evidence in support of investments in both
time and money. These factors work against the adoption of organizational learning. The inherent value of learning seems obvious. Yet, without an established, immediate, and obvious financial payback—or a clear
value proposition spelled out in practical business language—organizational learning can be dismissed or undervalued. Mike Hammer promised
that reengineering would yield real, near-term financial results. Some
companies agreed and so did Wall Street.

Iva: In contrast, organizational learning . . .

Bert: . . . doesn't do that. The closest thing I ever saw to something
that began to put organizational learning in the same category with
reengineering was an article about Peter Senge in one of the business
magazines. The title was something like, "You could learn something
from this man."

Iva: In the article I spoke about earlier Gary Hamel says, "I have long
admired Peter Senge's approach to action research with the MIT
Organizational Learning Center."[6] The fact that Hamel is a strategist, not
an OL expert, says a lot to me.

Bert: But you see the difference. I think we can find other examples where a new management idea has caught the interest of the
business world and caught the interest of Wall Street—and yet organizational learning has not. You could compare and contrast them and I
believe you'll find that the fundamental difference is that Michael
Hammer and other experts who are accredited by Wall Street talk in
financial terms.

Iva: Even when Hammer doesn't talk about financials *per se*, when he talks about concepts like value creation in management, Wall Street can relate to what he is saying. Wall Street understands what value creation is. If you talk in organizational learning terms, if you talk about such things as "building shared vision," you don't get the same response from Wall Street.

Bert: And that's the dilemma. The business benefit—expressed in clear business terms—has been left out of our discussion of organizational learning.

A lot has been written about organizational learning from a theoretical point of view, but until it gets expressed in terms that are acceptable to the financial community—which is to say, financial terms—it's very difficult to get a critical mass of enthusiasm behind it.

Iva: Exactly. We believe that there is a significant potential for business to benefit from organizational learning. Organizational learning clearly speaks to deep human needs for transformation of the workplace. We can imagine a workplace as a space where greater humanity, honesty, and personal fulfillment can be embraced. But, as you've said, since we cannot yet guarantee the benefit in financial terms, nobody listens.

Who Will Stand on the Burning Platform?

Bert: I suggest that a related aspect of the problem is that the "change masters" of organizational learning are naïve for the most part. Mostly, they're academicians who believe that this theory will, on its own, show value and merit and gain attention and investment.

But businesspeople look at organizational learning and, although they may like what they see, they know that an investment in organizational learning will not pass any rigorous marginal efficiency of investment criteria at present. In other words, it won't pass the CFO test. So we have a dilemma.

A strategy calling for an investment with no clear return can be promulgated only by people who are strong advocates, but that's not a winning strategy in the long run. If that remains the main way of disseminating organizational learning, then it is ultimately limited—and that is a terrible loss to the business community.

We need to create a greater awareness of this conundrum. The organizational learning community is now comprised of three subcommunities: academics, consultants, and businesspeople. We need to engage the academic and consulting communities as well as the business community in addressing this question. And what is the question, exactly? The question is, how do you build a bridge from current reality to a new reality?

We can't just declare that all business measures are antiquated. We can't just ignore business's requirement for a return-on-investment—because that ignores current reality. And one of the most fundamental aspects of creating shared vision in organizational learning is an acknowledgement of current reality, no matter how unpleasant we might think it is.

The Problem of Measurement

Iva: It is unclear how this vision can be realistically attained since the business world requires pragmatic, financial considerations to take precedent. How is it possible to bring these two goals into alignment?

Bert: The assessment and measurement of the effectiveness of organizational learning is a problem. While the business world craves predictability, a learning orientation is, by definition, concerned with creating something new. Therefore, success occurs in unexpected ways. The results of organizational learning efforts, while they can be significant, are often qualitative—they don't necessarily lend themselves to traditional numerical measures. Because of these differing sets of expectations, early organizational learning experiments seem to have had mixed outcomes.

So, while there has been some clear progress, the results have also been viewed as contradictory and controversial. The diffusion or transfer of learning and the sustainability of learning efforts also remains elusive and problematical.

Iva: We have focused on the need for empirical proof that organizational learning works, but perhaps all that is necessary is a good logical argument that links organizational learning with high performance. If you look at the history of TQM, it was the *logic* embedded in what Deming said, not necessarily the results that TQM produced, that engaged the early adopters of TQM.

In simplistic terms, we can say that businesspeople respond to things either because of need or because of greed. I don't mean "greed" in the Biblical sense, but rather the desire to make more dollars. By "need," on the other hand, I mean the sense that if I don't do this, then I'm going to lose the customer.

Bert: In other words, the motivation is either crisis or growth. We may wish there were other motivators, but that's the reality.

Iva: Now, if we look at TQM, Just-in-Time (JIT), et cetera, all these ideas were obviously supporting greed, i.e., making more money. The idea is that if you're faster than others, you're going to make more money. You know that if your quality is not as good as somebody else's the customer will leave you sooner or later.

If all the above is so, then does organizational learning help to satisfy need or greed? We don't really have an answer for that. So the essential question is, does organizational learning facilitate high performance, or is organizational learning to be pursued as an end in and of itself? If it's the latter, then do we take it on faith that performance will also be improved? Because, in the end, if it doesn't create wealth, it has no value to businesspeople.

Bert: Right. It has added value to the businessperson if it drives growth.

Iva: I would say it adds value if it creates *wealth*. I like that concept better than growth, Bert. Growth means nothing. You can grow and lose your shirt on the way. Creating wealth is a better concept. And by "wealth," we're not talking about just creating personal wealth.

Bert: No, we're talking about improving the value of the enterprise.

Iva: For *all* the stakeholders: the employees, the shareholders, and the customers. Everybody.

Organizational learning is like a new technology or a new product introduction. The risk is always much higher when you don't know exactly what the outcome is going to be. I submit that you have to take a lot on faith in the beginning. There's nothing wrong with that, necessarily. We take risks with technology every day. Look at all of the ventures that have sprung up because of the Internet, for example. In a sense, organizational learning could be viewed as just another new technology.

Bert: Let me make the pragmatist's argument: A degree of calculated risk is taken every day in normal business life. Both a new product launch and the introduction of a new technology require a certain degree of calculated risk. But organizational learning does not fit this formula. The unfortunate thing is that it is complex and not very predictable and—

Iva: There is no clear feedback loop.

Bert: With new technology, you generally have a way to get feedback. Your feedback tells you whether the new technology fundamentally works or doesn't. You know if it works partially, or if it works with certain criteria in certain areas. For example, in medicine you know whether a drug cures or doesn't cure, or if it cures with tremendous side effects. You look at the measures—

Iva: Bert, you're right in one sense, but there is a more fundamental issue and that is that *organizational learning may not lend itself at all to traditional measures.* Furthermore, the problem may not be with organizational learning *per se*. Rather, the problem may be that we are not measuring the right things in the right way.

We may need to change some of the ways in which we assign and assess value in business. Just think about the kinds of metrics we accept almost without thinking. For example, we talk about people as assets, yet we treat them as costs and liabilities on our balance sheets. What a contradiction.

Until we change how we measure, how we structure the balance sheet and the income statement, it may not be possible to use our traditional measures to assess to what degree an organization is learning.

Dancing with Paradox

Bert: Then it seems that organizational learning work is about two things that are in some ways contradictory to one another. In one sense we are trying use organizational learning to accomplish business results that are meaningful in the way we measure things now.

Iva: And the other is that organizational learning necessitates that we change what we measure and how we measure it.

Bert: It's about immediate gratification. It's that "ya gotta have return-on-investment," "Wall Street's gotta be satisfied," "I gotta have seven percent growth per year, every year, or I'm not viable."

Iva: And it's not at all clear to me that growth is always good.

Bert: Agreed. Agreed. But I would say that in America in general, bigger is better and more is better. And faster is better.

Iva: Yes, that's the motto under which our whole society is built. Everything we do, think, feel—

Bert: So that presents a challenge to us and to organizational learning. Either we're going to demonstrate that it's in sync with our present business goals, that it will enable us to get bigger and better with more on the bottom line, or—

Iva: Let me give you the reverse of that. What if it would be possible to create results that are even more in line with our deeper aspirations, rather than following the model of "better, faster, and larger?" What if organizational learning tools and methods can actually enable us to create those results?

If you look at what is happening in businesses today, you see that a lot of people are suffering from overwork, overstress, and overworry because they're trying to create bigger, better, etc. They're retiring early if they can or they're trying to create something different. Some are starting to get engaged with organizational learning work because they're realizing that the old way of working isn't worth it any more.

What if the deeper question is: Is there something about organizational learning that suggests that we have to "throw away" something that has been very useful to us? Is that the primary reason why we can't embrace it?

Bert: You're suggesting that organizational learning is going to change everything. My pragmatic nature says that's too radical, too revolutionary. I say that you have to work with the business culture that currently exists, whereas you're saying that we work on changing very basic assumptions—and maybe the culture of business itself.

I'm a bit scared of the latter because it's counter to a basic premise that I have, which is that you've got to work with a culture in order to change it. If you start by attacking the very tenets of the culture, then the culture tends to reject you.

Iva: Perhaps this is not a question that we can answer right now. Perhaps it is not a case of either-or. There is something else that I have learned from doing organizational learning work that may apply here. When you face a question like this, where the only apparent answers are unsatisfactory, there is probably another alternative. I have learned that it may show up if we just stay with the question.

The Crossroads

Savvy businesspeople have grown tired and suspicious of management fads. Is organizational learning just another fad? We do not believe so. However, the current situation presents a challenge to organizational learning because there is real danger that it may be dismissed as a fad unless some of the serious barriers to further proliferation are addressed. There is much work to be done before organizational learning concepts and practices can be widely embraced. Before that happens we must learn to live in a state of tension even as we work to continuously transform it.

Living in Creative Tension

In *The Fifth Discipline*, Senge uses the analogy of the stretched rubber band to explain the tension that exists between vision and current reality. When human beings experience this kind of tension we want to resolve it. There seem to be two ways: either we reduce the vision (allow the rubber band to spring back), or we work to change current reality in order to bring it closer to the vision. The latter is harder to do, of course, because we must hold the tension longer, but it illustrates how tension can be resolved by taking a *creative* approach rather than merely a reactive approach.

Ironically, the dilemma of organizational learning mirrors this tension. We are drawn to the promise that organizational learning holds, but we cannot yet prove its worth within the context of our traditional financially based measures. Thus, we are pulled back into the safety of our old system of thinking and behaving. Conversely, we sense that our old system, though safe, is inadequate to the needs, possibilities, and aspirations of the present and future. We want to stretch our old system such that it can validate new forms of measurement, but we find ourselves oscillating unsatisfactorily, caught between inspiring vision and practical reality, inconsistent in our thoughts and actions.

Robert Fritz writes that when you hold resolution in abeyance you can tap into the energy that is available during the three stages of the creative cycle: germination, assimilation, and completion. In the germination stage, you make choices about the results you want to create. In the assimilation stage, you allow for long periods during which it appears that nothing of significance is happening, knowing that momentum is building. Finally, you develop the capacity to successfully create your vision.[7]

People who have learned to be more creative rather than reactive are better able than most to tolerate the discrepancy between what they want and what they have. They know how to turn the tension of the discrepancy into a creative force. It becomes the engine of the creative process. They are able to tolerate a realistic assessment of the state of current reality and the distance between that and their vision without immediately attempting to resolve the tension.

This tension between vision and current reality is *not* resolvable within itself. It can only be resolved if we are able to hold the tension as we seek to replace the source of the tension with something else. The "something else" usually arises out of a shift in our belief system. The challenge is to hold that tension and see it as a source of creativity, rather than react to it immediately and try to force it away.

Will businesspeople be willing to meet this challenge? Will they respond to the challenge of remaking their world, taking on the many questions and dilemmas we have raised—particularly the question of measurements? Will they have the courage to embrace learning as a way of life despite the current barriers and risks? Will they be able to hold the tension?

In Part 2 we tell the stories of two people, Bert and Iva, who had the courage to step off the edge of their world and try.

Endnotes

1. Arie de Geus, "Planning as Learning," *Harvard Business Review*, March/April 1988, pp. 70–74.

2. Arie de Geus, *No Globalization without Learning*, speech given at Systems Thinking in Action Conference, 1999, audio tape available from Pegasus Communications, Waltham, MA.

3. Gary Hamel, "Strategy Innovation and the Quest for Value," *Sloan Management Review*, Winter 1998, pp. 7–14.

4. See Mary Walton, *The Deming Management Method* (New York: Dodd, Mead, & Company, 1986).

5. J. A. Byrne, "Management Theory—Or Fad of the Month," *BusinessWeek*, June 23, 1997, p. 47.

6. Hamel, 1998, op. cit., p. 13.

7. Robert Fritz, *Path of Least Resistance* (New York: Fawcett Columbia, 1994).

Part 2
The Journey

Warts and All

In the first section we presented our arguments for organizational learning (OL) and the promise it holds. We also discussed some of the challenges and dilemmas yet to be resolved. In the following section we explore some of the practical realities involved in implementing organizational learning in today's business world. We do so by sharing the very personal stories of our attempts to lead learning efforts—warts and all—and by interpreting those stories within a framework of theory. By so doing we hope to turn individual experiences into opportunities for learning.

Chris Argyris has written, "Anyone who has planned major change knows:

- How difficult it is to foresee accurately all the major problems involved;

- The enormous amount of time needed to iron out the kinks and get people to accept the change;

- The apparent lack of internal commitment on the part of many to help make the plan work, manifested partly by people at all levels resisting taking the initiative to make modifications that they see are necessary so the plan can work."[1]

These obstacles very much exist in the practical world of business organizations. As businesspeople committed to OL, our challenge is to develop the practical wisdom that will enable us to anticipate and work through these obstacles as they arise. Early adopters of OL must learn how to lead learning efforts effectively. While there is theory to draw upon, theoretical and conceptual thinking can only take us so far. We do not believe that it is an easy task to translate theory into practice within the dynamic context of real, live organizations. The real learning is in the doing. Out of that come practical knowledge, practical philosophy, and even practical wisdom. This is the key to lasting change. We think that the development of this practical wisdom requires the following on the part of businesspeople:

- **Faith**—Pragmatists and visionaries alike must start with belief in the premises of OL. This requires a moderate amount of faith.

- **Clear understanding of the theory**—Despite our practical orientations, businesspeople who engage with OL are, in a sense, engaging in research and experimentation. Despite Kurt Lewin's famous admonition that "there is nothing so practical as a good theory,"[2] we know that practical businesspeople tend to resist theory. Still, we must have a working understanding of the theory we are attempting to implement.

- **Active interpretation of the theory**—As businesspeople our task is to bring the theory to life; we have to try the theory out.[3]

- **Sharing of our stories and reflection upon our experience**—We cannot create practical knowledge without sharing our stories, which requires showing our vulnerability. But if more of us share our stories, that practical knowledge can be further refined and developed. Through sharing and then analyzing these stories with an eye toward learning from them, we can create a feedback loop. If we do this in community we can begin to close the gap between theory and practice. Together we reflect upon results and we inquire into each other's assumptions—each other's working theories. We invite feedback from outside our own experience. If we do so collectively, we can develop our practical wisdom.

These steps can be illustrated as a cycle, with faith as the entry point. As we move around this circle we participate in the stages that theorists such as David Kolb have described as the experiential learning cycle.[4] This cycle gives us a full view of the process of learning; it links ideas to experience, and action to reflection. In this cycle, abstract conceptualization (theory) leads to active experimentation, which leads to specific, concrete experience. Ideally, we reflect upon that experience, reframe if need be, and then go around the cycle again testing our new ideas.

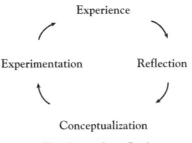

Experience

Experimentation   Reflection

Conceptualization

The Learning Cycle

An understanding of this process of learning is essential to bringing about OL in our corporations. It is also essential that we use that understanding of the process of learning to design our learning efforts and to make sure that we are able to learn from our experiences and share those learnings with others.

Bert and Iva's willingness to share their stories speaks to their commitment to this learning process. The stories illustrate how businesspeople can participate in the learning cycle. As they share their stories, we hope that the stories will stimulate your thinking and your sense of inquiry. Some aspects of our stories may resonate with your own experience, or suggest things to consider as you walk your own path. As you read, we hope that you will find yourself participating in what we believe are intimate experiences of the nature of learning itself. On our separate journeys, and in the time since, we have come to understand how the experience of true learning shifts expectations—particularly those expectations that have been shaped by the current business environment. We have learned that when one allows oneself to live in learning, one's basic assumptions are up for grabs.

And, as you learn about our experiences and our reflections upon those experiences in our own words, you are invited to consider what we might learn from these stories. We invite you to think about how you might design your own strategy, drawing on these learnings.

Endnotes

1. Chris Argyris, *On Organizational Learning* (Malden, MA: Blackwell Publishing, 1999), p. 123.

2. For more on Kurt Lewin's work please see Edgar H. Schein, "Kurt Lewin's Change Theory in the Field and in the Classroom: Notes Toward a Model of Managed Learning," *Reflections: The SoL Journal on Knowledge, Learning and Change,* 1999, Vol. 1, No. 1, pp. 59–74.

3. We are greatly indebted to Professor C. K. Pralahad for helping us to make these connections.

4. David A. Kolb, *Experiential Learning* (Englewood Cliffs, NJ: Prentice-Hall, 1984).

Chapter 3

The Compass

As we reflected on the two stories and what we were learning as we continued to review and consider, we realized that we needed a frame of reference—a framework— to help us interpret what happened. We needed a framework that could provide a container for all that we were thinking and learning. While both Bert's and Iva's change strategies had revolved around Senge's *The Fifth Discipline*, we found that we needed a broader framework. We needed to sweep in Senge et al.'s later work in *The Dance of Change* (1999) as well as the work of Chris Argyris, organizational culture theorist Edgar H. Schein, and others who have laid down some of the foundational ideas that make up the field of organizational learning. If we looked at the stories in this context we hoped to be able to find greater meaning.

In the Introduction to this book we offered a definition of organizational learning as "the process of forming and applying collective knowledge to problems and needs. It is learning that helps the organization continually improve, achieve goals, and attain new possibilities and capacities. It is learning that taps into employee aspirations, fueling commitment and creating the energy to change."[1] Now we offer another, more operational definition to help us in our analytical process.

Nancy Dixon has defined organizational learning as "the intentional use of learning processes at the individual, group, and system level to continuously transform the organization in a direction that is increasingly satisfying to its stakeholders." Dixon reminds us that all organizations learn. To some extent, all organizations "adapt to environmental constraints, prevent the repetition of past mistakes, and generate innovative new ideas." They do this by learning at all three levels: individual, group, and organization. Although such examples of learning occur, equally typical are situations in which learning is not achieved, that is, "organizations repeat their mistakes, fail to adapt to customer needs, and are unable to improve their processes to meet rising competitive standards."[2]

The conclusion we reach is that even when learning does occur, it is often *accidental* rather than the result of intention. Not only can some organizational learning be accidental, it can also be flimsy, weak, and depthless; organizations can learn the wrong lessons. Most organizations are, at best, inefficient learners and therefore much that could be learned is lost or missed. Why the inefficiency?

A primary difference between the accidental learning that happens in many organizations and organizational learning, Dixon says, is *intention*. Most organizations are inefficient learners because they operate with a learning deficit—they lack intentional processes that would help facilitate learning at all three relevant levels. Dixon also emphasizes *process*. If we in organizations want the outcomes that OL promises, we must engage in deliberate processes, rather than rely upon accidental learning.

Action Science as a Framework for Interpretation

How do we know that an organization has learned? According to Chris Argyris, an organization has learned when:

- The organization achieves what was intended. This happens because there is a match between its design for action and the actual outcome achieved.

- A mismatch between the intended outcome and the actual outcome is identified and corrected, so that the mismatch is turned into a match (Argyris, 1999, p. 67).

It should be a foregone conclusion that both of these forms of learning are needed in the business world. Yet, there is great variance in the ability to execute them. The field of organizational learning is concerned with enabling these forms of learning.

Single-loop and Double-loop Learning

Argyris writes that most organizations are reasonably skilled in what he calls single-loop learning. A single loop of learning occurs when an action designed to achieve a result works, or when an error is detected and is successfully corrected. In single-loop learning there is no questioning or altering any of the assumptions that underlie the design of the action. Argyris goes on to say that most organizational learning activities are single loop. Single-loop learning is quite appropriate for the routine, repetitive, everyday issue.

While single-loop learning can certainly be productive, it has its limitations. Single-loop learning may produce results in certain situations, but the problem is that it is not a sufficiently powerful form of learning and it is not appropriate for learning in more complex, nonprogrammable situations. It is inadequate for dealing with the increasing complexity that organizations are facing today. Argyris believes that organizations need to develop the capacity for double-loop learning because this is a more powerful form of learning and it is needed in order to bring about transformational change and to develop more profound capacity within organizations. The double-loop actions are the master programs that control the long-range effectiveness and, hence, the ultimate destiny of the system.

Double-loop learning occurs when mismatches between actions and results are corrected in a two-step process. The first step involves examining and perhaps altering those assumptions that guided the actions, and then, secondly, examining and altering the actions themselves. Argyris holds that more often than not it is the assumptions underlying our actions that are the more significant barriers to learning and profound change. Therefore assumptions represent important levers. However, they are often implicit and tend to go unquestioned.

Organizational learning tools and techniques can help to shift an organization from accidental to single-loop and then to double-loop learning. In sum, then, we can speak of three levels of possible learning in organizations:

- **Accidental organizational learning**—Learning that occurs without intention or process. This form of learning can be insubstantial or limited; organizations can even learn the wrong things.

- **Single-loop learning**—Organizations engage in an intentional learning wherein actions are deliberately designed and errors detected while the sources of errors, the embedded assumptions, go unquestioned or ignored. This type of learning yields results for certain types of problems and it may be easier for organizations to adopt, but it is limited.

- **Double-loop learning**—This involves a commitment to a deeper, riskier, and potentially far more rewarding process—a process that we will call "deep organizational learning."

As a starting place, we might think of an organization's learning ability as being located somewhere on a continuum that reaches from limited to single-loop to the capacity for double-loop learning.

Figure 3.1
Learning Continuum 1

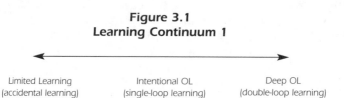

Limited Learning	Intentional OL	Deep OL
(accidental learning)	(single-loop learning)	(double-loop learning)

Organizations have the capacity to move from accidental, limited learning to more intentional, single-loop learning, to deeper, double-loop learning. If this is true, then those who would lead learning efforts must have a sense of where on the continuum the organization is currently and where it wants to go, and then devise a strategy for how it will begin that journey, whether the destination be only intentional OL or beyond. When embarking on an organizational learning effort, we believe it is helpful to understand this landscape so that we can design our strategies accordingly.

Why the Need for Deep Organizational Learning?

Argyris's research has shown that organizational change tends to focus on developing an organization's capacity for single-loop learning. Furthermore, he believes that even the field of organizational learning has been concerned with enabling single-loop learning. "Writers on the learning organization," he writes, "tend to focus on first-order errors," those due to "mistaken or incomplete action strategies and assumptions of the sort that practitioners ordinarily detect and try to correct."[3] What we don't tend to pay sufficient attention to are the deeper sources of errors: those factors that cause errors to be made in the first place and which, in turn, inhibit organizational performance.

Argyris says that we don't pay attention to those deeper sources of errors because people in organizations are often "systematically unaware" of them. Organizations tend to be permeated with defensive routines—mixed messages, taboos on discussing the key issues, games of control and deception, and other forms of organizational camouflage. All of these phenomena tend to create error and, ironically, also inhibit our ability to detect and correct error. These sources of errors are often systemic in nature and so we don't tend to see them, just as we imagine that fish don't realize they're in water—unless, of course, they're removed from it.

It is worthwhile to define what Argyris means by organizational defensive routines. Defensive routines are the policies or actions we put in place to prevent ourselves and our organizations from experiencing embarrassment or threat. The unintended consequence of these defensive routines is that they also prevent anyone from identifying and thereby reducing the causes of the embarrassment or threat.[4] This is why we all tend to collude in admiring the emperor's new clothes—and why we feel such a sense of chagrin when we realize that the emperor is, indeed, unclad.

Organizational defensive routines are "anti-learning and over-protective," says Argyris. The *Challenger* disaster is a classic example of how organizational defense routines can affect outcomes. Even though the major players certainly had the ability to recognize and report the O-ring problem, the "can do" attitude of the major players had them so focused on operational objectives that their ability to recognize and report problems was restricted.[5] In this example we can see what happens in many organizations: a "can do," winning attitude can blind people to seeing, and inhibit them from reporting and dealing with a potentially serious problem.

What causes these defensive routines and how do we overcome them? Argyris contends that they are a product of the limited learning system that we create in our organizations.

The Causes of Errors: Limited Learning Systems

In earlier work Chris Argyris and Donald Schön proposed that most behavior in organizations today is shaped by a common set of "governing variables." These governing variables are:

- Strive to be in unilateral control;
- Minimize losing and maximize winning;
- Minimize the expression of negative feelings; and
- Be rational.

These values lead to behaviors and actions that are primarily aimed at avoiding embarrassment or threats, such as:

- Advocate your views without encouraging inquiry (hence, remain in unilateral control and hopefully win);
- Unilaterally save face—your own and other people's (hence, minimize upsetting others or making them defensive);
- Design and manage situations unilaterally (in order to maintain control);
- Evaluate the thoughts and actions of others in ways that do not encourage testing the validity of the evaluation (and our own thoughts and actions);

- Attribute causes for whatever we are trying to understand—without necessarily validating them;
- Engage in defensive actions such as blaming, stereotyping, and intellectualizing to suppress feelings.[6]

Interestingly these variables don't necessarily match the values that people espouse (most of us apparently aspire to operate according to a "higher" standard), yet these variables tend to shape our behaviors, particularly under stress. Since business environments are often stressful, these values come into play most frequently, despite whatever values people espouse. Argyris and Schön call this constellation of variables and the actions that derive from them "Model I theory-in-use." (The term "theory-in-use" says that this theory can be inferred from our actions even though we may espouse a different set of governing variables.) Model I tells individuals to craft their positions, evaluations, and attributions in ways that inhibit inquiries into and tests of them with the use of independent logic. Furthermore, research has shown that Model I theory-in-use seems almost universal; it appears to cut across culture, age, gender, and economic status.[7]

The consequences of these Model I strategies are likely to be defensiveness, misunderstandings, and self-fulfilling and self-sealing processes. Like single-loop learning, Model I behaviors are useful in some situations—but are not useful in more complex situations where we must seek the best, most valid information. Errors cannot be readily detected in situations where everyone is colluding in saving face.

The crucial link here is that Schön and Argyris hold that human beings programmed with Model I—and that includes almost all of us—will create and impose a limited learning system on any organization in which they participate. In other words, we tend to create organizational cultures that reinforce these values and behaviors regardless of who comes or leaves. They term this an "organizational Model I learning system."

The paradox comes about because these Model I-based organizational learning systems reward limited learning and give rise to organizational defense routines. In fact, they are a type of defense routine. They also give rise to other negative consequences such as taboos and control games and mixed messages. So, without intending to, we start to create "Dilbertian" environments. And, as a consequence, our business results are not what they could be. Why? Simply put, because we are disabling intelligence that could be brought to bear on solving complex problems and making more efficacious decisions.

To compound the problem double-loop learning will not occur naturally in organizations whose structure is congruent with Model I. Model I learning systems discourage double-loop learning, because double-loop learning will result in questioning the assumptions that are the bedrock of the Model I learning system.

Why, despite the adverse consequences, do we all seem to act in accordance with Model I? First, because Model I is based upon values that were instilled in us in childhood and reinforced through most of our educational and work life experiences. This makes it very difficult to change because changing requires that we explore very strongly embedded values and assumptions within our own psyche. Few of us have the skills or courage to be able to do this alone.

Secondly, we have constructed a system that is self-reinforcing and self-perpetuating, making it extremely difficult for us to change the system unless we fully understand and confront it. To get to double-loop learning and deep OL, we must break the stranglehold that Model I has on us both as individuals and as organizational cultures. This is a deep sea, and we have only recently begun to wade, rather tentatively, into it.

The Way to Deep Organizational Learning

The stranglehold can be broken if we are able to engage a new set of governing variables and behaviors which Argyris and Schön call "Model II." Model II behaviors are governed by an entirely different set of variables than Model I, and they create an entirely different, more open working environment. In Model II:

- We value valid information over being perceived as "knowing" or being right. When we operate in accordance with this theory-in-use, all of our processes are open to being questioned. We are much less defensive.

- We value free and informed choice. We want others to agree and make decisions because they are informed and believe that the choice is right, rather than making choices based in control or coercion. This leads to tasks being controlled jointly, and interpersonal and group dynamics being minimally defensive. As a consequence, we can engage in double-loop learning, effective problem-solving, and decision-making.

- We value internal commitment to the choice (versus compliance) and vigilant monitoring of the implementation of the choice in order to detect and correct error. We now speak in directly observable categories, and seek to reduce blindness about our inconsistencies and incongruities. We operate according to learning-oriented norms such as trust and openness, and we test our theories publicly. Protection of self is a joint enterprise oriented toward everyone's growth.

People who recognize the value (and efficacy) of these variables can learn the skills necessary to design new action strategies. These action strategies include:

- Openly illustrating how they reached an evaluation or attribution; and
- Openly sharing how they crafted these evaluations or attributions to encourage inquiry and testing by others.

In essence, when people operate according to Model II, they begin to make the underpinnings of their thinking explicit, both to themselves and others. If the assumptions can be made explicit, then they are open to being questioned, tested, and changed. People's reasoning is productive rather than defensive. Operating this way gives rise to much more desirable consequences. The organization becomes a place where:

- Search is enhanced and deepened;
- Ideas are tested publicly;
- Individuals collaborate to enlarge inquiry; and
- Trust and risk taking are enhanced.[8]

These are the key elemental descriptions of an organization that is capable of learning what it needs to learn. The move toward openness breaks the cycle of the over-protective, self-sealing behaviors that systemically prevent the detection and correction of error. This leads to learning and learning leads to more effective performance.

It is important to note that Model II is not merely the *opposite* of Model I, but rather a vital new set of governing variables and resulting action strategies. The two are compared and contrasted in Table 3.1.

The Bad News and the Good News

Let us recap the ideas we've laid out so far:

- The evidence we use to determine whether or not an organization has learned is when an organization is able to produce the results that it set out to produce.
- This implies two forms of learning: the organization is able to design its actions effectively such that it gets the outcome it desires, and it is able to correct the design when the intentions and the outcomes are found to be out of line.

Table 3.1
Comparison of Model I and Model II Theories-in-Use

Model I	Model II
Governing Variables:	**Governing Variables:**
• *Always* be in unilateral control (so you can achieve your intended purpose).	• Valid Information
• Maximize winning and minimize losing.	• Free and informed choice
• Behave according to what you consider rational.	• Internal commitment to the choice and vigilant monitoring of the implementation of the choice in order to detect and correct error.
Implications: We:	**Implications:** We:
Design and manage situations unilaterally—In order to win we have to control situations—but one gains control by taking control away from others.	**Share power and co-create situations**—Rather than taking control away from you in order to accomplish *my* goal, we realize that we share in the responsibility for outcomes. Therefore we share power with anyone who has competence and who is relevant in deciding or implementing the action. We seek to build viable decision-making networks in which we maximize the contributions of each member, enabling the widest possible exploration of views.
Advocate our views without encouraging inquiry (to remain in unilateral control and hopefully win);	
Evaluate the thoughts and actions of others in ways that do not encourage testing the validity of the evaluation;	
Attribute causes for whatever we are trying to understand—without necessarily validating those attributions;	**Inquire**—We actively strive to test our theories publicly, making our inferences apparent; we actively seek to reduce blindness about our own inconsistency and incongruity. We try to find the most competent people for the decision to be made. We make fewer evaluations and attributions; when we do, we encourage others to inquire into them and test them.
Unilaterally save face by withholding information or making certain things "undiscussable" in order to minimize upsetting others or making them defensive.	
Engage in defensive actions such as blaming, stereotyping, intellectualizing. We use defensive reasoning: we keep our premises and inferences tacit, lest we lose control. To be rational means "to keep actions in constant alignment with our beliefs," but we believe it means "be logical by suppressing emotions." We fear effectiveness decreases as we become more emotional.	**We don't strive to save face** or protect ourselves or others by withholding information.
	Experience less defensiveness—People experience us not as defensive, but rather as facilitator, collaborator, choice creator. We seek to support each other's growth and evaluate every significant action in terms of the degree to which it helps the individuals involved generate valid and useful information (including relevant feelings).

Adapted from Chris Argyris, *On Organizational Learning,* 1999.

- All organizations learn to a greater or lesser extent. However, much of that learning is accidental.

- The field of organizational learning is concerned with developing the capacity to learn intentionally.

- Learning intentionally can result in single-loop learning. OL tools and methods can be used to build capacity for single-loop learning.

- Profound organizational change requires double-loop learning, but double-loop learning is deceptively difficult. It will not occur naturally in most organizations.

- This is because, at a very fundamental level, organizations have unwittingly constructed a learning system that both enables and disables learning. In the majority of cases, this learning system is based upon Model I theory-in-use, which emphasizes control, saving face, and advocating your point of view in order to win, rather than inquiring into the points of view of others. Model I-based organizational learning systems are currently pervasive in our organizations; they also profoundly constrain deeper forms of learning.

Breaking Free of Model I

Argyris offers hope that we can break free of Model I and that, if we do, we can create the organizations we want. As people learn Model II, Argyris believes that they will necessarily create an organizational learning system that then feeds back to reinforce their new Model II theory-in-use. In other words, *the process of individual and organizational transformation occurs simultaneously and is self-reinforcing.*

The link between individual and organizational learning and transformation is made explicit here. As the theories-in-use held by individuals come open to question, so do the assumptions embedded in the organizational culture, and vice versa. The transformation of the organizational learning system cannot occur without the transformation of individuals from Model I to Model II; likewise, individual transformation will be impeded unless the organization's learning system also transforms. The change processes are interdependent and coexistent and require deliberate processes with groups learning together.

When it comes to designing an organizational learning effort the essential question is, do we want profound change and optimum learning capacity, or are we willing to settle for moderate improvements? If we want profound change and optimum learning capacity, then it follows that the process of getting from here to there involves not just OL in the service of single-loop learning, but a deeper form of OL in the service of double-loop learning.

Tools for Developing a Model II Organizational Learning System

Argyris advises that creation of new learning systems requires a dialectical process in which participants can compare their theories-in-use and their embedded learning system with the alternative models. There are several organizational learning tools that can help us to practice Model II behaviors and to create a learning system more congruent with Model II. They are:

- Ladder of inference;
- Balancing advocacy and inquiry;
- Left-hand/right-hand column; and
- Dialogue.

These tools (described in Table 3.2) can facilitate generative conversations that help us to build improved organizational learning systems.

The Deep Organizational Learning Vision: Implications for Leaders

In theory at least, organizations have the potential of moving from accidental, limited learning to more intentional, single-loop learning, to deep OL with double-loop learning.

Figure 3.2
Learning Continuum 2

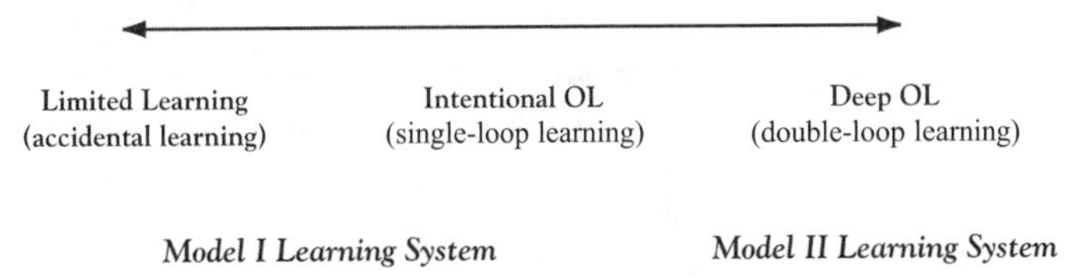

Limited Learning (accidental learning)	Intentional OL (single-loop learning)	Deep OL (double-loop learning)
Model I Learning System		*Model II Learning System*

If the people in an organization truly wish to break the hold of Model I, to free themselves from defensive routines, and to engage in double-loop learning, they must begin to construct a Model II-based learning system. This means that key individuals must learn the new values and skills necessary to create Model II and then endeavor to create learning communities, communities of practice. We try to bring the Model II learning system to bear in our organizations by entering into learning communities characterized by learning-oriented norms (trust, individuality, open con-

Table 3.2
Tools for Developing a Model O-II Learning System

Tool or Method	Description
Ladder of Inference	A conceptual tool designed to show how we tend to act on beliefs that are quite removed from observable data and actual experience, thus creating self-reinforcing belief and action systems. The lowest step of the ladder represents observable data and actual experience. The second rung of the ladder represents the data to which one chooses to pay attention, which is actually one step away from actual data and experience. The next rung represents the meanings one assigns to that selected data. At the fourth rung are the assumptions one makes based on those assigned meanings. Then rung five represents the conclusions one draws based on those assumptions. At rung six we have created a whole set of beliefs based on all that has gone before. At rung seven, we take actions based on our beliefs.
	When we operate according to Model I theory-in-use we tend to make attributions and evaluations of actions or events without sharing or testing our reasoning. The ladder of inference can help us be more aware of how our beliefs shape what we are able to see and how our assumptions constrain our actions, and it can help both individuals and teams be more effective.[9]
	When we are operating out of Model I we tend to advocate our positions so that we can "win." This strategy can fail us, however. When we are dealing with complex problems we need to seek out the best answers and learn from one another, but advocacy leads to defensiveness on the other side and thus to rigid positions on both sides. Arguments escalate without being resolved, and rigid thinking prevents learning.
Balancing Advocacy and Inquiry	Learning to balance advocacy and inquiry often requires adopting new conversational skills. We must reveal the assumptions and reasoning behind our own views (which makes us vulnerable) and also inquire into the thinking behind the views of others. At first, we may have a tendency to overcorrect, to focus on inquiry alone, but our goal is to find the balance between advocacy and inquiry, which fosters generative conversations about things that matter.[10]

Left-hand/Right-hand Column	Left-hand/right-hand column is a concept that helps people to become aware of the tacit assumptions that can get in the way of effective communication. Often people learn to use this technique by reflecting on a difficult conversation. In the right-hand column they write down what they actually said and in the left-hand column they write down what they were thinking at the time. By comparing the two they can see where their assumptions inhibited their communication almost instinctively. As people become more aware of those tacit assumptions, they can begin to test them and move into more productive conversations.[11]
Dialogue	Dialogue is a collective reflective learning process. In a sense, dialogue attempts to create a container or field in which people begin to perceive themselves, the world, and each other differently. At its best, dialogue gives rise to new insights and helps us to break through the assumptions and illusions that constrict our thoughts, actions, and aspirations.[12]

firmation on difficult issues). We invite double-loop learning and take actions to solve problems in such a way that they remain solved (versus "quick fixes"), and do so without creating defensive routines that reduce the present level of problem-solving effectiveness.

Argyris advises that efforts like this must start at the top because it is too difficult, if not impossible, to create a sustainable Model II learning system at the lower levels. We leave this to you to consider. We believe that leaders of learning efforts must have a sense of the dynamics we've outlined as a starting point. In a sense, they must understand what they are up against if they undertake such a learning effort; they must understand how resistant the organization will be to undertaking deeper forms of learning. This is largely because there is a systemic reinforcing process that keeps the organization—and the leaders as well—anchored in Model I.

Argyris cautions us that getting to Model II is not easy. It requires patience and an appreciation for time delays and the inevitable regression because, he has observed, individuals who value Model II and wish to learn it are unable to produce Model II actions during the early phases of learning. Learning Model II is going to be, he writes, "at least as difficult as learning to play, moderately well, a musical instrument or sport."[13] It takes a good deal of time and reinforcement before an individual is able to behave in accordance with Model II, and even longer before the organizational learning system can be transformed.

In the meantime, the old learning system will resist being changed. As Argyris points out, in order for double-loop organizational learning to occur, "individuals must be able to alter their theories-in-use and to neutralize the old learning system while simultaneously, and probably under stress, acting according to a new theory-in-use (e.g., Model II) and creating a new learning system." There are implications for leaders. The individuals who are leading this transition must straddle two systems, Model I and Model II, both at the individual and organizational levels. They will be required to monitor and guide their own internal transformation process. Contemporaneously, they will endeavor to nullify the existing learning system (in which others and the organization are probably highly invested) in the interests of creating another learning system which can easily be perceived to be too soft, too dangerous, or even unachievable. This is one of the reasons why Argyris believes that a learning intervention should begin at the highest level of the organization.

All of this is not to discourage us, but to heighten our awareness of the arena in which we are playing. For change leaders, there is a possibility of attempting too much without sufficient support or understanding—of letting our visions of what could be take us too far out on a limb. There is also the possibility of not attempting enough. It is relatively easy to give up on the potential of a deeper form of OL and to focus on enhancing single-loop learning. In fact, this may be a very logical first step, but we may be reducing the tension in the elastic band prematurely.

If we only attempt what the organization can obviously tolerate, then we run the risk of following blindly some unsuccessful—and perhaps very familiar—patterns such as the one described in the Introduction to this book.

Is reaching for Model II an impossible dream? Perhaps it is only a matter of courage, commitment, and community. Our disillusionment with the current state of our organizations may prove to be a gift if it opens the door to significant reform.

What does your organization want? What does it need? What is it ready for? What kind of a learning effort are you prepared to lead? We need to ask these important questions so that we can make free and informed choices about our own OL journeys. In the following chapters we tell the stories of Bert and Iva's learning journeys where these questions resonate. We then use this framework to debrief those stories discussing how these two stories may represent some typical patterns.

Endnotes

1. Steve J. Gill, *The Manager's Pocket Guide to Organizational Learning* (Amherst, MA: HRD Press, 2000), p. x.

2. Nancy Dixon, *The Organizational Learning Cycle: How We Can Learn Collectively* (McGraw-Hill, 1994), p. 5.

3. Chris Argyris, *On Organizational Learning* (Malden, MA: Blackwell Publishing, 1999), p. 6.

4. Argyris, 1999, op. cit., p. 58.

5. Chris Argyris, *Knowledge for Action: A Guide to Overcoming Barriers to Organizational Change* (San Francisco: Jossey-Bass, 1993), p. 17.

6. Chris Argyris and Donald Schön, *Theory and Practice* (San Francisco: Jossey-Bass, 1974); and Chris Argyris and Donald Schön, *Organizational Learning* (Reading, MA: Addison-Wesley, 1978).

7. Argyris, 1993, op. cit., p. 51.

8. Argyris, 1999, op. cit., p. 181.

9. Chris Argyris, *Overcoming Organizational Defenses* (Needham Heights, MA: Allyn and Bacon, 1990), pp. 88–89; and Peter Senge et al., *The Fifth Discipline Field Book* (New York: Doubleday, 1994), pp. 242–243.

10. Marcial Losada, "The Complex Dynamics of High Performance Teams," *Mathematical and Computer Modeling*, Vol. 30, 1999, pp. 179–192. Also, Peter Senge, *The Fifth Discipline: The Art and Practice of the Learning Organization* (New York: Doubleday, 1990), pp. 198–202; and Senge et al., 1994, op. cit., pp. 253–259.

11. Argyris and Schön, 1974, op. cit.

12. See William Isaacs, *Dialogue and the Art of Thinking Together* (New York: Doubleday, 1999).

13. Argyris, 1999, op. cit., p. 87.

Chapter 4

The Pragmatist's Path: Bert's Journey

Bert: I pride myself on being a pragmatist, but there are also things that I care very deeply about. Customer service is one of them. You see, I came up from the ranks. I spent most of my career in the line organization. I actually started as a telephone company technician, climbing poles and working face-to-face with customers.

The telephone company always had this ethic about doing the right thing by customers and I felt that we did the right thing in those days. For example, we were part of the community, we had local offices, we always took the customer's word when there was a problem with a bill, and we had the ethic of universal service. But in recent times we have evolved away from that ethic. Sometimes I thought we'd lost the heart and soul of what drives the telephone company spirit.

For example, I remember that when we changed telephone poles, we replaced the clotheslines that housewives attached to the poles. Now, when you change a pole, you're not supposed to put the clothesline back because, technically, the clothesline is an illegal attachment and if the lineman were to reattach it, he would expose the company to liabilities if anything happened as a result. That's very logical and very cautious—but it's not good service.

Our customer base is the community and the way I see it we are also part of that community. That creates a very special bond. People expect us to be there, not only in emergencies, but all the time. Although things are changing, people still trust us, at least to some extent. Some people still leave their keys under their mats for "the phone guy."

So I carried that ethic with me. I went back to school at night and got my degree in electrical engineering. I subsequently got a master's degree in business administration in finance and statistics and then I got up into management. All the way through my career, I never lost the ideas that I had when I was climbing those poles. I always believed that customer service was important and that we really needed to uphold that. I guess customer service was my driving idea—it was connected very much to my personal values. It was deeply ingrained. But as I was coming up into management, it started to get tougher and tougher to provide customer service in the same way because of financial constraints.

Backdrop: The Squeeze

Bert: I began my career in telecommunications in Canada. Eventually I took a position with a phone company in the United States. When I came into that American telephone company in 1979, the company was not in great shape financially for a variety of reasons. The company had had to undergo a lot of changes that were coming at them pretty fast and furiously. These changes had a big impact on customer service.

The first years that I was there were characterized by a tug of war between AT&T, who owned us, and the state regulatory commission, the Public Utility Commission (PUC), which oversaw all of our dealings with the public. The California PUC prided itself on having the lowest rates in the nation so they began reducing our rate hikes or cutting them totally. All of our funds came from AT&T, and AT&T started restricting our funds because the return on investment (ROI) was so low in California. The squeeze was on.

That was in direct conflict with our long-standing philosophy, which was, "customer service is number one." Our whole mentality was focused on service. This was an expensive philosophy, but we could afford it because we knew that the cost of service was reimbursable through a rate increase. Now that mentality had to change. We simply couldn't afford it because we couldn't raise our rates. We had to go into a belt-tightening mode.

Then came those famous rulings. In 1984, AT&T was split up through the consent decree of the Department of Justice. Things really had to change.

Outside Pressures Exert Their Influence on the Culture

Bert: With the AT&T divestiture came significant new pressures. There were major changes in three very crucial areas: competition, cost control, and regulatory climate.

First of all, we had been a monopoly but now, for the first time, we were going to have to compete for business. Did we know how to be competitive? We knew that if we were going to be competitive many things would have to change. For example, we had heavy bureaucracy, with levels and levels of approvals for the simplest things.

Also, when we were "The Phone Company," we told the customers exactly what they needed. We were in the driver's seat, not the customer. Now we would have to evolve a new vision of what "customer service" meant. But how do you change a culture that is so ingrained? That was a major challenge for us.

Then the regulatory climate became even more strict and controlling when the AT&T divestiture came. There was a climate of distrust. Now that we were going to be profit-making the regulators didn't think that we would have the best interests of the customer in mind. They still wanted us to retain our old style of customer service first—that philosophy that I had been accustomed to. To ensure that, the regulators took a certain position: "We guarantee you this rate of return so you need to do what we say. We're the regulator." But the company's view was that regulation was essentially a replacement for competition, and now that there was competition, the regulator role was no longer appropriate. This was a major source of tension and it was ongoing.

So now we had the pressures of competition and regulation coupled with the cost cutting that had begun earlier. We had to evolve a strategy for coping with all of these pressures.

In the 1980s (post divestiture) the focus was cost cutting and on growing the core business so that we were better able to cover costs. In the 1990s the focus shifted. The company was addressing questions such as: What business are we going to be in? What markets are we going to be in? What technology are we going to use?

The company perceived that we needed to go in a more technically advanced direction. Specifically, they wanted to invest billions in fiber optics and broadband. In order to do that, they had to take the money from somewhere. They decided to use the existing customer base—our core, traditional business—as a "cash cow." The idea was to milk the cash cow in order to fund starting up these other business ventures which might be more profitable. Therefore, there was an emphasis on reduced growth of the core; the core was to become more and more efficient in order to fund other growth opportunities. Naturally, that put a lot of squeeze on the budgets and put a lot of focus on finding places where we could save money. As a result, we probably did some good in some areas by trimming some of the budgets, but we also had a lot of discontent about service. Customer service was still a traditional telephone company value and there was still a strong desire to focus on the customer within the organization, but top management was focusing on finding dollars to invest in developing the business.

So, there we were. There used to be a mentality of service at virtually any cost, but now we came to believe that by cutting costs we could hone our monopolistic bureaucracy into a leaner, more competitive operation. We put pressure on people to cut costs. One of the things we did was put a major emphasis on reducing the amount of time that we spent with any one customer—because time is money, right?

Unintended Consequences

Bert: As a result of our focus on cost cutting, we did streamline our processes and we became, in many respects, a model of efficiency. However, this focus on streamlining had some unintended and unforeseen consequences. Over time, we put a great deal of value on the physical processes, on things we could quantify and measure, but we took it to an extreme and as a result we tended to lose the human contact. We forgot about valuing relationships.

You could feel this lack of valuing human relationships by listening to calls between our service representatives and customers. It showed up in our reluctance to just spend time with customers and help deal with their anxiety. It showed up in the mechanical way we'd relate to customers by just following a rote script. For example, a customer would phone in and we'd automatically say, "What's your phone number, please?" And the customer would say, "Well, I've been out of service, so I don't—" But we'd just repeat our script, "What's your phone number, please?!" We'd forgotten our roots, and I believed that we needed to get back to those roots.

Looking for a Way Out

Bert: As the cost cutting got tighter and tighter it became a question of: How can we save even more money? Yet, despite those pressures, some of us kept asking the question: How can we improve customer service within this climate? How can we improve *both* customer service and cost control?

In time I became the general manager of one of the business units. As I said, I had been interested in customer service from the days when I was climbing poles. Now I felt that I could finally begin to do something about the service issue. I embarked on the Quality (Total Quality Management, TQM) road. In my view, TQM meant "doing it the way the customer wanted." I hoped to be able to use TQM to find a way to bring customer service back into the equation. But how would I start?

There were a couple of things going on at the time. TQM had become viewed as a good thing at my company, but the approach we were taking was very conceptual and theoretical because it was being led by a staff person who was a very conceptual thinker. This conceptual approach didn't do it for me because it wasn't directly linked to our work. I was adverse big-time to theory for its own sake. I was in the line and I needed something that was tangible. I needed to see it in action, to see it actually working. Why do I need to reinvent the wheel or even create the wheel?

I was certain that we could learn from other companies who had already made Quality improvements, but I had some roadblocks. We had a major belief that you couldn't bring in innovations from another industry because the phone company was unique. Yet, we couldn't look to another phone company because none of the phone companies had particularly distinguished themselves in that regard. Because we'd all been part of AT&T, there wasn't a lot of fresh thinking. Then I heard about Florida Power and Light.

Florida Power and Light was doing some first-rate Quality work. They were the first and only American company to win the Deming Award. They were also instrumental in creating the Baldrige Award. When I looked at the company structure, I saw that they were very similar to us: they had business offices, splicers, trucks, cables, underground and aerial lines, linemen, unions, et cetera. They had all the process we had and they were also regulated. Power and phone companies have similar operations, and similar ways of looking at the world. Because they had been so successful I said, Let's go see what they're doing.

A Vision of How It Could Be

Bert: In 1990–91 I went to Florida Power and Light and met for about half a day with the president. He explained the visions and values and TQM principles that they had there. It sounded pretty good, but I was still a little skeptical. Then at the end of the day when I was leaving to go back home, I saw a Florida Power and Light worker working at the side of the road. I stopped and engaged him in conversation. I asked him some of the same questions that I'd asked the president. What was amazing to me was that I got the same answers.

Now, I'm not saying for a fact that the worker and the president used the same scenarios or spoke at the same level or scope, but the same phrases and words were part of both people's answers. I thought that was pretty good. For the first time I'd seen that what the executive rank was talking about, the working rank was also talking about, and that established that there was a golden thread linking all the goals and objectives of the company from top to bottom. That seemed rather unique because that wasn't my experience in my company. In fact, in my whole career I had never experienced that degree of congruity, the ability for the top-level management and the rank-and-file to actually articulate the vision, values, and quality principles in the same terms. That experience gave me a vision of what could be—and also told me that the vision was achievable. As a result, I introduced the Florida Power and Light TQM system into our company.

It was a rough road for a while. Our company version of TQM had eleven steps whereas the version from Florida that I was trying to introduce had only seven steps. So, instead of focusing on the essence of TQM, some people were fighting about which one was better and which one we should use. But I had a trump card. I was in a line position at the time and in this culture, the line position tended to have more weight than the staff position.

I also was reporting to a VP who was very well respected because of his grasp of the financial aspects of the business. We were facing major financial problems, as I mentioned earlier, so his expertise was very valued. Ultimately, he became the Chief Financial Officer. And since he was an officer—and in those days it made a difference—he had credentials.

So I was a line guy with the ability to speak through an officer who was a financial expert. This was a powerful combination. My boss became a champion of TQM and he made it clear to the rest of the organization that TQM was something that wouldn't go away. So, in our business plan, we made TQM the anchor of all the programs for the following year. He made it a fundamental strategic imperative for the business. At last I had some leverage to do the things that I felt were important. We had credibility.

Iva: So you were able to implement at PacBell the things you had learned at Florida Power and Light.

Bert: That's right. It was a Total Quality infrastructure.

Iva: This is sort of, I wouldn't say identical, but very much like what I did. I got into Senge's work from TQM. I thought Senge's work was going to help me with TQM.

Bert: That's exactly what I thought. The very next year, I went to the Program for Senior Executives at the Sloan Business School at MIT, a three-month, live-in course. We had a bunch of professors there from both inside and outside MIT, one of whom was Peter Senge who had recently published *The Fifth Discipline*. Another was John Sterman who had done a lot of pioneering work in simulations.

I was concerned that we were improving processes that had no business existing. After listening to Peter Senge and going through the courses, I began to see how organizational learning could complement our TQM work. I saw that we could use systems thinking to help us figure out whether our processes were really useful or not. *Then* we could use TQM to improve them.

There was something else that also clicked for me. I realized that we were potentially firing people because they weren't accomplishing certain things, when the failures really didn't have anything to do with them as individuals. It was the *system* that was creating the negative outcomes, not the individuals. It could have been anyone in the shop. After you do the Beer Game you find that out real quickly because you experience it yourself.

My colleague Dan Mlakar had some interesting insight into that issue.

Dan Mlakar, Project Manager: People often thought they could fix things by finding an individual to blame. The only method they had for solving problems was to shift responsibility, shift the burden, point the finger and find blame. They had no real understanding that there might be another approach.

TQM and Systems Thinking: A Powerful Combination

Bert: So, I could really see how both systems thinking and simulations could take us much farther on our Quality journey. Once I had a sense of what organizational learning was about, I asked Peter Senge to come to PacBell because I felt strongly that we needed to work together on this for my company. Peter responded, to my surprise, that he was already there. Unbeknownst to me, Peter had been brought to our company by one of our vice presidents. I told Peter that I didn't know at all what he was talking about, but when Peter mentioned the name of the VP, I recognized him.

That night I phoned the VP to find out what was going on and, sure enough, the individual said that he was engaged in an organizational learning project, and that it was a kind of "skunkworks" project. He also said that there was "lots of stuff around it" and that we should talk when I returned to California. That led to a discovery.

In a subsequent conversation with the VP I learned that the president of our company, who was very interested in the TQM movement at that time, had seen an article by Daniel Kim at MIT. The article suggested that systems thinking could enhance TQM; in fact Kim suggested TQM would fail without systems thinking.[1] After reading the article the president took a strong position against our getting involved with systems thinking because it would distract us away from the things that we were doing in TQM.

Iva: What was your own feeling, Bert, about this controversy, about TQM and the way that Daniel Kim had framed it?

Bert: Well, for me, TQM had to include a focus on customers. Yet, very often in our company I'd hear TQM being discussed in very abstract, numerical terms. I'd hear people talk about things like numerical TQM and statistical process control. I personally had the feeling that our approach to TQM was limited, so Kim's argument seemed logical. I still didn't understand the president's resistance—but eventually I figured it out.

You see, there was more to the president's resistance than just that article. We had had a unique experience in 1988 with a company-wide training program called Leadership Development. While the program was being implemented, a lot of the employees objected to it, but management did not listen or deal with those objections. As a result, the employees went public with their concerns. They went to the press and to our regulators with the complaint that "They're trying to brainwash us. They're trying to change our thinking." In fact, the Leadership Development program *had* been about changing our thinking and now there was a lot of fear in the organization about things like that. Then, some people made a connection between Leadership Development and systems thinking—and, therefore, between leadership development and organizational learning. I believe the president wouldn't embrace anything having to do with systems thinking because it might conjure up the memory of leadership development.

So, the president was very concerned that the TQM initiative would be diluted by the systems thinking work. Meanwhile, this VP was doing the skunkworks project without getting the president formally involved. It turns out, however, that the president knew about the project and was lukewarm about it. This came to a head and the VP left the company. The VP later said that he had pushed too hard at the wrong time and in the wrong place. As you might imagine, this had a major impact on my approach to organizational learning. I felt that this was a warning to me that this stuff was dangerous. I was fearful that I could lose my job.

After this happened, I faced my first challenge. Of course, I was aware of the risks, but I was still very excited about the potential of OL and I was confident that I wouldn't make the same mistakes. I went to my boss (who, thankfully, also had some background in OL) and said, *"I've got to do this."* I figured that I had certain advantages. On the plus side, I was a line manager, and in the culture of PacBell a line manager has a lot of say. That put me in a better situation politically than the previous champion who came from accounting, which is not seen as part of the mainstream.

But the irony was that my being a line manager didn't give me the opportunity to exploit OL work because my boss and I agreed that it was more appropriately done in staff at that point since the line is supposed to focus on day-to-day implementation, not company-wide process improvement. So OL went dormant for a while.

The Journey Resumes

Bert: About a year later I got a staff job. I became the Bold Goals and Customer Service Bureau Assistant Vice President. Our corporate journey in TQM had continued. My interest in OL had been sustained even though I hadn't been actively involved. I still saw a lot of potential in making the link between TQM and systems dynamics, but it wasn't until I actually came into the staff job and started working on some major corporate initiatives, which we called "Bold Goals," that I felt that I could resurface organizational learning. These initiatives aimed at making major changes in the business. I thought that OL could help us achieve those goals, so at that point I went around looking for what happened to it. I found that the skunkworks had sort of continued, but at a very minor pace.

I told my boss what I wanted to do and I also got the VP of Quality involved. To make it clear what the strategy was, I drew a diagram that basically showed that systems thinking was an extension of TQM, not anything which is antithetical to TQM. So OL work would not create any kind of diversion from the TQM path.

The VP of Quality and my boss decided to tell the president what I was up to in order to get his sanction. The president sent back the message that he wasn't crazy about it, but we could go forward as long as they gave him some guarantees that this would not be the preeminent part of my life. My boss's counsel to me was to go ahead, but cautiously. "Don't make it a mainstream event," he said. My boss also reminded me that I had a job to do and that I had business results to deliver. He also reminded me that my evaluation would not be based on how well I implemented systems thinking but on the metrics attached to the specific tasks that I had been assigned.

At this time, I believed that my new job function gave me a good opportunity to do more organizational learning work, and it did. We had four trial organizational learning projects during my watch. Two of them failed miserably and two were extremely positive. I learned a great deal from each of them.

The First Project Attempt

Bert: In the beginning my thinking was pretty idealistic in the sense that I was very enthusiastic about the potential for OL to have an impact on my company, but my thinking was also very practical. From my past experiences with TQM, I had learned that I needed a *practical platform* from which to launch OL. I had learned that one of the problems with TQM was that people didn't have time for it because they didn't perceive it as real work. They had their real job to do so they couldn't go to the Quality Improvement meetings. I always found this very exasperating.

One of the Bold Goals was something called "trouble report reduction." The objective was to drastically reduce the number of requests for customer service because a customer is experiencing trouble on the line. I believed that this initiative represented a genuine opportunity for collaboration between our company and the Organizational Learning Center at MIT (MIT OLC).

As it turned out, a staff manager who reported to me had begun some work on a service quality management flight simulator at the MIT OLC, but there was no momentum to keep it going. These circumstances triggered my interest in how a specially focused, systems dynamic-related project may be able to help reduce trouble reports. I wanted to get a field team together to validate the work, so I went in search of support. First,

I got support from my boss, an executive VP, and then I pursued the OL folks at MIT.

We engaged in a discussion about working together on a pilot project. Together, we hoped to build a service quality simulator to help us reduce the number of trouble reports. The next step was to get support from a line organization. The project never came about. I attribute this failure largely to the way organizational learning was introduced to our people. What happened was that some people from the Organizational Learning Center at MIT came out to meet with us for a so-called Project Definition Clinic. Our initial attempt at a conversation was, I believe, a fiasco. The clinic was too unstructured for us and our people got nervous. We were a bunch of top executives sitting around a table, and the OL people said, "Well, now we're going to discuss the undiscussables." From my training in OL, I knew that the idea of talking openly about things that are usually not talked about is important within the context of OL, but that was the wrong thing to do in our culture. We were not open to such an approach. Discussing undiscussables and dealing with culture first is the opposite of the way things worked in our culture. We were there to *do business.* So it absolutely did not go over well. The problem was compounded when the MIT folks told us that the staff manager and I had a lack of communication—which I felt was untrue.

The line people put up strong defenses against getting involved in the learning work. We had a subsequent meeting, but things got no better despite my best efforts. Then, during the meeting, the line VP stood up and said, "This better not have a negative impact on results." That was a warning signal. Then he said he was going to "play the devil's advocate role," and I knew that meant he wasn't buying in. I knew the project was dead.

I still didn't quit. After the meeting I talked with the line VP and explained to him how important this OL stuff was. I worked the whole road, you know? I said, "Look, you *gotta* do this." And what did the line VP do? He went to my boss and my boss backed down. My boss saw this as a test—and we didn't pass.

Now, my boss had shared with me that there was concern that this project was all I was doing. He knew this was dangerous because there were other more mainstream activities, such as Quality Improvement Teams (QITs), that were seen to be more important. He was concerned because he knew that others should view this not as something separate, but as part of a larger TQM initiative aimed at achieving the Bold Goals.

Naturally my boss saw the line VP's coming to him as a confirmation of my being too involved. So I lost leverage there. I remember being really upset at myself after that. I kept asking myself, "Why don't they see this?" I took it very personally. I felt responsible for not being able to make it work. I know now that I should have done it differently. I should have not pushed so hard, but I was so revved up and I believed that I needed to persevere.

Reflecting on it further, there were huge differences in perspective between the university people and our people. The OL leader's primary question was "How do organizations learn?" whereas mine was "How can a learning project benefit my organization and its goals?" In a sense, the OL folks' reaction to us reminded me of our old culture; it was their way or the highway. So perhaps these differences represented an insurmountable obstacle.

Then there was also the issue that programs targeted at modifying people's basic values, especially any with "thinking" inherently in the title, had became a taboo at Pacific Bell due to the fallout of the Leadership Development program. Another claim was that it was distracting them from doing their regular jobs. This was even truer in the line organization.

Learning from a First "Failure"

Bert: So, basically, my first attempt at gaining momentum around an organizational learning project was a fiasco. It was a total disaster in my mind. One of the factors was, in fact, my enthusiasm for what organizational learning could do for us. Because of that enthusiasm, I tended to overreach. I called Peter Senge to come. I brought out all the ammunition, the whole parade. I took the attitude, "I am bringing you the prophet from the mountain." I came in as the zealot and as a result I missed some cues.

For example, the vice president in charge of the line organization did not volunteer; I *asked* him to participate. At the time, the line organization also had 17 other initiatives that they were responsible for. So, of course, their commitment was very tentative.

Iva: That is a critical question. Can you create commitment or does it need to be there in the first place? And if you don't have commitment in the line from the get-go, should you even begin?

Bert: My colleague, Dan Mlakar, has the view that you absolutely need proactive, creative line people. He says that you need people who are "close to the resources and close to the results." These people need to be able to balance practice and performance. He believes that this is a prerequisite—creativity and commitment must be in the organization in the right place. You can't create it; it has to be inherent in the make-up of people. You've got to find the people and line leaders who have it already.

Iva: I almost agree. I don't believe that you can create commitment, but I do believe that, as a leader, you can create the conditions where commitment can take root. So I guess I believe that even if you don't have it at the very beginning, you still might be able to start something.

Bert: Perhaps, but it's a lot riskier. I also learned that OL was not going to fly on its own, that its inherent value was not transferable from all those OL meetings that I'd gone to. I had been persuaded in those meetings about how positive everything was. I'd set myself up in my own mind that all I needed to do was let these people know what this is.

It was at that point that I realized this stuff is dangerous for me. I also learned that the line folks wouldn't support the project because they saw the approach as being too unstructured and therefore they believed that it would have too negative an impact on the numbers. So, I realized that if I attempted anything else it better be supported by numbers.

Regrouping

Bert: I still had the Bold Goal of reducing the number of trouble reports. How was I going to approach this goal?

In order to decide on the best strategy, I felt I had to do some analysis work. I decided to do a SWOT analysis: I looked at the strengths, weaknesses, opportunities, and threats (SWOT) of our current situation overall. I came up with the information shown in Table 4.1.

First, I looked at what the company valued. At this time it was definitely cost reduction. In fact, the majority of Bold Goals were cost-driven, so I knew that cost reduction would have to be a major part of my strategy. But I held customer service in high value, so I did some analysis to see if there was a customer service angle and, of course, there was. When a customer complains about trouble on their line, cost reduction and service certainly overlap. Customers don't want to have trouble on their line, and every time they do we need someone out to fix it. That costs money. So, if we can find a way to reduce reports of trouble, then—theoretically, at least—both customer dissatisfaction and cost reduction can be simultaneously improved.

The next thing I did was I looked at our assumptions. There were some aspects to the way that we traditionally handled trouble reports that were considered to be "Motherhood." I mean, they were just unassailable. For example, when we had a customer calling in with a report of trouble on the line, we'd dispatch a technician and then measure how long it took the technician to fix it. We held each individual tech responsible; we never looked at overall patterns. We'd get reports daily on how long it was taking each of our techs and whether or not they were able to fix the problem. Then we would have a formal review.

During the review we'd actually drag in the technician who worked on the customer order and we'd grill that person for having screwed up on a customer call. We used to call these the "TELSAM barbecues" (TELSAM stands for Telephone Service Attitude Measurement, a survey that was considered to represent the voice of the customer).

The barbecue was our method for reducing trouble reports. I learned from the Beer Game that it doesn't make a difference *who* you put in there. Given my background as a service technician, and my experience

Table 4.1
Bert's SWOT Analysis

STRENGTHS:	WEAKNESSES:
<ul><li>Results driven</li><li>Customer-oriented</li><li>Employee technical ability</li><li>Employee loyalty</li><li>Dominant market presence</li></ul>	<ul><li>Reaction-time driven</li><li>First-cost driven</li><li>Regulatory confrontation</li><li>Shadow of Leadership Development</li><li>Business unit fiefdoms and rivalry</li><li>Hierarchical decision making</li><li>Monopoly thinking</li><li>Line versus staff friction</li></ul>

OPPORTUNITIES:	THREATS:
<ul><li>New union-management relationship</li><li>Frustration with current results</li><li>New idea champions</li><li>Industry technology innovations</li></ul>	<ul><li>Competition</li><li>Legislation</li><li>Customer disenchantment</li><li>Regulatory sanctions</li><li>Declining profitability</li><li>Adverse financial rating</li><li>Higher than expected employee early out</li></ul>

with the Beer Game, I knew that this wasn't the answer, but what was? I believe that we could learn something about this if we applied OL to this Bold Goal.

The SWOT analysis helped me clarify my working assumptions. I identified some leverage points and came up with some strategies to deal with them. For example, our focus on results meant that we could not participate in learning for its own sake; learning had to be tied to results. First and foremost, we were cost driven so we had to make sure that the initial cost for learning was very low to nothing. There was friction between line and staff, so we didn't do anything that exacerbated that. We were hierarchical in our decision making. The implications were that we had to make sure that we involved our peers and didn't ever go over their heads to their bosses or we'd alienate them.

Also, the Leadership Development experience had left a shadow so I knew I should distance myself from any comparison to anything like it. I also knew I had to be careful about how we brought OL in, because it can look pretty foreign to our culture. I took that into account. For example, I determined that we should eliminate all the OL jargon except during our core group meetings.

That's how I processed all the weaknesses and threats. The opportunities represented the possible portals—the openings for learning. I perceived that those openings were small now, but they could grow larger as our frustration with results increased.

Finally, I believed that I needed to get some protection for myself. After all, things had *not* gone well for the early proponents of OL and I didn't want to find myself without a job. I had a real heart-to-heart talk with my boss and told him what happened from my perspective. I said, "We've got to work out air cover around here because this is good stuff, but it ain't easy to introduce." "Air cover" is a term we used to describe getting some protection from someone higher up in the organization. The role of your air cover was to listen to any perceived negative impact of things you were doing and to tell you the things that weren't being said to you directly.

My boss agreed to provide air cover and he also gave me the confidence that I wasn't going to be fired, but that I had better learn from this experience. "Major in the majors," he said. "Don't try to make this mainstream." My boss was smart in the sense that I don't think he was totally convinced that this was good stuff, but he had enough wisdom to let me find out for myself. So now I knew I had to find a different approach. And I did.

Going Undercover

Bert: I decided that I would begin again by forming a team and then practicing organizational learning within my own group, rather than try to involve an outside group. So I put together a team around the concept of the spokes of a wheel. I found people who had different areas of expertise. They represented the different spokes. My job was to stay in the hub and remove barriers so that they could do their jobs to the best of their abilities.

We started developing a learning group, or a "community of practice" to use the jargon. In particular, I decided that I wanted to use causal loop diagrams to help us come up with a diagnosis of the situation and then a strategy for intervention. My plan was to pull in a line expert and an expert in causal loop diagramming and have them talk to each other.

As we were working together, practicing some OL techniques, I began to notice a rather dramatic change in the group. For example, our culture was very hierarchical—like the military, the number of "stripes" you had defined your reality; people would defer to the ranking individual. It could be a very tense environment. I used to have a pet phrase that described it. I'd say, "My boss is a six and I'm a five and a six beats a five any day of the week." But within our group that wasn't true anymore. One day when we were at a meeting somebody commented that we were listening more. And that we were challenging each other more, but we were challenging the *ideas* without challenging the individuals.

People began to see that there could be another interpretation of reality, there could be another way of being. We also began to see that we were no longer as competent as we thought ourselves to be and that the methodology by which we had been promoted to our vaulted positions was not necessarily the methodology that was going to be successful in the future. All that made people very willing to listen.

We had new insights. For example, we had a problem with our cables getting wet and so we put a lot of effort into extracting water. We realized that a better approach would be to work on preventing water from getting into the cable in the first place.

We also got more into group decision making. I believe that we actually made better decisions. We used the OL language, we all understood each other. So in that sense, it was good.

The Second Project: A Major Success

Bert: The trouble report reduction project required us to find a line manager who would work with us and allow us to do some field investigation. My job was to cultivate this line hero and create a relationship that would enable us to do the manual tracking of data that was required to support our theories. In this way, we went around the hierarchy.

Once I found the line hero we had all the pieces. We had an expert from the line and an expert in systems thinking diagrams, so we had someone to tell the story and someone to draw the diagrams. We began to draw systems diagrams of how things were *really* working out in the field.

It was like playing detective. We started with the TELSAM barbecues because I was really convinced that we were picking on the front line and I didn't think that was right. I learned from the Beer Game that it doesn't make a difference *who* you put in there. And we were killing these guys. It had to stop. I was convinced that they were not the problem.

So, if our TELSAM results showed that customers were saying that we weren't making repairs fast enough, what could be other reasons besides the speed of the actual repair guy? That question led us to look at how the repair guys fix things. When the systems diagrams were done, we all looked at the pictures. We saw that all the arrows were coming into one spot. It was crystal clear what was going on.

It turned out that how the repair guys fix things was driven by *policy*. The policy was driven by a set of assumptions that we now began to question. The company believed that customer satisfaction in this area was a function of how quickly the repair was made. Therefore, the official policy was to make the repair as quickly as possible. The unspoken policy was that we'd punish—or barbecue—our technicians if our TELSAM results showed that customers weren't happy with our repairs.

The trouble was that we unknowingly created a system wherein neither the customers nor the technicians could win. That was because we didn't really understand what our customers wanted.

Aha!

Bert: The systems diagrams helped us discover that our customers weren't looking at *how long* it took us to fix a single, isolated case; they were looking at whether the problem was fixed *for good*. And, due to our policy, it very often wasn't. The reason was that we never really repaired the problem, we just switched them to a new line. We focused on a quick fix rather than identifying the root cause of the problem and solving it. We didn't look for the root cause of the problem because that would have taken more time and more of our critical resources—at least in the short run.

Then we had another "Aha!" We realized that as we continued to switch customers over to new lines without making permanent repairs, we were reducing the capacity of the cable. Eventually we ran out of cable. That meant we had to go and place a new cable—which meant that we shifted the burden again, this time from one organization to another. Laying more cable was Engineering's problem; it no longer belonged to Repair. The burden shifted from one organization's budget to another's—and yet we kept blaming individuals.

The causal loop diagram in Figure 4.1 was a seminal document. It told the story, showing how the TELSAM measures, customer satisfaction, the barbecues, and the physical issues of the trouble reports all interacted.

This shared, systemic picture of reality gave the team the ability to challenge the TELSAM barbecues because it showed very clearly that the way we were interpreting TELSAM was wrong. For example, customer comments like "Not fixed the first time" were made *not* because the technician screwed up, but because of our policy. We "repaired" a customer complaint by switching the customer to another twisted pair in the cable—which meant that the problem wasn't really fixed for good. It would occur again. Sixteen percent of our customers said, "Every time it storms, I lose my telephone service." A customer's comment that the repair "took too long" was based on *their* definition of time versus *our* definition of time.

Not only that, we were exhausting all our repair forces and at the same time creating more work for Engineering! It was all right there on the systems diagram. The diagram also showed that the TELSAM barbecue was the result of this inappropriate measurement. It focused on the technician, not the experience of the customer.

The other thing that became clear was that customers didn't understand why all this happened. And the truth was, we could anticipate these problems. The reason we didn't was because we looked at each of these trouble reports as individual, isolated cases, not as elements in a pattern. Could we, in fact, find out about the problems ahead of time? The answer was, "We never really looked, but sure we can!" This is the issue of preventative versus reactive maintenance, which eventually became a key focus of our intervention.

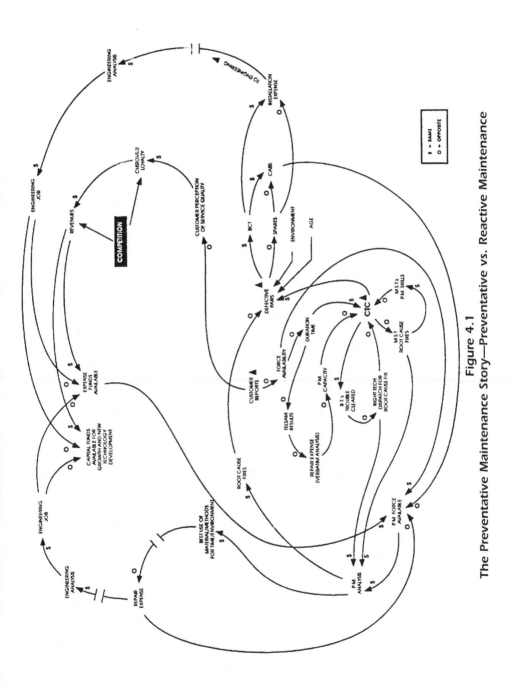

Figure 4.1

The Preventative Maintenance Story—Preventative vs. Reactive Maintenance

Our next step was to go out into the field to verify this picture. We talked with the people in the field and asked: "Is this really what happens? Is this really how we do it?" They helped us confirm that our picture was correct.

Once we verified everything in the field, we had the ammunition we needed to challenge some assumptions. Our measurement system was considered to be sacrosanct, but we started saying to people that there were flaws; it wasn't necessarily measuring what we thought it measured. We had been misinterpreting the results and coming up with bad policy as a result.

> **Dan Mlakar:** People began to acknowledge that the measurement contributing to the TELSAM persecution in the field was broken. Until it was fixed, you couldn't improve service. You needed to break the cycle of blame, to speak with data and facts, and to bring in another method of improving service beyond TELSAM.

Proving Our "Hypothesis"

Bert: One of the VPs was a big proponent of TELSAM and we argued about it. He challenged me and I said, "You've got to trust me on this." But he said, "You prove it to me." So I said, "OK. Give me a group in the field and let me direct them. We *will* prove it. Let's watch those results." That was the whole ethic of the business at that point. *You prove it and you can go somewhere.*

This VP had confidence in me because I came from the line, so he gave me the field group. Of course, this was a risk. My credibility would have been zero if this hadn't worked, but I believed in what the data was showing. Especially when I saw everything coming together on the systems diagram. I also believed that I had minimized extraneous risk by pulling in competent people to drive it, because you always run the risk of having the right idea, but implementing it badly.

So I took the risk and it paid off. We did a pilot based on our theory and it worked. It came through like gangbusters! We got a 26 percent reduction in trouble reports, and saved the company millions of dollars.

As a result, we changed the practice of the TELSAM barbecues, which had been our method for dealing with trouble reports for years and years. It was finally abandoned because we were able to use systems dynamics to show that the practice was actually counterproductive and did not solve the trouble report problem. Instead, preventive maintenance became a big thing. We identified a number of interventions and we did most of them.

This project worked because we had all the ingredients of success:

- We had hard data.

- The project was done by a line group though it was directed by the staff group.
- We had theory behind it (shown in the causal loop diagrams) that drew on practical expertise.
- We had demonstrable results.

These were all things the company valued.

Because of this work, I was made Service Policy and Quality Vice President. Our achievement made me even more certain that *proving it* was the secret to success. But I was about to learn that even that conviction was up for grabs.

In Search of a Strategy: The Challenge of Diffusion

Bert: Because we ended up being very successful with the trouble report reduction project, I wanted to take it to the next step. I wanted to give all our district managers the means to get those same results. My enthusiasm for this came out of the highest principle of TQM, which was to share and replicate. So my next step was to find an effective diffusion strategy.

Dan Mlakar, who had been the systems thinking guru on our team and was also very committed to OL, suggested that we engage all the district managers in a learning process using the causal loop diagrams we had created as a tool to facilitate their learning about the patterns we had discovered. I didn't agree with that approach. I didn't think it would lead to a successful diffusion. First of all, I knew that "learning" wouldn't be considered mainstream and it would therefore be suspect. Secondly, I didn't want to take this causal loop diagram around and try to explain it to each of them. We had tried that when we first went out in the field, but we found that people found the diagrams very confusing. They weren't accustomed to thinking in loops and they were concerned that drawing diagrams wasn't "real" work.

Again, I was assessing our culture. My view was that you have to build your change strategy on the working model of how change actually happens in your organization. Therefore you have to see the culture you're operating in as clearly as you can and accept that culture as it is. I have a strong belief that you need to work *with* the culture, not against it. I've long been a believer of the biological rejection phenomenon.

My assessment was that our organization had an immediate gratification-type culture. There was a very low tolerance level for trusting any kind of process that people didn't easily understand—like systems diagrams. Secondly, my organization was geographically dispersed throughout California, and I knew it was very difficult to replicate a successful practice from one location to another, largely because of resistance. Everybody feels that their area is different.

On top of that, my working assumption (based on my SWOT analysis) was that there were only two reasons why this company would ever adopt anything new. The first reason was because somebody in authority said to do it. That's the "push" strategy. Anything that was blessed from on high had a better shot at getting done—although even that didn't always work because, again, there was lots of resistance on the local level.

The other reason was because somebody got tremendous results doing something different. That's because this culture was very success-oriented. It was a very "show me" culture. It required a lot of data and results. And it was more averse to risk than you would normally expect. The good part of that was that once you had the data to prove that you had results, the innovation tended to be adopted and readily diffused throughout the organization. But until that time, it only took one or two people, at any level, any place, to shoot it down—and there was a natural tendency to shoot it down. The devil's advocate position was alive and well.

I wanted to create that "pull." That's why I had to first prove that it could be done—and we did. My initial theory of change was pretty simplistic, and it was also idealistic. It was something like the movie *Field of Dreams*. You know, "build it and they will come." And it seemed to be working. After we had the original success with the trouble report project a lot of people said they were interested in getting those same results. But then I realized that it wasn't that simple. That's when it became clear to me that they wouldn't try it unless I could prove to them that they could be successful with it as well. How was I going to do that?

I got the idea that I had to get our innovation packaged into some kind of vehicle that would enable the results to be easily mass-produced yet at the same time be customizable by the various field groups. I thought I could accomplish that by developing a simulation. My thinking was that if people saw a simulation—a model—that they liked, and if they saw that it could bring them better results, they might go for it.

I was personally very excited about the potential of simulations in our company. A simulation could get to people's personal belief systems. I believed that I already had a lot of intellectual, conceptual agreement at the company to the fact that we had lots of examples of poor decisions and no way to simulate the results beforehand. So my plan was to create a simulation model that would enable us to spread the innovation we'd had with trouble reports to all of the business units.

We spent a lot of money and a lot of time working with someone from MIT, but it all came to naught. In the end, the model couldn't meet expectations—despite a whole year of work. That was very disappointing because a lot of line people came to see the model as it was progressing and they indicated a high degree of interest. I really think that if it worked we could have broken through.

That failure of the simulation put a negative spin on organizational learning. It came down to a simple equation: If OL can give us the right results, then it is good; if OL can't give us results, then it is bad. I wasn't able to leverage the positive results that we had with our trouble reports. I believed that our success was directly attributable to OL, but we were not able to make the results replicable. I was really disappointed.

Learning, Again

Bert: I realized that I had become so excited about the success with trouble reports that I made a big jump. We had proved the concept! We published results and I got a lot of people hepped up about it. We saved millions and millions and customer satisfaction went up and everyone got a reward. We were heroes! I was so euphoric about the success that I wasn't disciplined in my thinking. I made some assumptions. In particular, I made the assumption that I could use a simulation to replicate the work my team had done in the pilot. This was a major leap because when we did the pilot my team and I went out in the field and gathered a lot of new data. We worked directly with people to make sure that we were capturing all the accurate data. It was very laborious, very hands-on, and manual as hell.

We couldn't do that for every district, and the other district managers refused to do all the manual data tracking that we'd done in the pilot. They said, "We're downsizing. I'm not going to take on a manual tracking process." So we were in a bind. I had to develop a simulation but I didn't have the data. So what did we do? We tried to build a simulation without sufficient data.

In my view, it was a disaster. I didn't understand that it was like going from a laboratory environment to an industrial strength environment. We really had dual requirements: to make it user friendly, and also to make it data rich. Because the model was incapable of dealing—or we were incapable of dealing—with those dual requirements, the simulation fell down. Dan Mlakar has another perspective on what happened.

> **Dan:** The problem was that the people in the field didn't really want a simulation; they wanted a black box that would tell them exactly what countermeasures would produce these kinds of results for them. They wanted to be able to bank on it.
>
> We didn't have the data to do that for them so we ended up building something in between a simulation and a black box. I think we realized there was tension between the black box that everyone wanted and what we could actually deliver.

Iva: So the original idea was that each of the district managers could select his or her individual variables and come up with a formula that was right for him or her?

Bert: Right. And customize it.

Iva: Was there another approach you might have taken?
Bert: As I said earlier, Dan had suggested another approach.

Dan: Theoretically, we could have taken more of a learning approach. Rather than try to turn the simulation into a black box or a decision support tool, we could have used it as a *microworld* for trying out policy and strategy with Bert's peers. Then people could have thought about what they needed from the top and the bottom of the pyramid to make it happen.

It's hard to position anything successfully like this "down in the mud" because people in the mud are going to be looking for answer machines.

Iva: I see a dichotomy between a) taking a learning approach—which says, if we all learn together we can better deal with the world we're in—and believing enough in your people that they'll respond to that, versus b) short-cutting the learning and providing people with the answers. Maybe I'm being simplistic but that seems like what you were trying to do.
Bert: I was very convinced that taking the learning approach in this environment would get us nowhere. In fact, it might get us in a lot of hot water. So I wasn't going in that direction.

Dan: We didn't have the freedom to expose people's thinking and to ask questions like, what do you think is going on here? We didn't have the freedom to expose mental models or double-loop learning. We could only take it as far as Bert was willing to take it. And I guess we knew that a generic learning experience would go over like a lead balloon, so we tried to move toward something we called a decision support tool (DST) that would help people make decisions and see the impact if they spent money on countermeasures. We tried to build something too comprehensive and because we lacked real data we guessed how to quantify things. We got caught in the middle. You don't want to be caught in the middle in terms of any kind of market positioning.

The simulation was not successful because the field people wanted a black box. They wanted so much more in the model than we could ever build. They wanted to know things like: What is the cost-benefit of each countermeasure? We couldn't deliver that, although we tried.

But Bert was very clear about his approach: Build it and they will come; prove it and they will come. I understood this approach and we stuck with it. So, that's the road we went down.

The Challenge of Building to Critical Mass

Bert: All the while I was thinking that here was this success, but it was isolated to the technical world. Yet, I was still holding in my mind this corporate transformation that I wanted to have. I realized that in order to have any real effect on the business you have to involve the whole delivery chain, those departments that are each other's customers. So I began to invite people from various other groups to go to OL training.

The intent was to try and seed OL throughout the company. I thought if I could build support in other organizations, eventually I could build critical mass. Yet it seemed that OL would attract only a certain type of person—the ones who are already open, or at least searching for something beyond the normal way of doing business. The rest really require that the value of OL be proven to them, in terms they understand and relate to. So I kept trying. That's why I tried to get a project going with AT&T.

The Third Project: A Failed Collaboration

Bert: My third try at an OL project was an attempt to create a partnership between our company and AT&T. Now that we were divested, we had problems dealing with them. AT&T complained that we weren't giving them a lot of business. But we were fearful of dealing with them because we didn't know how to approach them. Were they a customer? A supplier? Or were they a competitor?

I knew AT&T was also involved in OL, so I thought this was a natural. I thought that by bringing OL tools to bear on these questions that we could bring more clarity to the relationship. We began a series of meetings between representatives from our company and representatives from AT&T. The purpose of the meetings was to discuss the relationship between the two companies and to look at how we can best work together as supplier, competitor, and customer.

After the first two or three meetings, an AT&T representative came back and said, "The AT&T people don't want to play any more." The AT&T representatives were all salespeople. They were measured on sales in the short-term and they did not see how this conversation contributed to that.

Upon reflection I realized that I thought having these conversations was a viable idea because both of our organizations were involved with organizational learning, but I forgot to look closely at the motivation on the other side. I learned that everybody around the table has to see value in what you're trying to do and that you have to be really open to the fact that what's good for the corporation isn't always the same as what's good for individuals. We didn't do sufficient planning.

So, I'd had another disappointment and another miscalculation on my part. I was learning a lot. In fact, I guess one way of looking at it was that I was doing research—by trial-and-error—into what the critical success factors for introducing organizational learning were.

The Fourth Project: A Moment of Truth

Bert: My next challenge arrived on a burning platform: competition. Now that the industry was deregulated, competition was really heating up and at the same time our customer satisfaction was declining, and we knew that meant trouble competitively. There was also pressure from the regulator to improve our service. How were we going to improve customer service *and* be more competitive? Executive management was pretty desperate for ideas and therefore they were willing to try almost anything.

By this time I had service policy responsibility and, of course, service had always been my driving idea. Now it was a formal charter from the company president and the business council.

Again, I had to do quite a bit of up-front analysis to come up with a strategy. I knew that competition was on the horizon. I'd had a lot of experience in operations in our business offices, and I remember a number of customers saying that when they were upset with us, they would love to have another option, but they didn't have a choice. And now I was faced with the fact that for the first time, customers did have a choice.

As I was reflecting about this challenge, an idea began to dawn on me. My sense was that we had to redefine our idea of what "service" was. We had been a monopoly for a long time and, to me, the ultimate image of monopoly was the image of the old Fords. The adage that so aptly described Ford at the time was, "You can have any color you want, as long as it's black." I could see the parallel in our own company. We'd been so used to being a monopoly that we always seemed to be *telling* our customers what they should want and how they should want it. We didn't really have a strong model of putting the customer's wants and needs first.

While reflecting on that, I was struck by the fact that we also had a tremendous history of being superb at service during any kind of crisis—earthquakes, fires, all those things. I mean, we really outshone ourselves and people know that. But it was in regard to the day-to-day operations of our world that our customers were dissatisfied and were therefore saying that they wished they had somebody else. They never said that when there was a crisis, because in a crisis we always did the right thing by the customer. That led me to a very simple conclusion: *Doing the right thing seems to be the answer.* But how could we reawaken this value in the culture so that it was present all the time? And, could we do it without "giving away the store?"

Searching for a Strategy to Shift Culture

Bert: Now that I had the basic idea of what I thought we should create, I went looking for a way to create it. I looked for a strategy and I made the link to TQM. One of the defining characteristics of TQM is respect for people, particularly the people on the front lines. The belief is that the people who are actually doing the work are the people that probably have the answer to how to fix something.

I recalled a story I heard in a "Management for Success" seminar. Gary Heil, the consultant who led the workshop, was marveling at how a certain department store deals with irate customers. He described the usual process where when the customer wants to return something the salesperson and the customer both have to wait for the salesperson's boss to authorize the transaction. Yet, almost inevitably, when the boss comes to sign the authorization, he or she never even looks at it! He or she just signs it! So, the question Heil posed was, "Why do we do this?" It really is absurd—and it's wasteful, not to mention disempowering for the salesperson. And what does it say to the customer, who's kept waiting? Well, we did the same thing. And I thought, "This is the wrong paradigm."

I began to put all that together. I concluded that we really needed to empower—and I hate to use that word because it's becoming such an overused word—*but we really needed to enable the people who are at the front line to do the job that's right for the customer.*

Then I happened to read a book that was written by an individual named Jan Carlzon. It was called *The Moment of Truth* and it was about the transformation of a Swedish airline.[2]

Similar to the telecommunications business, the airline industry has also gone through deregulation. There were many parallels to what our industry was going through—the shake-ups, the competition between the big airlines and the little airlines, and stories about the companies who subsequently disappeared. Everywhere you look in strategic matters the telecommunications industry is being compared to the airline industry, so, it was a good analogy.

I believed that we could build upon Jan Carlzon's approach, similar to the way we had built upon the learnings at Florida Power and Light.

So, for a host of reasons, whether you took it from a strategic point of view or a TQM point of view or a personal point of view, it all came together and I said, "We gotta do this. It's our business to lose. We've got to do this." That's what gave birth to a program that we also called "Moment of Truth." The Moment of Truth (MOT) program was about empowering our employees to serve customers, to do "the right thing" by our customers.

Working with the Culture

Bert: Now that I had a vision and a basic approach, I knew that I had to have a strategy for implementing this idea in our culture without triggering that "biological rejection" phenomenon, an intervention that's rejected by the host. I focused on two key things: finding champions and generating data.

I was able to find a lot of data that backed up my theory. I showed how expensive it was to recover customers that we lose because they're not satisfied. The market literature concluded that it is twice as hard and five times as expensive to recover customers once you've lost them. We also did a lot of statistics work with our own customer service data that supported this idea. So, the conclusion was that in this new, competitive world, it's going to be really important that we develop customer loyalty. The statistics also showed that when we were really good with customers, they appreciated us. And, that translated into repurchasing and recommending us to others.

Taking a Different Tack

Bert: We knew that it would take even more data to convince people of this approach, so we had to find a champion who would support our going into the field and doing some trials so we could get more data and a proof of concept. However, when I initially tried to find support for this Moment of Truth idea there weren't many takers. Of course, I felt disappointed, but I was still sure that it was the right thing to do.

In the meantime things happened; there was a reorganization that slowed us down, but brought in new players who became our champions. Now we could start to make it real. We began by interviewing our frontline folks, about 240 people. We asked our service reps what barriers prevented them from providing good service—and they told us. They talked about how they didn't have enough information because we had cut back on training in order to cut costs. They told us that we had such a strong emphasis on keeping them on the phones that they didn't have any time for meetings where they could share ideas or learn new things. This statement really rang true because we had a measurement we called "accessibility," which tracks how available reps are to answer the phones when our customers call. We drove that measurement very hard. However, there were unintended consequences of driving that number so hard. To improve access we tried to reduce the average time that reps spent with customers which, of course, had a negative impact on customers' service.

One of the key things the frontline employees expressed in the interviews was that they were often caught in a conundrum. They felt like they couldn't satisfy customers because doing so was contrary to some policy we had. For example, we had something called a manager "take-over," which means that when a rep had a customer with a problem, he or she would call in a supervisor to take over the call. When that happened, the supervisor usually did something to placate the customer. Well, there's no reason in the world why the service rep couldn't do that him- or herself, except that, historically, that's not how we did it. It was just like the story the consultant told in the management seminar I spoke of earlier. We automatically invoked the hierarchy while we needlessly kept the customer waiting on the phone.

So we told the reps, "If you know what the right thing to do is, then you do it." All the vast majority of service reps needed was some reassurance that this is what was expected of them and that it was OK for them to do the right thing by customers. The number of manager takeovers dropped dramatically as a result and the frontline people felt much more effective.

One Moment of Truth Leads to Another

Bert: It was a long road from where we were to where we wanted to be. The frontline employees had been through a lot, with downsizing and cutbacks on training and, of course, they were veterans of the "another fine program" syndrome. But because we put the emphasis on telling the truth and on drawing on the strengths inherent in the frontline employees—and because MOT wasn't ever driven from the top down like all of our other programs—we got strong support from the rank and file. One of the most important things that we did in MOT was feed the data back to the people who gave it to us. We did it in a verbatim manner so they could see that we didn't "clean up" the data, that we didn't filter it. As a result, people began to feel that they could trust, and that was the beginning of real change. Even the union helped quite a bit. This was one of those rare occasions where we had both the union and management talking the same talk and walking the same walk. The employees took heart and they started working on removing some barriers to service that we had inadvertently created. It was like what I saw at Florida Power & Light. Management, the union, and the front line were all speaking the same language. I finally got there—in one small, specific case.

We followed our guiding principles; we empowered the front line to get out of the box and take the extra step with customers, to shift their mental models. And in terms of organizational learning, we especially relied upon Dan, our project manager, who became a very proficient networker. He engaged with the line people about some of the OL tools such as ladder of inference, creative tension, and whatever else might have been appropriate in terms of what they were trying to accomplish. Despite the not-invented-here (NIH) barrier, the field offices began to learn from one another about how to serve customers better. When one of the local supervisors translated the MOT idea into a very fundamental approach called "Just Say Yes," it created a big shift in momentum because it built a lot of credibility and was a very viable tool for people to get the idea of what could be and what one could do. That was a milestone. It led to our videotaping service reps who had new ideas and sharing those testimonials across the company. That encouraged new learnings to be transferred.

Again, we were able to change policies, but this time we were also able to affect culture and personal values. I believe that Moment of Truth was very successful.

One Journey Ends

Bert: Unfortunately, our company was not doing so well financially. The huge investment we had made in future technology had drained our resources and as a consequence, we negotiated a "merger" with another, larger company. Although it was referred to as a merger, we were actually bought by the other company—and, of course, things changed substantially. The new emphasis was on growth and sales. Because all the service initiatives now took a back seat to sales, MOT did not continue. I left the company shortly thereafter.

I moved to a fast-paced technological company in Silicon Valley, but found that I was not able to integrate my passion for TQM and learning into that culture, so, regrettably, I chose to leave. It was a pragmatic decision because I assessed that the readiness for learning and continuous improvement wasn't there yet. And for me, that's now becoming essential.

I've learned a lot about what it takes to do organizational learning work. I believe that you have to balance your enthusiasm for this work with pragmatism because it's important to pay attention to the financial aspects of the business. If the underlying fundamentals of the business are in jeopardy and today's success is the issue, then you have to deal with those first so that your organization survives and you are still around to deal with tomorrow's challenges.

It's important to assess your culture and use what you've learned about the culture to make incremental progress rather than trying to lead people where they don't want to go. Though you may not always achieve your loftier goals, above all, leave it better than you found it and take comfort in any step forward, no matter how small. If there's a message that I want to give, it's do that. But I can't tell you how. There's no formula. Just keep looking and assessing. Learn about the system in which you are embedded and how it works. Find out what's sacrosanct and find a way to deal with that. Use champions judiciously. Do the systems diagrams. Develop a working theory. Then try things. Learn from your mistakes. Regroup. Remember.

Endnotes

1. Daniel Kim, *Toward Learning Organizations: Integrating Total Quality Control and Systems Thinking* (Cambridge, MA: MIT Sloan School of Management, 1990).

2. Jan Carlzon, *Moments of Truth* (Cambridge, MA: Ballinger Publishing, 1987).

Chapter 5

Debriefing Bert's Story

What can we learn from Bert's story? How can it help us to learn more about how to change our organizations? First, let's review some of the issues that Bert faced in his organization.

- The divestiture from AT&T and the rise of competition triggered confusion over identity, core values, and competencies.

- Bert perceived that the company tended to be a closed system; within the larger system were many other, smaller, similarly closed systems. He saw this as having both positive and negative consequences. The positive consequence was that the company—and the business units within the company—protected themselves from quickly adopting bad ideas. The negative consequence was that there were major barriers to sharing innovations and learning. The not-invented-here phenomenon was alive and well.

- With divestiture and competition came a need for new ideas, but also a tendency to reject them. Some ideas could be sanctioned and brought into the culture, providing they were proven successes on the outside. TQM was a good example. But even these ideas had difficulty taking root and growing. Ideas tended to be championed by someone—an executive—but then dropped rather abruptly if and when the champion moved on. A kind of "another fine program" or "flavor of the month" mentality began to develop; new ideas began to be viewed with the skeptical attitude of "this too shall pass."

- The system functioned through the use of legacy processes that had not been tested in a competitive environment.

There was pressure to improve, but that often translated into assigning blame. In lieu of a better approach this became a method for solving problems. As a consequence, poor processes were perpetuated and the culture tended to be punitive.

- When the company embraced TQM, it opened the door for finding root causes, reasons that were outside the individual and embedded in processes. But, as Bert observed, TQM was necessary but not sufficient; it did not have all of the tools necessary to evaluate a process and make lasting improvements, especially from a systemic point of view. TQM alone did not have the tools to deal effectively with high levels of complexity.

- Systems thinking held the potential of finding points of leverage not only for improving processes but also for moving the organization beyond its crises, but there was a major barrier. Systems thinking and organizational learning arrived at a time when the company was recovering from a public embarrassment over a recent attempt to recover and create collective meaning, identity, and values: Leadership Development.

The Organization's Learning System

There is some anecdotal evidence that Bert's organization had a limited learning system. A strong command-and-control environment tends to reinforce the values (i.e., governing variables) and behaviors that instill a Model I learning system. Through Bert's eyes, we can observe these other cultural realities that constrained—and helped create—the organization's learning system. For example:

- Assumptions, such as the view that customer service necessitated increased cost, were generally unquestioned. The assumption that "time is money" is a case in point.

- Another prevailing—and unassailable—assumption was that "you got the results you measured." However, in some key instances, the measurements that were in place did not measure what people thought they were measuring. Consequently, the results obtained were the opposite of the results desired. Still, questioning those assumptions did not come easy.

- Problems (such as the high number of trouble reports) were often solved by finding the individuals who were thought to be responsible and blaming them—rather than finding the root source of the problem, which was often embedded in methods or processes. Another method for resolving problems was to shift the burden (a systems archetype) from one department to another, as in the case of shifting the responsibility for cable utilization from Repair to Engineering.[1]

- The organization seemed to create undiscussibles and had no tools for making them discussible again.

- There was some evidence of defensive routines. Bert believed people could not communicate negative messages so he had to seek out what he called "air cover," someone who could find out and tell him what people were really thinking.

- The fallout from the Leadership Development program seemed to indicate that there was no infrastructure to support acquiring a deeper understanding of what happened. Instead, the organization seemed to learn that organizational change efforts were potentially dangerous and programs that involved "thinking" were to be avoided.

Limited Learning

The fallout that Leadership Development experience provides helps us see how limited organizational learning systems work. Bert's company's reaction to their experience with Leadership Development looks like learning. The company's leadership found itself swept up in a movement that was actually so disturbing to some employees that they went public with their protests. As a result, executive management learned to be highly suspicious of any sort of sweeping, charismatic program that endeavored to change their thinking. Therefore, by virtue of the use of the very term "thinking," systems thinking became suspect.

Did this reaction constitute organizational learning? Or did it represent something else? We might interpret these events by suggesting that Bert's company created a defensive routine to protect itself from experiencing further embarrassment or threat. In a positive sense, the organization protected itself from being swept away by similar evangelical programs. However, the unintended consequence of this defense routine seems to be that it prevented people from identifying and dealing effectively with the deeper, root cause of the embarrassment or threat. As a result, the organization may have limited its own learning.

Values as a Source of Vision

It's within this context that Bert sought to begin his organizational learning work. The desire to create change often comes with an initial dissatisfaction that transforms into creative energy. Bert's source of creative energy was rooted in his personal values. Bert had a central driving idea and core value: customer service. This driving idea was deeply rooted in his personal value system. It had stood the test of time; it persisted even when the organizational values could not or would not support it.

Bert: I wanted to transform the direction the company was going. The cost cutting, the reduction of service to the customer, the hurt the employees were having, the antagonism with the union, all these things were irritants to me. I wanted us all to grow together and have personal goals and corporate goals be in alignment. I thought that was the key to success.

I saw the beginnings of that alignment at Florida Power and Light. While I didn't talk to them about how they handled such things as downsizing and cost cutting, I did look into how they handled customer service and I was amazed. They had a very intricate system that allowed for customers to directly impact their policies. For example, one of their earlier corporate policy statements did not include the number one concern that customers had, which was nuclear safety. They put that in only after they did an investigation into customer concerns. But the point is, they did it. I saw the customers really influencing company policies and I thought it was the way things should be done.

There was flow there. I saw that. When the value system and the personal and corporate objectives fall in line, it's powerful.

Bert's Challenge: The Dichotomy of Service vs. Cost

Bert also had a central core belief—a working theory: he believed that good customer service made good business sense. He did not believe that the adoption of this value would take the business away from bottom-line results but would instead support greater profits. Bert also believed that OL was the pathway for bringing personal and corporate values into alignment.

Bert: I believed that you could have both customer service and economic viability at my company. Based on my experience with TQM I also believed that the people closest to the work have the answers. The challenge is to value and include them.

Because of the emphasis that OL has on being open to listening to people, I thought that OL was the way to create that win-win scenario. That was why I thought the trouble report project seemed so good, because I thought we could reduce the dissatisfaction of customers and save money at the same time. We could also help employees because they were sick and tired of working crazy hours to fix problems and then being "barbecued."

Bert's thinking was directly opposed to the assumptions that seemed to be driving his company. How had this come to be?

Bert recalled that in the old AT&T culture, the operating philosophy was "service at any cost." This philosophy was workable because costs were directly reimbursable through rate hikes. Essentially, the customer bore the cost burden of service. Then, with crisis, came cost cutting. The prevailing assumption was that cutting back on cost necessitated cutting back on service, since service had always represented added cost. Also, a new strategy had been put in place: Harvest the core to fund new business ventures. The crisis and this new strategy seemed to create a disintegrating sense of identity and confusion over core values within the company. All of this had consequences for customer service. An overcorrection developed which was self-reinforcing.

- A compliant workforce, produced by the traditional command-and-control culture and reinforced by metrics, conformed to the cost-cutting ethos by tending to protect the company from customers, leading to lowered customer satisfaction;

- The primary focus on cost containment was reinforced by a new focus on measurements and short-term performance. A form of measurement was needed by the company to help determine how it was faring in the new competitive environment; the measurements provided an important feedback loop. Now measurement became the focus and the real issue was forgotten. The intention was to contain costs, but numbers became so important that the focus was on them.

- As a result, customer service suffered. The impact could be measured, but the path to correction was unclear.

Good measurements can support the Model II governing variable of valid information. Ironically, however, if quantitative measurements become exclusive or all-important, the focus on these quantitative measures can disable other important capacities. The consequence in Bert's company was that culture began to only value the things that can be measured; the value placed on human relationships—once a traditional strength of the company—began to diminish. Question: How many times do we overcorrect for one problem and then experience unintended consequences?

We often see values as opposed to business results. Bert believed that this was a false opposition and he wanted to change it. But Bert was not operating purely out of humanistic ideals. He sought proof. And in this way he was very much operating by a Model II governing variable: valid information.

Bert's Initial Strategy and Tactics

Senge notes that most business managers usually begin change projects with some implicit theory of change in mind. Although he would be loath to use the word "theory," Bert was no exception. Like any successful executive, he was interested in what factors would be critical to his continued success. Bert based this strategy on his experience. He had seen ideas become adopted when a guru was brought in to sell them. They subsequently became the "flavor of the month."

Bert also believed that personal relationships were a key to making things successful. Enthused and excited about the potential of OL himself, he was sure that a spark would be ignited in others from the company if he could just bring the prophet to the flock. Therefore, his initial, quick survey of the territory led him to two tactical decisions. He would:

1. Bring in expertise that is recognized and validated on the outside.
2. Use personal influence to bring a prospect (a line VP) to the table.

Bert believed that he had identified the proven engines of change in his organization.

Bert's Theory of Change

Underlying Bert's strategy was a working theory of how thing worked in his organization. As part of his SWOT assessment, Bert concluded there were only two reasons why his company would ever adopt anything new: "One reason is because somebody in authority says so, therefore it's blessed and anything that's blessed from on high gets done. And the other reason is that if they can see that somebody's doing something different and it's giving them a tremendous result, then everybody wants to know how they did it." Bert further mused, "My initial theory of change was something like the movie, *Field of Dreams*. You know, 'Build it and they will come.'"

In *The Dance of Change* (1999), Senge says that most managers have an implicit theory of growth and change that he calls the "better mousetrap theory." When managers operate according to this theory, they tend to believe that if an innovation or change initiative is successful, interest will spread; i.e., "our results will speak for themselves." Senge says that it generally doesn't work this way. What happens is:

1. Innovations, in fact, don't spread;

2. Innovators are often at risk even when they produce results; and

3. This theory causes people to focus on picking "low hanging fruit," i.e., they constrain their learning efforts, constructing them such that they can get practical results quickly.

Senge goes on to say that operating according to this implicit theory of growth is not *wrong*, but it tends to blind leaders to the deeper issues that their changes will eventually reveal and to their inability to deal with these issues. Thus, they fail to develop the learning capabilities needed to sustain change.[2]

Essentially, then, Senge holds that this implicit theory of growth will not be effective. It will not result in diffusion even if practical business results are achieved quickly. Not only that, but their success and visibility may put an innovator at risk despite producing good business-relevant results.

Strategy: Identifying the Wellsprings of Transformation

In *The Dance of Change* (1999), Senge et al. also express the view that one needs to take a biological perspective on change. Senge posits that there are three fundamental, interdependent, self-reinforcing processes that sustain profound change by building upon each other. Therefore, by definition, any organizational learning change process must start by creating conditions whereby these processes are set in motion. What are these reinforcing processes?

- **Personal results**—Senge says that once people experience living their lives more closely to the way they really want to live, their passion will emerge and it will be a self-sustaining source of energy.

- **Networks of committed people**—Galvanized individuals are necessary but not sufficient; they must also be organized into networks. The reason is that networks are key to helping innovations diffuse; as agents of diffusion, networks are superior to hierarchical channels.

- **Improvement in business results**—Finally, besides the personal commitment and the network organization, OL change efforts must be linked to business results. It is insufficient to simply feel good.

Linking organizational learning to business results may be the most critical source of reinforcement, but it can be problematic. As we stated earlier, the impact of OL on business results is often hard to assess, difficult to attribute, and, because learning takes time, there are often significant delays before any kind of result occurs. How long will the organization wait? If you perceive that the organization cannot wait long, you can begin by eliminating wasteful practices, Senge suggests, but "even if a pilot group becomes acknowledged for achieving significant business results, the larger organization can respond by killing the innovative process."[3]

Along with setting in motion the three reinforcing processes, in *The Dance of Change* Senge et al. describe four challenges that often arise at the beginning of an OL effort. These four challenges are:

- **No time**—There is no time to do this.

- **Not relevant**—This "learning stuff" is not relevant to our "real" work.

- **Walk the talk**—You're saying all this stuff about change but your actions don't match up. You behave the same way you always did.

- **No help**—We don't have the help we need to get going.[4]

These challenges must be worked with in order for the change effort to take root. To what extent does Bert's theory of change and his experience bear out what Senge says?

Interpreting Bert's Approach

Unfortunately, Bert's first experiment failed so utterly (in his mind) that he had to seek reassurance that his job was not in jeopardy. Could things have gone differently on that first project attempt?

Bert had seen the tactic of bringing in a "guru" to sell an idea work in the past—or had it? Ideas brought in by gurus seemed to become the "flavor of the month," but they did not necessarily have a lasting impact. Was there a deeper reason why such ideas did not stick around, outlasting their champions? Could this fit the pattern Argyris has identified? (See the Introduction.)

Our recognition that good ideas become "fads" and "flavors of the month" indicates that we may be making some fundamental errors in the way that we introduce new ideas into organizations. In particular, if we try to force-fit learning into that pattern we may kill it before it has a chance to take root. Even more to the point, learning is in direct conflict with this approach. The implication is that leaders must make the shift at the very beginning, that their very first action must show that they are opening up a space for learning. It is not easy to come to terms with this because fear will arise: the fear of being clumsy as well as the fear of rejection, of appearing to be too different. Yet, there must be a moment when the leader makes a definite decision to follow a different path—a learning path—and to do so with both subtlety and humility.

The need for subtlety and humility seems to show up in the way people in Bert's organization reacted to the suggestion that they begin the meeting by talking about the "undiscussables."

Seen within the context of Argyris's work, this may have been important, but it was also premature. It felt like an attack because neither the values nor the skills for moving from Model I to Model II were in place. Nor had people agreed to begin this learning. The ability to abandon the need to save face or to question deep assumptions had not been cultivated and therefore the suggestion (by the people from MIT OLC) would certainly be challenged.

Another factor contributing to the collapse of Bert's first project attempt was that Bert did not engage any other sources of support (such as those identified by Senge et al.) that might have helped his initial idea catch fire. As a consequence, there was no pull. No one was able to see how they would achieve personal results, nor was it clear how business results would be achieved— and, while Bert tapped into his personal network, there was no strong network of people who were inherently committed to a learning approach.

Learning from the First Project Attempt

Bert didn't have the benefit of Senge's thinking when he encountered the early challenges described in *The Dance of Change* in his first project attempt. Thus, he responded to them in his own way. Essentially, he reacted to them rather than anticipated them, and the solutions he devised tended to be defensive rather than generative. For example, the negative reaction he experienced from the line VP reinforced his determination to connect OL to business results so that OL would not be seen as irrelevant. Similarly, when the line people pushed back on the issue of time, this may have triggered him to overcompensate by trying to do too much himself.

In terms of finding help, Bert had thought that he could just rely on personal relationships as an engine for change, but that backfired. While he might have engaged in a process of inquiry to understand why and to perhaps get at some deeper assumptions, he instead leapt to make a correction in his strategy. He determined that if he couldn't rely on his network of relationships to support his getting a learning effort going, then he would go underground, focus inward, and build a small learning team. Bert did seek help in the form of "air cover." He asked his boss to tell him when and if he overstepped his bounds, but he did not seek help with the larger question, how do I initiate learning in a culture that is highly suspicious of unfamiliar ideas?

Bert also determined that he had to be careful about how he introduced OL into the organization, because it was foreign to the culture and that would most likely result in its rejection. So one of his first steps was to eliminate all the OL jargon in order to make OL look more like the existing culture.

Learning and Limitations

After his first project didn't get off the ground, Bert did a SWOT analysis that told him there were limits to what he could attempt. Bert was not at the top of the hierarchy and he had determined that support from the top was minimal at best. Therefore, it would not have been politically prudent for him to attempt too much, such as addressing the organizational learning system directly. Rather, he tried a more indirect strategy: he attempted to use the culture to change the culture. In other words, by acknowledging the limits of the culture's learning system, he could find ways to leverage that learning system in order to get the results that he saw were in the long-term interests of the firm. In essence, Bert found a "work-around."

In many respects, this was an ingenious strategy, one that dealt exceedingly well with Bert's current reality. However, the strategy created its own conundrums and paradoxes. In trying to work around the limitations of the organization's embedded learning system, Bert was trying to do the learning for the organization. This is very apparent in the simulation project.

Simulation: The Failure of Diffusion

Bert's trouble report pilot project was a success in the business's terms. He successfully investigated and challenged some loosely held assumptions, an excellent example of double-loop learning. Yet he was convinced that the rest of the organization wasn't ready to learn in this way. After the initial success he went on to develop a strategy for diffusing the learning. However, he ran into roadblocks. He sensed that people in the organization were not invested in learning about how to get the results themselves, so he essentially tried to devise a strategy whereby the simulation (or black box) could do the learning for them. This dilemma sensitizes us to the ways in which limited learning systems can impede getting results. It also shows us how, as leaders, we can leap into making heroic attempts rather than taking the risk of trying to engage with others in collaborative problem-solving.

Dan Mlakar added, "We took Bert's approach which was 'Prove it and they will come.' But I do think that you have to generate personal results and business results. I still believe that's true. How you get there is a real big decision."

In Dan's view, you cannot begin an OL effort as a "lone ranger"; you can't single-handedly lead a learning effort. Nor can you use OL to create commitment and creativity in people if it isn't already there. The better approach is to find people who are inherently committed to a learning approach and then begin to activate the development of a mutually supportive network:

Dan: The bottom line is that you need proactive, creative people who are both close to the resources and close to the results. They need to balance practice (with learning tools and techniques) and performance. This is a prerequisite. Creativity and commitment must already be in the organization in the right place. You can't create this commitment with OL; it has to be inherent in the make-up of people. You've got to find the people, the line leaders who have it already.

The key learning for me was that you can't circumvent the learning. You don't even have to build a microworld to start the learning. Just start with some causal loops on policy exploration, decision making, understanding assumptions, side effects, etc. You need to explore mental models in a casual, friendly way.

I am convinced that if Bert had gotten his potential early adopters (district managers) in a "hostage" situation with some systems thinking experts, things might have been different. These systems thinking experts were just magical in their ability to take a complex situation and scope it out using causal loop diagrams. If we'd done that some of our guys may have begun to see the value in learning and thinking this way. The reason I think this is because the Beer Game is such a powerful tool. It's a real eye-opener. It's a concrete experience in a risk-free environment. And it works. Everybody learns from the Beer Game.

But people have to be committed to getting a sense of policy and strategy; they have to be committed to double-loop learning. There is some important foundation stuff that has to be there. People have to be willing to engage with mental models and deal with the ladder of inference because those are the fundamental tools to explore why you do what you do. That foundation is required (but it wasn't there).

Dan's suggested strategy takes us in the other direction. Rather than doing the learning for the organization by creating a black box (as Bert attempted to do), Dan suggests that key people in the organization can be enticed into learning if they can personally experience its benefits. In other words, if they begin to experience personal results, learning might become valued. This is similar to a strategy that Senge et al. describe in *The Dance of Change*. When facing a diffusion challenge they suggest bringing together a group of key, yet diverse people to engage in a skillful, facilitated discussion about the diffusion challenge. This is a suggestion that could have enabled Bert to share the responsibility for diffusion rather than shouldering it all himself. But did Bert and others have the capacity to engage in such generative conversations? As Argyris has pointed out, managers often have communication difficulties in these areas. The inability to communicate well up and down a hierarchy and across divisions is a major threat to successful change efforts.[5]

Another aspect of Bert's theory was the conviction that you had to "use the culture to change the culture." Bert used this idea to remind himself not to challenge the organization's culture directly. The area of culture and its relationship to organizational change and learning needs much more attention than we are able to provide here, so we only pose a question: Would it have been helpful to Bert's change effort if he had been able to do a more extensive cultural assessment?

The Third Project: A Missed Opportunity

Bert's third project, the attempt to create a mutually rewarding relationship with AT&T, was defeated early on by not meeting the initial challenges of relevancy and time. The AT&T participants did not see the relevancy to their performance, which was measured in the short-term, and therefore did not believe they could devote the time to the conversations.

Learning efforts all require a certain amount of what we call "ground zero preparation work." We need to spend the time to prepare the ground for learning. In particular, we need to balance our advocacy with inquiry, asking the questions that need to be asked before we begin, questions like: What do we want to create? Who should be involved? How can we all benefit? The reinforcing growth processes that will bolster the development and sustainability of the project also need to be uncovered and nurtured. In this case the reinforcing growth processes identified by Senge et al.—personal results, networks of committed people, and business results—did not appear to be in evidence. The challenges to initiating that Senge has also identified, relevance, time, etc., also need to be anticipated. Due to a lack of understanding and the rush to do the project (because that's what businesspeople are good at), Bert did not do all of the ground zero work to ensure that the project had a chance of succeeding.

The collapse of this collaboration shows how Model I learning systems can prevent us from getting the results we truly want. Issues of relevancy and time can sometimes provide handy

excuses for not working the tough issues. We often let an inefficient, painful, or even absurd situation continue rather than to
challenge the conditions that keep it in place. The limited learning system undermines commitment and, of course, the lack of
commitment reinforces the limited learning system.

The Fourth Project: Moment of Truth

The Moment of Truth (MOT) project was Bert's most successful
project, primarily because crisis created an opening for a new
approach. Management was out of ideas and something new had
to be tried. Crisis had weakened the existing learning system.

MOT also had the following:

- A well-thought-out theory of change that kept evolving
  based on feedback.

- At least two of Senge's reinforcing growth processes were in
  play from the beginning. Both business results and personal
  results seemed possible on multiple levels. These results
  were beginning to be experienced by some executive and
  line managers, the front line, and the union.

- The project was able to find and connect the people who
  had a sense of commitment to the project. Therefore it could
  bypass the early challenges of initiating: no time and not relevant.

- They found champions who truly did walk the talk. In particular, the VP-level champion was willing to reveal that he
  did not "know all the answers."

- There was sufficient help in the beginning stages and
  throughout.

- While the idea for the program began with Bert, the program
  itself took on a very grassroots flavor rather than be a program that was rolled out from the top down. The VP-level
  champion was obviously and openly committed to providing freedom of choice. Without explicitly saying so, he advo-
  cated the Model II values and behaviors.

- As a result of the proven interest in obtaining and sharing
  valid information and allowing freedom of choice, a network of committed people, including the union, evolved. In
  a sense, MOT validated the power of Model II and revealed
  how readily it could be set in motion—providing the conditions were right and the proper values were in place.

These were strong initial conditions. Senge et al. have also
identified challenges that can hinder a learning effort in the later
stages. These challenges didn't seem to pose significant threats

because fear was acknowledged and discussed openly. Also, because of the deliberate openness and choice—a hallmark of the Model II theory-in-use—there were no "true believers" in the threatening sense. People were free to do what they thought best. However, Senge et al.'s challenge of assessment still proved somewhat problematical. Evidence of results was looked for, and measures themselves were looked at. Although the program made sense in every other way, it was hard to prove that empowering front line employees to do what's best for the customer was the most effective business strategy from a financial perspective.

Although the MOT program was not in place that long (perhaps just over a year), it began to have an effect on the organization in which it began. In effect, the program began to address the challenge of governance by implicitly and explicitly questioning the long-embedded tendency to invoke hierarchy. More decisions were made at the local level and at the front line level. Local organizations had the latitude of choice which was antithetical to the traditional approach of one-size-fits-all. There were also several successful transfer-of-learning efforts. Ultimately, however, MOT was not sustained. It met up with the challenge of strategy and purpose when the buy-out/merger occurred. It did not survive the merger.

Learning and Leadership

Without ever naming it as such, Bert was sensitive to the aspects of himself and his culture that reflected Model I. Of course, this dissonance did not show up as a theoretical construct. Instead, it came to him as a feeling that something wasn't quite right and that potential was being lost.

> **Bert:** Most of the people who worked for me in the early days would say I was a Theory X manager.[6] But then different things started happening that bothered me. For example, I perceived that the company was actually being run as if it were made up of fiefdoms. Each of the fiefdoms was sort of a closed club. Everybody was running their fiefdom; they followed the party line and they were very much control freaks. Although I had elements of that in my personality as well, it wasn't really satisfying and I didn't think it was in the best interests of the company. But I wasn't sure what the alternative was.

A logical consequence of Model I theory-in-use in the business environment is that fiefdoms form. Individual managers are concerned with controlling and winning; there are battles over turf and people advocate their points of view. These behaviors can continuously bolster each other, creating a self-reinforcing system. In this atmosphere, concern for the collective well-being is minimized. In Bert's view this was characterized as typical command-and-control or "Theory X behavior." Why did Bert begin to turn away from this style of management?

Bert: I really started to feel differently when I went to the executive program at MIT in '91. I was in a class of 47 people from 22 countries and we had 3 months of intensive living together. We were all assigned "buddies" and my buddy happened to be from Japan. I realized that he had a whole different perspective on the world. His basic issue was whether or not things were in harmony. He used the word every day. For example, he would draw a Venn diagram. The three circles represented family life, personal life, the corporation. He would show them overlapping and talk about their being in harmony. That just stayed in my mind.

So when I got back to work I wanted to try to change some things. And since I was having good results, I was given a certain amount of leeway. But it was a hard transition. It was much easier to be successful by being the way everybody else seemed to be. But it just didn't feel good anymore.

Bert's shift began when he first sensed discomfort, but his real change effort began when he had a close and prolonged encounter with someone who had a different perspective. He began to sense that his present lens was not the only way of looking at the business world and he began to consider an alternative. As a consequence, his commitment to bringing personal and corporate values into alignment grew stronger. Yet, being pragmatically oriented, Bert chose to act on that conviction only when he thought there was a viable approach (such as OL) that could produce positive business results *and* when he thought he had sufficient clout and credibility to begin.

In moving forward, however, Bert encountered one of the most difficult challenges facing change leaders: How do you become the type of leader who is embodying the change you wish to bring about? This is the challenge Senge calls "walking the talk," but that term may camouflage its inherent difficulty. When Bert began his own learning group he seemed to be trying to shift his own leadership style, as Dan Mlakar observed:

Dan: Bert was always a Theory X manager looking to be Theory Y. That was the conclusion a number of people in our group reached. I think he was always caught in the middle, asking himself the question: How can you act like Theory Y when you really are kind of Theory X? I think that was his big challenge.

Our mental models constrain the way that we can think and act. For example, we tend to think in terms of dichotomies, so when we think of Theory X or Theory Y management styles they feel like binary categories. So, then, how do we change from one style to the other? We try to act differently, almost as if we could just flip a switch. Then, because we can't consistently stay in our newly adopted style, we tend to oscillate between seemingly binary choices, often confusing others and ourselves.

However, if we think within the context of Model I and Model II we may start to see that the transition is not just a matter of jumping categories; it is a learning process. We no longer expect to make this transition without the benefit of a supportive learning process that would enable us to inquire into and learn more deeply about our leadership styles. We need to be reminded that the journey from Model I to Model II is a collaborative learning process, not a matter of throwing a switch or reprogramming ourselves in isolation from others. Like many leaders, Bert expected himself to be able to negotiate that shift in isolation without feedback, support, or process.

Learning from Bert's Story

Bert's story is about taking a relatively pragmatic path through the uncertain territory of a limited learning system. If Bert's story tells us anything, it focuses us on the importance of values. Values can be galvanizing and they can sustain us.

Bert's story also illustrates the choice that senior managers who are embedded in a Model I learning system (and who are not top management) must make. They must ask themselves a series of questions: First and foremost, do they attempt an organizational learning effort? Are there sufficient conditions to support their doing so? Are there significant signs—as there were in Bert's organization—that deviating from the Model I system is a risky venture? If there are more apparent risks and threats than opportunities or sources of support, is it worth the risk? We have to go even deeper and ask ourselves: Are the risks *real* or are they only apparent? If we don't go to a deeper level of inquiry and if we don't check our conclusions with others, we may be colluding in limiting our own sense of aspiration. We reduce the tension by lowering our vision.

If these potential learning leaders say "yes" to learning, then there are more questions. Are they drawn to this challenge for the good of the organization or because they have a need to be heroes? Do they attempt to bring about learning within the constraints of the existing learning system—or do they attempt to "stretch" toward Model II, invoking the proverbial creative tension? If they choose to attempt learning within the existing (limited) system, how do they avoid reverting to the old ways of limited and accidental learning? Conversely, if they attempt to stretch the organization toward a Model II learning system, how do they create conditions so that they have sufficient support?

Because these questions weren't as yet articulated, Bert was caught in a gap. In his moments of unalloyed pragmatism, Bert accepted the Model I learning system as a given and adjusted his tactics accordingly. Yet, Bert wanted the Model II governing values to be in place; he wanted the organization to operate on the basis of valid information and informed choice. However, he believed that if he deviated too much from the cultural norm he would place himself at too great a risk.

Not surprisingly, the limits in the organizational learning system were mirrored in Bert's own capacity to learn. He needed to have a clearly articulated theory of change that was also open to question. The assumptions underlying that theory of change needed to be open to question as well. However, overall, Bert's personal learning tended to be single-loop (in other words, the detection of error and correcting without questioning deeper assumptions) even as he was attempting to lead an OL effort. Throughout the four projects, Bert was continuously acting, evaluating, and then trying something different. To the extent that his next tactic got him the results he wanted, he was continuously learning because he was able to detect an error and correct it by designing a more effective action. But Bert did not explicitly engage with double-loop learning. Nor did he seek support for this deeper learning process.

This is not to single Bert out for criticism. Studies show that when managers confront open-ended situations, they have a very widespread tendency to use single-loop learning, as Ralph D. Stacey points out in *Managing the Unknowable: Strategic Boundaries Between Order and Chaos in Organizations* (1992). Stacey goes on to say that managers "seldom activate the second loop of reflection." Yet, "When consequences are unknowable and cause-and-effect links extremely unclear, it becomes vital to inquire into the manner in which one is perceiving what is going on. Many problems that managers have with strategic thinking may be traced to their use of an inappropriate kind of learning."[7] Ironically, it is when we most need to do reflection that we are most likely to shy away from it.

By relying on single-loop learning, Bert may have circumscribed his potential for success. The constraints Bert tended to put on his own learning mirrored the external constraints that Bert experienced. There's an insight here that could help other leaders of learning. If leaders want their organizations to truly transform, they must *begin with themselves*, because, as Argyris and Senge both say, individual transformation and organizational transformation go hand-in-hand. As leaders engage in the process of collaboratively learning Model II values (i.e., governing variables) and skills, this learning will begin to create the new system.

Bert's story shines a light on the modest heroism that learning leaders must demonstrate when they are working within the confines of Model I, particularly when they are not at the very top of a hierarchical organization. The resources of such leaders are limited and their options are often constrained. They have to work with what is at hand. There are real risks involved with taking on leading change. The risk has to be worth it. In the middle of the night, when you can't sleep because you're worried that you have it all wrong, you have to feel that in your heart-of-hearts, it's worth the risk.

While Bert's story raises some key questions about leading change, Iva's story raises others. We turn to that next.

Endnotes

1. For more on systems archetypes, please see Peter Senge, *The Fifth Discipline: The Art and Practice of the Learning Organization* (New York: Doubleday, 1990), pp. 378–390.

2. Peter Senge et al., *Dance of Change: The Challenges of Sustaining Momentum in Learning Organizations* (New York: Doubleday, 1999), p. 42.

3. Senge et al., 1999, op. cit., p. 53.

4. For more on "The Challenges of Initiating," please see Senge et al., 1999, op. cit., pp. 67–237.

5. Chris Argyris and Donald Schön, *Organizational Learning: A Theory of Action Perspective* (Reading, MA: Addison-Wesley, 1978), pp. 246–249.

6. For more on Theory X, please see *Leadership and Motivation, Essays of Douglas McGregor*, edited by Warren G. Bennis and Edgar H. Schein with the collaboration of Caroline McGregor (Cambridge, MA: MIT Press, 1966), pp. 5–21.

7. Ralph Stacey, *Managing the Unknowable: Strategic Boundaries Between Order and Chaos in Organizations* (San Francisco: Jossey-Bass, 1992).

Chapter 6

A Visionary Voyage:
Iva's Learning Journey

Iva: Peter Senge's *The Fifth Discipline* has had a profound impact on my thinking about business management and organizational learning. My experience as a business leader has confirmed to me the importance of the principles set forth in this book. In particular, I have learned through practice that to successfully grow a business, one must take into account the interests of multiple stakeholders, and not just the actual shareholders and investors. Customers, suppliers, and employees are all crucial participants in any business operation, and their needs and capabilities for contribution must be accounted for in the business plan.

Deep Aspiration Becomes a Driving Idea

Iva: Although I very much consider myself an American, I was actually born in Europe—in Yugoslavia. From the age of 10 I had a vision: I wanted to leave my homeland because I wanted freedom. I was exposed to the fear and the suppression of people's voices that was so intrinsic to the Communist agenda, and I knew that I did not want to stay in Yugoslavia.[1]

For some very deep reasons, then, freedom is very important to me. Everything that I have done in my life and career—particularly my attempts to change the corporate environment—came from the desire to create greater freedom for myself and for others. However, over time I have learned that freedom is a far more complex concept than I had originally thought. I wanted freedom so much, yet that does not mean that I knew how to be free.

As president of Philips Display Components (PDC), I initiated work on organizational learning. The goal was to create a workplace that would respect the needs of all stakeholders. My hope was that we could put in place an infrastructure that would support learning and, by so doing, we

could create a workplace that was both kinder to people and more productive all around. These efforts yielded small successes in some areas,
and unexpected consequences in others.

Organizational learning was actually the third strategy that I put in
place in the hopes of sustaining the company in the face of enormous
competitive pressures. The story begins with describing those other
strategies in order to set the context. While the other strategies do not
deal with OL *per se*, they describe the challenges we were facing and the
events that finally turned my thinking toward OL as an optimal strategy.
This story also includes the voice of Phil Fazio, my former Chief Financial
Officer. I asked Phil to comment on my story because, as a CFO, I believe
he will offer a pragmatic and balanced perspective on what happened. I
offer this narrative as a "learning story" from which we might draw some
lessons for leading change efforts in the future.

Background

Iva: I joined PDC in the spring of 1983 as VP of Engineering. PDC was
a maker of color picture tubes for use in television sets, which was a very
competitive, global market. At that time PDC had about 2,500 employees
and $250 million in sales. There were two factories, one in upstate New York
where PDC headquarters was also located, and another in rural Ohio.

PDC had been acquired from Sylvania by PDC's new parent company,
North American Philips, in 1981. In turn, North American Philips was 52
percent owned by Philips in the Netherlands with its headquarters and
management located in Europe. At the time, PDC was not fully integrated
into the global Philips business.

I was excited about the opportunity because I had a strong conviction that Philips had the financial and human resources necessary to get
the consumer electronics industry, in particular the components industry
in the U.S., on its feet so that we could be successful global competitors.

First Strategy: Integrate Fresh Ideas, New Technology

Iva: As Engineering VP, I was responsible for product and process
design, product and process implementation into manufacturing, and control of manufacturing processes.

My boss and I were keenly aware, however, that PDC had been
neglected; the previous owner had not made capital investments in quite
some time. The factory was old and had not been upgraded. The equipment
was old, the picture tubes were manufactured using different, less efficient
kinds of processes than those used in other Philips factories, and production
yields were lower. Costs would have to be cut. Capital investments would
have to be made.

We also made the assessment that certain critical technical competencies were lacking.

Therefore, part of our initial strategy was to bring in competence from the outside. I began hiring people from the competition and set about trying to improve our processes.

First Learnings

Iva: Because of my exposure to the Japanese methods while working at my previous company, Zenith, I felt very strongly that TQM would be the path toward achieving some of our objectives. However, there was a lot of resistance to change. The not-invented-here syndrome was alive and well.

I remember sensing the climate at PDC at that time. The company had been acquired by its parent company two years earlier and it was still feeling the effects. The former Sylvania employees saw the Philips people as "conquerors." After they experienced the first sense of relief that comes from knowing that the doors are not going close, they began to realize that the new owners were bringing change and new culture. All of this was not welcomed.

As I began to try to integrate new ideas, I also began to realize that we really did not have a full appreciation of what needed to be done to integrate people, processes, and the machines with which we produce the product. Our focus was totally on technology—which is not surprising since both my boss and I were technologists.

In 1984, after I had been in my job for about a year, the parent company's previously taken decision to move most of the manufacturing to Ohio was implemented and 1,000 people lost their jobs in the town where the factory was located.

Seeing Red

Iva: In 1986, I became president of PDC. When I took over as president I had my work cut out for me. I quickly realized that the projected budget for the company was not achievable. Although we had tried so hard to turn the company around, we still had red ink flowing. We were losing both money and market share.

I believed that the state of the business was such that we had only two choices: either radically restructure the business or close it. I wanted to attempt a radical restructuring. To achieve a turnaround the PDC management team and I needed to marshal all the resources and knowledge that we could. With the approval and support of my European management, I evolved a plan that included bringing both human and financial capital to the enterprise, implementing traditional restructuring, and introducing the principles of total quality management (TQM) as a management philosophy. But the first step involved downsizing.

The Turn-around Strategy

Initial Tactics: Downsizing and Moving

Iva: I offered upper-level management a stopgap strategy to get us out of our immediate problem. The first step in the turnaround was the elimination of the New York factory—which after the first consolidation in 1984 still employed about 400 people—and to consolidate the remainder of manufacturing into our one larger factory in Ohio. I also moved the headquarters in New York closer to the Ohio plant.

I recognized that this was to be another downsizing for the company, and that there had been a lot of downsizing before I became president. I was able to justify it to myself and to the company and its people, however. I believed that, as president, my first and foremost task was to stop the flow of red ink. After completing the downsizing, my task would be to rebuild by aggressively integrating the parent company's and PDC's technology, while also improving product quality and customer service so that we could be competitive again.

I believe that teamwork and management sensitive to people's needs helped smooth the factory closing and the HQ move. I believe that we downsized in as humane a way as possible. And, when we moved the headquarters, everyone was given the option to move. We explained the reasons for the move; we gave people adequate notice; we helped them sell their current homes and get new mortgages; we offered financial assistance for moving and other expenses; and, we had career counseling for spouses. For those who didn't want to move, we offered outplacement services. Approximately 50 percent of the employees moved with the company.

There's a difference between reducing the number of people in a facility and closing the doors and leaving town. I was the one who closed that facility. I still believe that it had to be done and I still believe that people can learn a great deal about themselves from adversity, so sometimes things like this can actually serve people's growth and learning. But it is not easy stuff and I did not want to ever have to downsize again.

Meeting Resistance to the Integration Strategy

Iva: During this time I continued and expanded my initial strategy of infusing fresh ideas, now bringing in technological know-how from the parent company in Europe into PDC.

Again, there was resistance. I perceived that there was mistrust on both sides. Those who were responsible for technology development in the European headquarters were not ready and willing to transfer that technology because they were not sure that we were competent to receive it. They were also very concerned that the technology would leak to the competition, especially the Japanese, whom they greatly feared. So a dance, a kind of tug-of-war, began.

There were also divisions *within* the company that hampered overall productivity. I discovered that the engineering department did not feel responsible for either the costs nor any losses incurred in manufacturing its designs. In other words, they were never asked to take responsibility beyond design.

Creating Culture as a Tactic

Iva: As we were working on the many issues that beset us, I also became aware of the role that corporate culture was playing—or not playing—in our effort to recreate the company.

The company I previously worked for had what I call a "street-fighting culture." It was a free-for-all. If you had the opportunity to grab something, you did, because that was the only way you could make something happen. I was comfortable in that kind of a culture, and thrived in it.

By contrast, as I assessed the organizational climate, I saw that PDC was acting like a very hierarchical, very traditional command-and-control organization. In general, people did not speak out or act until they were told to. In addition, the management at PDC had been isolated from the employees and there was little trust. In the midst of factory closings and layoffs no one would tell management anything important. The employees were silent, waiting for direction. Morale was low.

It also seemed to me that there were a number of cultures now operating within PDC after Philips acquired the company. There was the Philips culture and there was the culture of the acquired company, which seemed very typical of company cultures in a regulated industry. (General Telephone owned Sylvania before Philips acquired it.) Although some were keenly aware of the competitive forces arising out of globalization, particularly Japanese competition, there was a lack of knowledge of how to deal with that effectively. There were also some cultural issues introduced by some of the new senior managers, including myself, who came from "superior" companies such as Zenith or RCA. Decisions and actions taken by these newer members, though appropriate and necessary, tended not to sit well with members of the old culture. And, of course, there were the differences embedded in the various subcultures such as manufacturing, engineering, and so forth.

So when the PDC management decided to move the company headquarters to a location closer to the factory, we spent much time thinking about the kind of culture we wanted to develop in the new location. In our view, this sort of thinking ahead was essential not only for saving the company but also for growing it. After much thought, 25 people (out of 350 at HQ) developed a company credo.

PDC's Credo

We, the members of Philips Display Company, are dedicated to:

- Recognizing that the customer must always be satisfied.
- Striving for excellence by producing quality products and services.
- Communicating company strategy to each level of the organization, so individuals can make knowledgeable decisions to support those strategies.
- Driving decision making down to the organizational level that has the most information on the subject.
- Encouraging teamwork throughout the organization.
- Being enthusiastic leaders acknowledging that each decision is made to further our common goals and communicating this enthusiasm to everybody.
- Being attentive to listeners to enhance two-way communications.
- Recognizing that we, the employees, are the foundation of our business. That each person contributes in accordance with his/her skills to the success of the business and that each contribution is important.
- Nurturing an environment that encourages creativity, experimentation, and risk taking, understanding that mistakes and failures provide opportunities for learning.
- Celebrating the success of an individual or group; recognizing achievement; having fun while celebrating.
- Respecting all workers by treating each individual as you would want to be treated.
- Fostering the growth of employees through training and support, to provide maximum opportunity for contribution and achievement.
- Integrating these goals to achieve satisfactory results.

This credo was developed many years before the parent company in Europe started a corporate initiative on corporate values. It grew out of our work in TQM and expressed my expanding vision, which was to provide the opportunity for more people in the company to create what they truly desired. The credo reveals what these people desired to create.

We made the credo a part of our orientation for new hires and we were successful in creating a culture at the headquarters that was very much aligned with the credo. The credo was also distributed throughout PDC, but that was not sufficient to result in its being adopted by everyone in the company. Since the people in the factory did not participate in the development of the credo they did not feel ownership—and that would play a role in what was to happen later.

Culture and Conflicts in Leadership Style

Iva: As I continued in my new job as president, I found myself both pushing people for compliance to my ideas and vision and working toward getting genuine cooperation. Most of the time I felt as if I were on a teeter-totter. This was not a good feeling. I also believed that for us to be more competitive, we needed to develop from that hierarchical, command-and-control organization into a high-performance, participatory organization. But the pathway between here and there was unknown.

Yet, I believed that we were making progress—albeit very slowly. I realized that we had to create a communication link between engineering and the factory. This required some retraining of staff and opening up the communication channels between the engineers and the factory. This effort took years.

As I dealt with these issues I began to become very interested in the field of organizational development. I began to seek out more information, coaching, and training in organizational development. At the beginning of my career, I had not given much thought to integrating what I call "social technology" into the process. Given my background as a technologist, it's probably no surprise that I didn't have a good understanding of how to put people, machines, and technology together. Now I wanted to develop my own abilities in this area.

A New Tactic: Focus on Developing the Management Team

Iva: I reasoned that if I built a strong management team—a team that really acted like a team—then management would actually be living and modeling the behavior we wanted and that behavior would trickle down through the ranks. I had a very exact definition of "team." In a team, everyone in the group is supportive and sensitive to all its members. That creates an environment where it's OK to make—and learn from—mistakes. Having traveled to Japan many times I had picked up some insights about the Japanese view of management. I saw that if you only reward and encourage individual achievement, you'll get contributions only from the most individualistic and self-confident members of your staff. Since those people only account for a small portion of your staff you end up limiting overall company performance. Most of us in management were trained to develop individual skills, but we had little training in how to make better teams.

It was equally important for us to accept the fact that, as an organization, we had not effectively used the ingenuity of all of our people. We had to learn to break the tradition of, "You are told what to do, and that's all you do" or "Check your brains at the gate." This sounds like a simple and clear thing to change, but it's fraught with many difficulties that come from past history, individual expectations, fears of being discovered for not knowing something, lack of trust, etc.

We worked closely with a consultant recommended by the people from the Center for Creative Leadership who coached us and helped us with team-building, in particular within the management team that led PDC. In the years to come the management team, including myself, made a lot of progress toward building a better understanding of what team-work was all about. At the same time I was surprised at how difficult this transition would be and how long it would take.

A Failed Tactic: Developing a Better Relationship with the Union

Iva: The union leadership and management had some confrontations during this period, but we did make some progress and, ultimately, I knew that we needed to evolve the relationship beyond the current confronta-tional one. To that end we entered into a collaboration with an industry relations and human research center at Cornell University. The goal of this collaboration was to merge our TQM effort with a parallel attempt to cre-ate a sense of partnership between management and the union. The man-agement team and I had great expectations for this collaboration; we believed that we would see real business improvements.

The partnership didn't materialize as we hoped for reasons that, in retrospect, I can see were very typical of the way we went about things. For example, we created a steering committee comprised of selected people from the factory and headquarters to work on a project that would create multifunctional jobs with the objective to reduce the num-ber of classifications then enacted by our union contract. They developed a comprehensive plan for how we were going to implement it and every-thing looked fantastic. Then, when we rolled it out to a pilot group, it blew up in our face. It was wholeheartedly rejected.

In addition, during the same period in which we were making progress with the union leadership, that leadership was voted out of office. This happened because of the perception among part of the unionized workforce that the union leadership was "in bed" with man-agement. A small group of unionized workers went on a campaign to change the leaders, and they were successful in making it happen. As a result, we had to start the process of engaging the union all over.

More Learning

Iva: I learned a lot from this experience. I learned that the people who did not participate in the original thinking and planning would not buy in because their inputs were not taken into account. I had thought that we had had a pretty representative process, but then I realized that the people who represented the unionized workforce didn't really represent them because they didn't have the skill to ask people questions.

I guess this was my first major lesson in how to bring more demo-cratic ideas into the workplace. I learned that you have to get inputs that are truly representative. I also learned that even when I think I have rep-resentation it's very likely that I'm wrong. When I'm sitting at the top of the company it can easily look like somebody (a manager) represents somebody else (another manager or an employee) in a way that makes it possible for a project to be implemented, but true representation is very difficult to obtain. I learned that I needed to be very sensitive to that, but I didn't know exactly how. This is a lesson that I didn't learn well enough at the time—and it would return to haunt me.

And still, I didn't want to give up on the idea of a greater sense of partnership with the union.

Crisis Leadership Yields Positive Results

Iva: The turn-around process took three years. We moved the compa-ny HQ in 1989 without skipping a beat. As a matter of fact, that was the first year we made a profit. The quality of our products improved overall, and we stopped the flow of red ink. Sales volume increased by 50 percent and the company became profitable. In fact, we were on a par with even Japanese companies doing business in the U.S. PDC moved from last place in the industry and joined the ranks of the best among its competitors. There were a few people who called this period a "bloodbath," but I believed that all of it was necessary to save the company.

I know that it was also necessary to use traditional command-and-control tactics to get the results we got. In fact, when *BusinessWeek* magazine ran an article on women in high tech they praised my efforts as follows:

> When Iva M. Wilson took over as president of Philips Display Components Co. three years ago, the TV picture tube maker was fighting for its life. Low-cost Asian producers had flooded the U.S. market, and the company was in the red. The first woman ever to head a division of Dutch electronics giant Philips, Wilson moved decisively. She shuttered a plant in Seneca Falls, N.Y., slashed employment at another facility, while investing more than $30 million to modernize production. Last year, the com-pany broke even for the first time in five years on an estimated $300 million in revenues.[2]

Simultaneously, we began putting in place plans for a new, state-of-the-art factory.

Looking to the Future

Third Strategy: The Dream Factory

Iva: Despite all the strides we had made, we still felt that we were caught in a kind of winepress. We were in a highly competitive, commodity-type business with low profit margins. At one end of the supply chain, a key component of our product was in short supply and the price was climbing. I saw that as out of our control. At the other end, over 80 percent of the picture tubes we produced were sold to a single customer, a customer also owned by the parent company. In sum, we were being squeezed between the pricing of the product, which had to be kept low, and the cost of materials, which was continuously climbing.

Furthermore, due to increases in our product quality, we were also experiencing a period of high demand, but we were simultaneously limited in our ability to produce. Also, if we were able to produce larger picture tubes (called "jumbo" tubes) we could have gained more profit, but our factory did not have that capability. We needed a way out.

While at Zenith I learned about the Japanese way of management, Japanese processes and equipment, and their innate capability to integrate those into a whole system. Out of that learning a vision of a new, state-of-the-art factory emerged. I believed that building such a factory was the strategy that would enable us to achieve long-term prosperity

My reasoning was as follows: I believed we needed to grow the business and take leadership position in the market. I was also convinced that we would not be able to accomplish this merely by upgrading the existing factory. In order to do that, we needed to expand our capacity for producing products for the future, using the best technology available from Philips in Europe. I also realized that this would require a change in the way people thought about and performed their work. Our efforts in making these changes within the existing business infrastructure were, in my judgment, not fast enough. The reason went beyond the technical issues. I believed that the culture of the factory was a critical barrier.

I believed that we needed to change the workplace environment at PDC. If we were going to attain a quantum leap in performance we had to alter the way people at PDC thought about and performed their work. We needed to create a new level of empowerment in the unionized workforce that was resistant and hostile to anything new. We thought that a new factory would give us a clean slate. It would be a Greenfield—in other words, a new location with new equipment and new people. In a new environment we would be able to show by example what a "different way of working and leading" meant.

In this factory we could bring together new technology, new ideas about how work should be done, and new models for managing people.

It was our belief that the new facility would promote the change faster than pursuing TQM in the old factory.

After a long and tedious process, we got the approval from Europe and started construction of a new manufacturing facility. Unfortunately, during this time period (1989–1991) Philips encountered major financial difficulties. The consequence was that our factory project was eliminated.

There was also a lot of restructuring going on at a higher level. The management model of the company was changing and the worldwide Philips HQ in the Netherlands now required us to report more directly to them rather than to the U.S. HQ. There was more fallout from the cancellation of the factory. Also, we were about to enter into labor negotiations. The new factory would have given management some leverage with the union, because there would have been a second factory. Now, since the Ohio factory was still the only shop in town, we had no choice but to rethink our strategy.

Turning Inward

Iva: The loss of the new factory was a great disappointment, a real letdown for me. Yet, in my mind, it was not a terminal blow because it is not in my character to ever give up. I was deeply engaged in the business and its people, customers, and products, and I did not want to leave. Looking back, I can see that this event probably signaled the end of our autonomy from the parent organization, but at the time I did not want to face that. I continued searching for another strategic solution.

Now that our dream of a new factory had vanished, I knew that I had a real challenge in front of me. I had to face the fact that the reason I wanted the factory so much was because I didn't know how else to generate fundamental, profound change in the existing factory. I remember standing in the old factory one night, thinking to myself, "What are we going to do? Is there some other way to renew the company and to make it more competitive in this fierce global environment?" I realized that our relationship with our hourly workforce needed to drastically change, yet the skills of that workforce did not seem to make that possible. It wasn't the skills of producing picture tubes that were deficient. In my view, it was the listening skills, and the ability to inquire rather than advocate—all the skills necessary to create a good union–management relationship seemed to be lacking.

I remember long evenings and weekends of discussions with my management team and many others from the company about what to do. We needed to rethink our entire strategy and come up with something that would work within the existing manufacturing infrastructure. It was during this time that I became especially intrigued by the possibilities of organizational learning.

Organizational Learning: A Radical New Commitment

A New Set of Strategic Tools

Iva: It was during this time that I became aware of Peter Senge and his associates' work at the Organizational Learning Center at MIT. I was intrigued by the application of systems theory to management science.

What struck me immediately was how systems dynamics—which I was familiar with from a technical standpoint—could be extended to human systems. This was extremely exciting! For a long time I had thought that there was too wide a gulf between the technical aspects of the business and the behavioral aspects, the so-called "soft stuff." I thought these two things needed to be integrated, but I did not know exactly how. The essence of OL is that it joins together, integrates, the technical nuts-and-bolts of business with the behavioral aspects. This, I believed, was the framework I needed to build upon.

I had had a sense that there were aspects of the business world that seemed inexplicable. For example, business organizations are systems but, unfortunately, we do not see them that way because we have a strong tendency to a reductionist way of thinking. Because we have that reductionist view, we only look at parts, rather than the whole system. As a result, we tend to focus on creating shareholder value, thinking that if we satisfy the shareholder, everything else is going to fall in place. And it's not that simple.

A more systemic view of business organizations says that their purpose is to satisfy human needs. Shareholders are humans, customers are humans, suppliers are humans, employees are humans, et cetera. That focus on people is much more conducive to creating more wealth and better economic conditions, but it's much harder to put into practice because you have to deal with more complexity—which we tend to fear.

Our tendency to be reductionistic comes from a "mental model" of the universe that we inherited from the Industrial Age. We have learned so much more from the work that is being done in the new physics, yet this Industrial Age thinking is still the prevailing view, particularly in the West. As long as a corporation is viewed as a mechanical system instead of as a living system, we will continue to use strategies like downsizing to remedy our problems and we will suffer from those choices.[3] All these things will not change much until our mindsets change.

That connection with organizational learning started another phase in my professional career. I saw another way, a better way, to create a new strategy for PDC, and I was deeply convinced that this was the path forward.

The Strength of My Convictions

Iva: I strongly believed that "learning" was the right path for us. My personal vision was very clear, but how could we develop a shared vision for the organization? I had long believed that there was no way we'd ever succeed unless we changed our way of working. At first I thought that we could accomplish that if we built the new factory, but that dream was ended. Then, in reading about OL, I began to believe that perhaps we could accomplish the same result if we began to learn together.

The learning tools described in *The Fifth Discipline* seemed to offer us a unique opportunity to develop a new business strategy that would make us more competitive than ever. In fact, many of those tools seemed ideal for broadening the Total Quality Management philosophy at PDC, and for increasing the company's capacity to generate the new ideas we so desperately needed to hone our strategy.

I believed that the OL conversational tools, such as Dialogue, would help us to make better decisions. When we made decisions, we needed to learn to distinguish when we base our judgments on data and when we based them on assumptions or feelings. We also needed to understand the assumptions that underlay our actions. If we could understand where our assumptions came from, how they are supported by our belief system, and how they might have developed, then we could see our judgments more objectively, and we would be better able to suspend judgment and thus come to a better decision. The Ladder of Inference as a tool provided a real opportunity to start thinking deeper about the assumptions we held, why we held them, and how to sort them out.

It was also my firm belief that Systems Thinking would give us the very tools we needed to rethink our business. This approach seemed a huge improvement over the kind of linear, reductionistic, cause-and-effect thinking on which PDC had based most of its decisions in the past. I also believed that, in our technically oriented culture, systems dynamics would prove easy to understand and implement. Systems Thinking, which has its roots in systems dynamics, would be understandable to both technical people and nontechnical people.

Defining a Change Strategy

Iva: It seemed quite clear to me that developing learning capabilities and applying learning disciplines in our company would require a different kind of commitment from the people in the organization. So, I felt that the pertinent question was: How do we create that kind of commitment?

My change strategy was one of deployment. I chose to deploy the learning effort through the HR and Quality departments and with their respective vice presidents. The rationale for that was relatively simple. First, the two VPs were very interested and involved in learning and applying the tools of OL. Second, I felt that the tools of OL would provide the opportunity to improve on existing Quality processes. Daniel Kim's MIT working paper from 1990, "Towards Learning Organizations: Integrating Total Quality Control and Systems Thinking," made that possibility very evident.[4] Since the OL tools required that people become engaged in the business in a way that would change the way they think about themselves and the business they are part of, it was natural to use HR as the other function to lead the deployment process. Only later did I realize that this was another major flaw in my strategy.

The plan was to gradually expose the people in our organization to the learning tools and to thereby develop their skill in applying those tools in their work. I believed that people in all functional units needed to be exposed to these tools, and that we needed to simultaneously expose people on various levels in the organization, so that the deployment could be faster and more efficient. I also believed that we needed to expose these tools to a diagonally cross-functional group of people who could then take this process further and engage the rest of the organization. I expected to achieve this through the educational programs the MIT Center for Organizational Learning offered, project support from researchers and consultants associated with the Center, and interaction with people in other sponsoring companies.

This was similar to the strategy I had used previously to bring new ideas into the company from competitors and Europe. I had met with resistance when I pushed those new ideas. I had also found myself teeter-tottering between two leadership approaches: pushing for compliance and working toward getting genuine cooperation. As I galvanized this change effort, I did not anticipate that this same pattern would return with even greater ferocity. We embarked on our organizational learning journey in 1992.

First Tactic: Voluntary Deployment

Iva: Because my management team and I wanted to emphasize that we were no longer operating from a command-and-control mentality, we decided from the beginning that the initial training would be voluntary. The plan was to train the most interested people who would then, in turn, take the change process further by engaging the rest of the organization.

As it turned out, those people who had the most interest in leading and supporting this change work tended to come from the salaried and nontechnical workforce. Few of them came from manufacturing, the function that had the most direct impact on PDC's performance. During time of high demand for picture tubes there was intense pressure on our manufacturing function to pump out more tubes, despite PDC's limited manufacturing capacity. As a result, the overworked manufacturing staff had little interest in investing precious time in the change effort.

Reflecting on this time period, I question how voluntary this selection process actually was. All the desired participants knew that the president of PDC was supporting this effort. We were also still walking around in the residue of a command-and-control culture. Therefore it is quite possible that they considered participation in the program as mandatory, or at least, "a good personal policy."

First Challenge: Commitment from the Line

Iva: I knew that there was little hope of real organizational change without the commitment and involvement of people from the line. But how did we manage this? We did an assessment of the cultural differences between the headquarters and the factory (our two locations).

> **Phil Fazio, former CFO of Philips Display Components (PDC):** The factory culture was very pro-union brotherhood, solidarity, and distrustful of management. They kind of had the view, "We've been doing this for forty years, don't tell us anything new. We've been through all these fads. Just give us good equipment, good pay, and leave us alone."
>
> It was very much a midwestern, rural culture with strong family values, strong religious beliefs, and not really any interest in too much change. And a few could lead many.

Iva: We concluded that despite the significant cultural differences between the two locations, it was paramount to include both in this process. We anticipated that the importance of interdependence between the two, already stressed through our Quality drive, would minimize any problems emerging during the new initiative.

Unfortunately, because the first people to attend OL training were primarily from HQ, the factory people framed it right away as the president's project, "another corporate initiative." They concluded that it had nothing to do with what was going on in the factory, so they wouldn't have to worry about it.

Second Tactic: Using Dialogue to Improve Conversation

Iva: As more of our people began attending the OLC course, the PDC management team encouraged them to use organizational learning tools as much as possible in all aspects of their work, such as in the strategic planning process, product development, and so forth. These tools included team learning and conversation tools such as:

- Balancing advocacy and inquiry
- Left-hand/right-hand column
- The Ladder of Inference.

The first group to be trained in OL was charged with figuring out how to introduce OL into the organization. They decided to focus on Dialogue.[5]

I was particularly committed to Dialogue for the following reasons. We have all experienced conversations that lack focus, as well as those that generate new ideas and move the creative process forward. To develop the "conversational muscle" necessary for what Senge terms "generative conversation" in an organization, we need to understand the mental models we create through our thinking. However, without sharing our aspirations and building them into a shared vision, it is difficult to create outcomes that support both individual and collective aspirations in the organization. Dialogue as a process supports creating more effective conversations.[6]

Early Resistance

Iva: Initially, it was difficult to get Dialogue to be accepted in our cultural environment. We were a very crisis-oriented company. We tended to react to the most immediate problem and converge on solutions quickly, rather than set priorities and maintain a course of action that deals with the long-term issues. We were also very task-driven. Dialogue slowed us down—and it was seen by many of our technical and line people as being too consuming of precious time and too "soft"—not sufficiently linked to business results.

Then there was the issue of trust. Many people were afraid to be as open as Dialogue required. They wanted to play it safe, especially because management was present at the Dialogue sessions. I very much wanted there to be openness and for people to speak their truth. I very much wanted to create an organization where people could feel free to say the truth in public, rather than just in private. I tried to model that behavior, but as much as I wanted people to be open, I also turned out to be part of the problem.

Phil Fazio: Quite honestly, I think people were afraid at the time to say a lot about specific problems in the factory with Iva there. Iva was perceived as a very intimidating person. She was really strong in her conviction and I think as a consequence they missed a lot of things that she was trying to get them to learn. They also knew that if she wanted to do something, that you lined up and you did it. That was "the early Iva." That was before Iva did some learning herself and managed differently.

Challenging My Leadership Style

Iva: This was a time of tremendous learning for me. As a result of the Dialogue sessions, I began to get glimpses of how I might be acting in a way that was contrary to my beliefs, and I tried to make changes. I tried to be more reflective, to be increasingly more accessible to people, to be more the creator of an environment in which people could feel freer to be open. However, I would slip into my old command-and-control style; I would "backslide." This would do quite a bit of damage because then, in some people's eyes, I would undo the good work that had come before. Yet, there were others who could see that I was genuinely trying to embrace this new path.

Expanding the Organizational Learning Effort

Iva: I strongly believed that OL was the way out of the situation we were in. In early 1994, I made the commitment to implement the learning tools on a companywide level. This meant that OL became more than a corporate program that no one in the factory had to concern themselves with; it was a mandate for the organization. I also began to push some of the OL techniques, tools, and teachings up into the Philips organization in Holland. I pushed pretty hard and had the VP of HR and the VP of Quality engaged in the process.

Resistance and Faltering Results: The View from the Factory

Iva: We wanted the Dialogues to be representative, so we had the people from the factory come for the sessions, which sometimes involved up to 30 people. I felt that this was very important for our growth as a whole organization, but it was also true that the people from the factory were on the horns of a dilemma. On the one hand, they were under great pressure to produce. On the other hand, they were being asked to give up their time for something they did not see as being specifically job-related. If they were only there because they were merely being compliant to my wishes, then that went against our long-term goal of participatory management.

Phil Fazio: Around this time, performance was starting to deteriorate. We weren't selling as many products. We lost a customer because of an internal quality problem. There was a lot of internal pressure because most of our tubes were being sold to our own internal sister company and they wanted price reductions. We started having performance problems in the factory with scrap being up and yields being down. So there was a lot of stress in the organization.

Some of these issues came up in the Dialogue sessions, but I cannot remember a time when any action items came out of dialogue or any decisions were made on those actions. It was always presented as getting things off your chest, putting things out in the middle, and not necessarily worrying about solving them. And that drives factory people crazy.

As far as being an effective tool for opening people up and getting feelings out, I think Dialogue was very successful—but it was very disjointed. There was nothing systemic in place to deal with some of the issues that surfaced in Dialogue. And some of these things were emotional and people were spilling out their guts—then it was "Let's all go back and get to work." It was a difficult time. People didn't know how to handle those things.

I was concerned that we were only doing Dialogue. I used to tell Iva, "Look, we're only doing one of the learning disciplines. We're focusing so much on Dialogue that people are feeling that all we do is talk and we never made any decisions." Furthermore, the European HQ was beginning to have much more influence—and what had previously seemed like "influence" was now shifting to "orders." There was more need to justify our actions.

Fourth Tactic: A Project in Process Management

Iva: We had been actively looking for a meaningful project to which we could apply organizational learning. So, I continued pushing and we eventually had a project, Process Management (PM), that I felt gave us the steps to not reengineer, but to recreate our processes. The next step was to bring OL tools to bear on a process improvement effort. The idea was to use reflection and Systems Thinking to help the Process Management team think through the "why" of a process before rushing to revise it. We called this "process re-creation." We were looking to shift from discrete process improvement to a mentality of continuous process improvement. The work was beginning to show signs of success. At the same time I was bringing all these ideas to Europe. My peers from other regions, such as South America and SE Asia, seemed very receptive and supportive to me.

However, as we went about this process, the more technical tools of Systems Thinking, such as simulation modeling, were not being employed nearly as much as the other tools. This was because, as mentioned earlier, the initial round of people who expressed interest in organizational learning came from nontechnical backgrounds and felt most comfortable with less technical tools. This imbalance would have important ramifications later.

A Sea of Conundrums

Iva: During these early stages, several challenges arose. The European management did not understand why, given the bottom line results, there was a push for Dialogue, which they saw as just sitting around in a circle, talking, with no actions being taken. This was certainly not their model for how you deal with business problems. That began to add strain to how they perceived the company was performing as well as their perception of how the management of the company was performing.

In the background, there was a kind of "tug-of-war" going on—a struggle between PDC's desire for autonomy and the parent company's desire for more control. The desire for control kept getting stronger and our ability to control our destiny seemed to be diminishing. There were also tensions in the business relationship between PDC and its main customer, another Philips company, which sparked resentments and criticism on both sides. Both companies were facing an especially challenging time owing to the relentless lowering of TV set prices at the retail level. We gave this customer a sizable volume discount, but they never felt that it was enough. We felt that we couldn't reduce our costs any further unless we made further capital investments. The parent company would approve these only if PDC increased its profitability. We were locked in a not-uncommon catch-22, a vicious cycle. This not-so-merry-go-round would drag on for years. There was a lot of blame flying back and forth, but very little willingness on either side to grasp the underlying causes of the friction or to join forces to find a win–win solution.

As a result of my work with OL, I thought I had a fresh perspective on this rivalry. It was clear that the situation could not continue on this track without causing serious damage to one or both companies. I wanted to explore the root causes of the two companies' conflict because it might unveil leverage points for improving matters. I was not able to act on this intuition, however. I had an excellent relationship with the president of the company that was our biggest customer. We respected each other, we trusted each other, and were therefore able to speak about the things that troubled us the most. We shared our views with Peter Senge and elicited his support, which resulted in his recommending a consultant to work with us. We both decided that this process needed to be led by the customer and not the supplier, i.e., the other president had to take the lead. However, we both also decided that the conditions were not yet right to start reshaping the relationship, and so the tensions between the two companies continued to worsen over time.

The First Setback

Iva: The first setback came as a consequence of a worldwide job satisfaction survey of Philips employees. When the results came back, PDC's results turned out to be lower than our peer divisions. The parent company management took note of these survey results and a negative picture was beginning to form in some people's minds. A former peer had recently become my new boss and he was watching our performance closely and becoming critical.

In response, I asked that one of our external consultants help to interpret the results. We knew that we were the only division that actively encouraged hourly workers' participation in the survey. In an effort to include everyone, we actually paid overtime to the unionized workers so they could respond to the survey. This was an unprecedented move and now it began to seem politically naïve on our part. When we analyzed our survey responses, we discovered that the unionized workers' responses were much less positive than those of our salaried workers, which greatly biased the results of the survey. The unionized workers had never been surveyed before, so they naturally took the opportunity to voice their concerns. Although we tried to explain the disparity to upper level management, their opinions seemed to have already been formed.

Success Brings Some Unintended Consequences

Iva: Yet, I was not overly concerned. The parent company was going through a difficult period, yet I believed that we at PDC were making progress in Quality as we received ISO 9000 certification in the latter part of 1994.

Due to our TQM work, PDC had become a leader in Quality, winning high ratings in a peer evaluation. Our customers were now demanding ever more deliveries—but we did not have sufficient capacity because our new factory was never built. The continuous struggle to fill deliveries with our limited production capabilities put a huge strain on the entire organization and, because we could not meet all of our customers' needs, our reputation was beginning to suffer.

In response, the only thing we were able to do was drive our workforce harder. We tried to increase production by adding more working hours, working people in the factory with overtime to their maximum capability. The pressures were unbelievable, but we had no other choice— or at least we did not know how to look for other choices. And although the hourly workforce were making more money because of overtime, the morale and the satisfaction in our factory were dwindling.

The Strike: A Crushing Blow

Iva: Then, in the fall of 1994, the stress between management and the union crystallized. A conflict with the union arose because we wanted to add an extra shift. Unionized employees were divided between those who supported unlimited overtime, and those who preferred not to work overtime and supported an extra shift instead.

In the spirit of my new leadership style, I had delegated the contract negotiations. I had also changed another key element of the negotiation process: my personal involvement with the unionized workforce. This was the first time that I chose not to meet with the entire unionized workforce before the negotiations. Previously I had always engaged with them personally. I shared management's reasoning about what was in the contract and answered their questions. Several other things were different this time also and the outcome was not what everybody had been assuring me it would be. By a small margin, the unionized workforce decided to reject the contract and they went on strike for the first time in 25 years. The strike only lasted a week, but it had a significant impact on the business. When the strike occurred, inventory was down and we did not have reserves. The factory had to be shut down. This was the first strike in PDC's history. It was a surprise to me and, more importantly, a surprise to my bosses in Europe.

What Can We Learn from This?
Healing through Learning and Dialogue

Iva: Not only did the parent company take notice, but the strike had intense repercussions within PDC. During that summer, an oppressive sense of unhappiness blanketed PDC's labor force. The manufacturing staff seemed particularly dispirited.

Everything that I had learned by doing the work within organizational learning told me that I must stay on the course that I had begun. I knew that if I came down with repercussions and "punishments" for the strike that I would destroy everything I'd built so far. I still believed that if I continued using the OL tools and methods that I started implementing in the company, we would find a way out of this morass. I also believed that everyone involved—the management, the salaried workers, and the union members—needed to grasp how all our actions had precipitated the strike.

I found myself thinking about ways in which the company could learn from this disaster. So I gathered a group of 60 people, from both headquarters and the factory, to take part in a facilitated Dialogue for this purpose. The Dialogue went on for an intense, emotional two days and surfaced many profound insights. Obviously, a lot of people on both sides, management and the union, were deeply hurt by the strike. Many salaried employees resented the union for taking those steps. There were also conflicts within the unionized workforce. Conflicts often involved family members, friends, or neighbors pitted against one another.

I believe that the use of Dialogue methods helped reduce the amount of blaming despite the intense pain that people were feeling as we discussed these issues. Management began to acknowledge some of the mistakes they had made during the negotiations. We acknowledged our ineffective communications, and our lack of true understanding of the reasons why employees were divided on the issues of overtime and the need for an additional shift to increase output. We had not fully understood the impact of our demands on personal lives of employees. Amazingly, no one lost his or her job during this grueling analysis.

A New Beginning?

Iva: We used this learning the next spring, 1995, when we reopened the contract negotiations. During the subsequent 6–8 months the organization was deeply involved in the work leading to a better understanding of the system that created the conditions for the strike and finding the leverage necessary to take the next step. I felt that the tools of the learning organization enabled us to successfully ratify a contract within six months from the strike, a feat that was previously deemed impossible. The new contract gave us the opportunity to increase the factory output. It also opened the door for improving working conditions within the factory and creating a more satisfying environment for our employees. I therefore believed we could easily justify to management above me that our new initiatives could bring results.

During this period we also made great strides with Quality. In 1995 we passed Philip's Peer Quality Audit. This award gave PDC significant recognition for its pursuit of Total Quality Management, which had included the application of the tools and methods from *The Fifth Discipline*. In fact, the Philips Quality Auditor who visited our plant noted how committed the factory workforce was to their customers and how proud they were of their company. This surprised him because he expected to find a different attitude after the strike. This was a great sign of progress and confirmed my belief that it was only a matter of time before my boss would also "see the light" despite the strike and the survey results.

After the strike, however, several people on my management team urged me to go underground with organizational learning, but I didn't listen. I was optimistic because I believed that PDC's management and union members had scored some major successes in their resolution of the strike. I was still confident that I could make significant changes in the company and that I could persuade my boss by giving him evidence of how these learning organization things are really making a difference. I was confident that if I showed positive results I would be home free.

Fiddling While Rome Burns: The View from Above

Iva: I had been very vocal about my commitment to organizational learning. I'd taken the message to Europe several times and was an advocate for everyone else embracing these ideas. Now I was totally exposed.

The strike caught the attention of upper level management. Management from the European HQ began frequent on-site visits.

Phil Fazio: Two levels of upper management came to PDC to get debriefed about the strike. They said things such as, "You say you're doing all this good learning, you're getting in touch with the workforce, you're driving cultural change—then you have a strike. If you're doing all this great stuff with the people, we can't understand how the heck you can have this kind of a problem."

Their perceptions went to judgment. They flat-out said that Iva was doing a bad job by focusing the company on the wrong things. They would come from overseas and go directly to the factory, skipping the PDC HQ, and form their own opinions based on what they saw and heard. The management of the factory actually made presentations to some of the management from overseas. In these presentations they showed that a decline in yields in the factory was happening at the same time that all these other initiatives on learning and other things were going on, and making a cause-and-effect relationship between the two. This was a deflection tactic; they probably exaggerated this relationship.

Now there arose in PDC the strong perception that if you were too visible in supporting some of these things that the president was promoting, you were at risk for your job. The perception was that if you were working on "that soft stuff" while Rome was burning, you couldn't be very valuable to the company. You're driving the agenda away from where upper level management thought it should be. There was division on the management team.

A House Divided

Iva: In late 1994, after I realized that our organizational learning efforts were not necessarily creating the intended consequences, I decided to have a three-day off-site meeting to discuss this with the management team. Those were very difficult days in the history of the management team, but also very gratifying for me because I was able to use what I learned in the past several years and apply it "in action." I believe the same was true for others on the team.

An outside consultant helped us to discover that my management team appeared unable to agree on the relevance and importance of specific initiatives, particularly the learning and process management efforts. The management team appeared to be divided into two camps, each with its own priorities. One camp, consisting of people associated with staff functions, championed and promoted the learning organization activities. The other camp, which consisted of operational people, was concerned that the organizational learning activities took too much time and diverted energy and attention from critical business priorities. The managers in this camp sought to avoid activities that weren't focused on production.

We also learned that these two camps didn't trust each other and this distrust affected the ability of the management team to set consistent priorities. Moreover, we learned that they didn't believe that they could tell each other the truth. And—even more critical—they didn't believe that I would listen if they said something with which I disagreed.

Phil Fazio: When Iva became the president, the company was in terrible shape and she really turned it around. People will tell you that that was when Iva was performing her best in the president's role and that it wasn't until she got involved in some of these other things that performance began to deteriorate.

My perception is that there wasn't enough of a balance. The pendulum had swung too violently in another direction—toward OL, let's say—and that gave the perception that management had taken its eye off the ball and was not addressing the immediacy of the problems.

We all had that feeling at some point in time and we would have discussions about it, and try to tell Iva. But the points maybe weren't made strong enough, or they weren't heard, or they weren't communicated properly—whatever—they didn't sink in. There became a great division on the management team. It was perceived that a small group had influence over Iva and they were actually driving her away from a focus on the business activities.

Iva: It is entirely possible that the "breakdown" in my management team was actually foreshadowing a "breakthrough" to a greater level of honesty. They were now willing to openly tell me what was going on—and perhaps, for the first time, I was willing and able to listen. I felt that we experienced a significant change in the level of trust within the organization. This created an opportunity to expose the disagreement with new initiatives. Unfortunately, we were running out of time. Word of this dissension had been informally communicated to my boss in Europe. It had been reaching him, but I had not heard it until then. When those comments, with best intentions, were made to the management above me, it created a good reason for my boss to question those initiatives led by me.

Our management consultant also uncovered that people in the factory believed management was delivering mixed messages about the value of organizational learning to the workforce. As a result, there was a split in the organization between those who supported the OL effort and those who did not. The lack of support came primarily from two sources: lack of understanding and lack of agreement. Those views continued to create conflicting messages and, with time, further eroded my boss's confidence in the validity of the approaches applied in PDC.

Phil Fazio: The perception that the initiatives were driven by the HR and Quality functions did not help because they were seen as being outside the business, outside the guts of the operation. So it seemed that there really was a separation. There was the part that worries about running the business and the part that does other stuff. It really became divisive among the team. It became dysfunctional.

Iva: As a result of these discussions, we decided to initiate a project to assess the organizational issues within PDC and its relationship to the global business. I felt we needed to deal with some fundamental differences between my boss and myself regarding how the business in the U.S. should be organized. Unfortunately, I did not appreciate how serious the disagreement with my boss had become. I compounded the situation by refraining from direct communication with him and instead communicated with the three consultants who were performing the organizational assessment. I thought that these individuals had the professional understanding of the efforts we were introducing, and the ability to communicate with my boss in a way that would help him understand the fundamental thinking behind the effort. Upon reflection, I realize that this decision had numerous unintended consequences—as I once heard Dee Hock say, "not all intended consequences of our actions materialize, but all the unintended do!"[7] Still, I remained confident that we would reach an agreement.

After a four-month-long study it became clear that the recommendation was to reorganize PDC to be more in line with the organizational structure of the parent company. Among other things, the factory was to be given increased autonomy from PDC HQ. In addition, the responsibilities of the VP of HR and the VP of Quality were greatly reduced since the corporate function was restructured. Responsibility and accountability for human resources and Quality in operations were fully transferred to the newly established position of Business Team Leader (formerly the VP of Operations).

No Latitude without Results

Iva: As far as results were concerned, we were lagging behind other Philips plants around the world in terms of return on assets. Because of the strike and the messages my boss was receiving about the pressure on the people to be engaged with organizational learning, my boss was becoming convinced that my interest in organizational learning was distracting me from focusing on the parent company's priorities.

I could rationalize this. I believed this shortfall to be caused by the lack of capacity in our old factory and outdated processes that we were attempting to revise through our process management efforts. I could see that the parent company wanted more immediate gains from the factory, but I was convinced that our efforts would yield better gains in the long term. We were completely out of synch in our thinking about time.

When my boss and I finally sat down face-to-face to discuss the reorganization plan, I learned how things looked to my bosses "from above." In summary, my bosses had become unhappy about my leadership of the business. They decided that I would not be able to do what was necessary to increase the business's profitability, such as laying people off in order to reduce costs and improve PDC's bottom line.

They were right on that point. In my view, laying off people does not necessarily lead to a reduction in a company's overall costs. We generally think there is a direct correlation because our view of labor costs is simplistic at best. We only take into account things we can easily measure. We'd have a better picture if we could take account of not only the wages we pay them, but also the quality of the work we get from their full participation in the process. It was more important to me to use our learning from successes and failures in order to create efficiencies and better output. I therefore committed to our workforce that I would not pursue a strategy of restructuring by laying off people. Instead, I focused on improving our business processes and creating a learning environment so we could achieve better results. So, my bosses were right. I was not going to agree to lay people off.

My boss also questioned my leadership. He deemed my new management style too "soft," citing that I should have fired a few people after the strike. As he often said, "You have twenty-first-century ideas, running a twentieth-century company, and this will not work. You have to do something more traditional first." He believed that the people who were responsible for OL, the VP of HR and the VP of Quality, should go. I did not agree. Together, we decided that I should leave PDC by the end of 1995. Quite rapidly, organizational learning disappeared without a trace.

Staying with the Commitment

Iva: I was appointed the Senior VP of Manufacturing Technology for Philips U.S. I did not abandon my beliefs, I continued pursuing my vision.

While in this position we developed a Manufacturing Training Program for all Philips manufacturing plants in the U.S. that contained many of the learning disciplines. We might not have advertised it as such, but the people who got the training were very enthusiastic about what they learned and expressed how helpful this was in managing their jobs and people more effectively. The program is still being used today.

I retired from Philips at the end of 1996.

Epilogue

Iva: My first organizational learning journey lasted about four years (1991–1995).[8] That was a period of tremendous learning for me—learning which continues to this day in an even more robust phase. Whether the efforts I initiated while working for Philips should be called a "success" or a "failure," I believe I learned a lot in the process of struggling to implement—and especially in the process of reflecting on it since.

Phil Fazio: There was no major transformation of the organization, but the success, I think, is with the people who learned a little about themselves, a little about some of the tools and techniques, and are using those things in the places that we are now. It is in the way we behave and the way we are in meetings. I can balance advocacy with inquiry in difficult situations. I can now use creative tension. That's where I think the success was: with the people that took the time to actually learn. It changed some people and gave them a different tool set that they didn't have before and I think some of us are pretty successful where we are today.

Personally, I feel I've been very successful and a lot of it has been because of some of the things I learned as a result of this exposure to organizational learning. That isn't bad.

Iva: One of my biggest questions has been: "What would I do differently if I had a chance to do it again?" Unfortunately, we do not often get the opportunity to apply the lessons learned from our mistakes, even though we all know that this kind of learning is the most powerful one. On the other hand, by sharing what was learned somebody else might learn from our mistakes.

Phil Fazio: I've learned that for a leader to be successful over the long haul, it's very important to have a vision, a core philosophy, and to be true to that vision—to follow it and live it. But you also have to have flexibility in your strategy. You can be totally committed to your vision, but you shouldn't be totally committed to your strategy. You have to look for opportunities and then show flexibility. Your strategy and tactics can change. If your strategy doesn't fulfill your vision, change your strategy, but not your vision. Don't change your core belief.

I think where things failed with OL at Philips was that it was very much a vision and a core philosophy that Iva developed. She was successful in getting it passed down to certain members of her management team. But she was not flexible in the strategy or tactics for implementing. That I believe, in hindsight, killed it and it caused catastrophe for many people. That was a hard lesson to learn.

That doesn't mean that people didn't think it had value or didn't like participating. But I don't think it was ever perceived as a way to solve problems or a way to drive change or deal with culture. I think that's because we didn't do the whole program using all five disciplines. We focused on Dialogue. We primarily used one tool and people really could not understand the whole program.

Iva: I very much value Phil's perspective and I have learned from it particularly about the need to plan for how to use all the tools of organizational learning even if some seem to be more compatible with the culture than others.

Ever since I left Philips, I have worked to deepen my understanding and continued the practice of implementing these principles in my work. This has not been an easy path, because reflecting on the past created many opportunities to recognize my errors and mistakes, but the learning that came from it made it all worthwhile. It has been a real joy to see how this learning has impacted the results I have produced since. I am now convinced even more that the world will continue on this path of change.

Endnotes

1. For a deeper insight into the subject, please refer to *The Learning Curves in Business,* Jeff Mortimer (ed.), (Troy, MI: Momentum Books, Ltd.), pp. 371–394.

2. Emily T. Smith, et al., "The Women Who Are Scaling High Tech Heights," *BusinessWeek,* August 28, 1989, pp.86–88.

3. For a more in-depth understanding of how a corporation can be defined and viewed as a living system, refer to Arie de Geus, *The Living Company* (Boston: Harvard Business School Press, 1997).

4. Daniel Kim, *Toward Learning Organizations: Integrating Total Quality Control and Systems Thinking* (Cambridge, MA: MIT Sloan School of Management, 1990).

5. Iva Wilson, *Organizational Change at Philips Display Components*, Innovations in Management Series (Waltham, MA: Pegasus Communications, 1999).

6. For a better understanding of Dialogue as a process and its application, refer to William Isaacs, *Dialogue and the Art of Thinking Together* (New York: Doubleday, 1999). Also see Daniel Yankelovitch, *The Magic of Dialogue* (New York: Simon & Schuster, 1999).

7. In his book, *Birth of the Chaordic Age* (San Francisco: Berrett Koehler Publishers, Inc., 1999), Dee Hock describes his work in creating VISA. This is a good example of a practitioner's experience in applying the concepts and tools of organizational learning, although he does not characterize it that way.

8. In order to get further details about the learning journey, it might be useful to the reader to refer to the learning history of that part of the journey: JoAnne Wyer and George Roth, *The Learning Initiative at Electro Components* (SoL Publications, 1997; online publication found at www.sol-ne.org/res/wp/index.html).

Chapter 7

Debriefing Iva's Story

How does Iva's journey illuminate the pathway for others? Iva's OL change effort was not "successful" in a conventional sense. The change effort was shut down. New management was brought in. Nothing diffused. But this is a success story in the larger sense, because it gives us a rich opportunity for learning and exploring deep questions about large-scale change. Furthermore, there were pockets of awakening. Real change takes time. Profound change may well have been occurring, but we lack the measures to prove it. The only guideposts we have are the instances of resistance. Each signal of resistance can also be interpreted as a sign of progress. Change happens even as it is being resisted.

Iva's Early Change Strategy: Turn the Ship Around

When Iva assumed the position of president of PDC, she quickly realized that she had inherited multiple challenges. From her experience with Japanese companies, she also had a vision of what a competitive organization looked like—and, in her mind, there was an enormous gap between that vision and what she saw at PDC. Yet, she also saw great potential.

Iva's first priority was triage; she had to apply tourniquet measures to stop the flow of red ink. These turnaround measures involved closing a plant and moving the headquarters: in effect, downsizing. While Iva attempted to do these things with as much sensitivity as humanly possible, downsizing always carries with it certain baggage. The ghosts linger; feelings of anger, resentment, or fear are stoked. So, while there is on the one hand this great desire to create something, to set people's aspirations free, the first step involves a walk through the fire. How did people in the organization perceive this first major move by its new president? Were they truly able to rationalize that this was being done for the greater good of the organization? On the other hand, did Iva have any other alternatives?

These are hard questions and there are no easy answers. The point is that they are organizational realities. All actions beget reactions. Some predictable and intended, others not. When we must take an action, it is a good idea to take a hard look at the assumptions that we are basing those decisions on, and to test those assumptions with others. Then, look for the reactions. Look with new eyes; notice what surprises, not just the confirmatory outcomes.

The Organizational Context

Iva's change strategy was to be implemented within a context that had many sources of conflict and tension. A quick survey of the situation shows that there were internal divisions and structural tensions on multiple levels. For example:

- The parent company and the subsidiary (PDC) were resistant to accepting each other's technology ideas; eventually, the tension between the two escalated into a struggle between autonomy and control.
- There were tensions between the supplier (PDC) and its primary customer, also a subsidiary of the larger parent company.
- There was long-standing animosity between labor (the union) and management.
- There was also a related tension between the culture of HQ and the culture of factory.
- There was growing but covert distrust on Iva's management team, particularly between staff and line, which ultimately led to a split on the executive management team.

The existence of so many multiple tensions raises some questions: Can learning efforts be effective when they are seeded in such shifting ground? Conversely, can learning efforts be the source of resolving these tensions? The energy devoted to holding these tensions at bay—to keep from flying apart—gets in the way of having enough energy to deal with organizational learning and change. Can change leaders help organizations balance and "hold" these tensions while simultaneously attempting to undergo change efforts?

Iva's Challenge: Turn Shell Shock into Creative Energy

Now that Iva had stopped the hemorrhaging, she had to ask herself another question: What was the key to turning the dying patient into a vigorous, thriving entity? Her first solution was the dream factory. When the new factory was cancelled, Iva found new hope in organizational learning. She believed that the future of the firm lay in creating the conditions within which people could flourish. In a sense, this was Iva's implicit theory of change: *create the environment in which aspiration can take root—and the business results will follow.* A time delay is implicit in this approach.

In Iva's view the gap between her vision of a high-performance, participatory, vigorously competitive organization and PDC's current reality had two facets. There was the technological gap brought about by the long-standing lack of investment in factory operations and there was a "culture" gap. This perceived culture gap was characterized by the existence of multiple subcultures such as engineering, marketing, and the factory. These subcultures did not communicate well with each other nor did they function interdependently as a cohesive whole. In addition, Iva inherited a disempowered workforce. The previous management of the organization had been very much command-and-control. The takeover by Philips exacerbated the submissiveness of many of the employees; it left the organization defeated and even more compliant. The organization's life force—its creative energy—would have to be rekindled. What was the way of being that would enable and engender this transformation? The issue, then, became one of strategy and tactics—and something more.

In response to this assessment of current reality, Iva's overall change strategy was multifocal. It began before she became interested in organizational learning and it encompassed the following:

- Iva addressed the conflict between HQ and factory cultures by attempting to develop a new corporate culture.
- She attempted to address the union-management relationship through repeated efforts to evolve and improve the relationship.
- She also made an attempt to address the relationship between her company and their chief customer. However, the customer company wasn't ready or able to respond to her overtures.
- Great effort was made to improve the capability of the management team to work together as a team. Iva also was working hard to develop her own leadership abilities.

- Because of the technical focus of the company, there was a gap in "soft skill" knowledge and skills. Few conversations were skillful or generative. Iva hoped to develop those skills by introducing many in the company to the conversational tools that supported organizational learning.

Interpreting the Change Strategy

If we look at each of these efforts, we can see that the attempt to develop better relationships between the different factions is a recurring theme.

One way of interpreting the passion that Iva had for trying to transform her organization is to view the situation through the lens of Argyris and Schön's Model I and Model II theories-in-use. As we have said, Model I is characterized by defensive behaviors. In environments shaped by Model I, people tend to advocate and don't seek to understand the positions of others through inquiry. Model I values and behaviors tend to create a reinforcing loop which in turn creates an organizational learning system that reflects Model I. That learning system in turn limits the learning potential of both individuals and the organization. The system perpetuates defensiveness and is a closed, self-sealing system. It does not support the questioning of assumptions and therefore does not support double-loop learning.

In actuality, Iva was not explicitly trying to create a new organizational learning system based on Model II. However, we might see Iva's efforts as emanating from a Model II framework in that she was attempting to cocreate situations and tasks and to share in the responsibility for outcomes. She was seeking to build these factions into a viable decision-making network and to maximize the contributions of each member enabling the widest possible exploration of views. These are all hallmarks of Model II. Had Iva been able to see her actions within the context of this framework, she might have better understood, anticipated, and responded to the difficulties that arose.

In Iva's mental model, relationships were the foundation, the bedrock, of effective functioning. In her view, if we have a good relationship, we will have openness and trust. And if we have openness and trust, then of course we will be inclined toward Model II values. The first step, of course, was to develop the trust and the skills to act in accordance with Model II. Hence, Iva's initial focus was on the OL conversational skills and dialogue.

In Iva's mind, the connection between the importance of relationships, the efficacy of conversation, and the end goals of Model II behaviors was implicit and self-evident. In her vision, there was a clear connection between what the organization was attempting to learn and the development of PDC into an organization where:

- Search is enhanced and deepened;
- Ideas are tested publicly;
- Individuals collaborate to enlarge inquiry; and
- Trust and risk-taking are enhanced.[1]

In other words, Iva envisioned PDC as a learning organization.

Awakening Aspirations

In our view, the primary theme that threads through Iva's story is her struggle to awaken in others that which had been awakened in herself. Whereas Bert was consistently in touch with his devotion to customer service, waiting patiently for the time and place to be right so that he could put his ideas into play—which he believed OL provided, Iva's experience with organizational learning was even more cathartic. Beyond seeing OL as a strategy for the long-term viability of the firm, OL also reawakened her aspirations and put her in touch with that which she truly believed.

Iva: When I got involved with Senge's work I saw that there was another way to lead. It was like a light bulb went on. My body responded to it. I felt this enormous energy. And when I have energy, I act out of energy. That propels me into the future.

Senge very much believes that people in organizations need to aspire to things they care about; organizations need people's aspirations. Iva's story crystallizes for us what deeply felt aspiration looks like. Iva's change effort was animated by her deep desire to create greater freedom in the workplace.

Without completely realizing it, Iva had long been on a path of discovery. Iva was clearly a "lifelong learner" who embraced new ideas easily, particularly when these ideas helped her make new connections between other ideas. Her naturally inquisitive mind sought ways to make connections between seemingly opposite ideas, such as technical knowledge and so-called "soft skills." In the systems thinking approach described in *The Fifth Discipline*, Iva saw that Senge seemed to have masterfully crafted that connection, creating a bridge between two worlds that did not effectively speak to one another.

Even more powerful was the possibility of freedom, of honest dialogue, of being able to speak the truth openly within the walls of a business organization. What might we be able to create if such speech were possible? How much creative potential do we lose by *not* being able to have such conversations?

Often, as in Iva's case, our aspirations come from our own lived experience. Some people know what their aspirations are; they are close to the surface. For others of us, though, finding our true aspirations is a long journey in and of itself. When one discovers what one truly believes in, one will have found a wellspring of creative energy, as Iva did. Then one must begin the difficult work of managing the effect of that creative energy on others.

The systems that we create can constrain the activities of the people within them. And, if the systemic forces are not well understood, people can be defeated by the systems within which they are acting. But the essential thing to remember is that we have created these systems and therefore, through sustained effort, we can also uncreate them and build something better, more life-enhancing. This is easy to say, but far more difficult to do because it will require us to unlearn and unlearning is just plain tough. We are just beginning to come to terms with what learning is. How well do we know how to unlearn? The theme of unlearning weaves its way through Iva's story.

Vision as Wellspring of Change

As we discussed in our debriefing of Bert's story, Senge says that most managers have an implicit theory of growth which he calls the "better mousetrap theory." According to that theory, if an innovation or change initiative is successful, interest will spread; i.e., "our results will speak for themselves." Bert's strategy was very much in line with the better mousetrap theory. Iva's approach to change also resembled the better mousetrap theory although it differed significantly from Bert's.

Iva believes that her implementation of organizational learning lacked deliberateness. She wasn't explicit about her theory of change nor her change strategy. The primary growth engine of her change strategy was her vision; she was also trying to inculcate in the organization the capacity for creating shared vision, which is one of Senge's five disciplines.

Iva: We did not have the plant capacity to compete effectively, yet we were facing enormous upheaval in our industry. Globalization was bringing increased competition, and it was like we were involved in a giant international chess game. I looked at everything that was happening and I realized that in order to become competitive I had to create a new vision for the organization.

Because of my exposure to organizational learning, I decided that that new vision would not be created by just me and my staff, it had to be created by the whole organization. And that's why building the capacity for creating shared vision became an important part of my strategy. That's why I trained people not only in the five disciplines, but also in Covey.[2] My philosophy was a variation on *Field of Dreams.* My philosophy was, "Expose people to the ideas and they will come to see the value in them."

Iva relied primarily on her own vision as an engine of growth—but can vision act as a reinforcing growth process? Vision is a powerful catalyst, but it must be mutually shared in order for it to be an effective, self-reinforcing growth process in the same league with the growth processes that Senge has identified: personal results, business results, and networks of committed people. As Iva herself has said, "Vision that isn't shared is only a dream."

Unfortunately, the majority of the organization did not share Iva's vision. This was not so much because they rejected the vision, but more because they either didn't understand it or they were threatened by it. But, if the desire to create shared vision was so strong, why did the vision fail to be shared? We believe that the answer lies in understanding Iva's strategy. There were at least four factors that impeded the strategy:

- A limited theory of change: Critical reinforcing growth processes were not put in place and effectively nurtured;
- Resistance was underestimated: The "challenges" were not anticipated nor handled successfully;
- The larger system was not supportively engaged in the transformation; and
- The leader's personal transformation was critically linked to the organizational transformation.

A Limited Theory of Change

What about other sources of growth? As we discussed previously, Senge et al. (1999) have described three potential sources of growth for an organizational change effort: personal results, business results, and networks of committed people.[3] To some extent all of these were present, but in a problematic way. For example, some people began to experience personal results, but this had unintended consequences. Those who were experiencing personal results were either starting to feel somewhat distant from the parent company or were being perceived to be somewhat distant. The perception arose that OL was some kind of "cult."

Second, the link to business results was clear to Iva herself, but it was long term and not well understood or accepted by many in the line nor by upper level management. Third, a network of committed people did begin to evolve, but the majority were staff, not line people. Increasingly, these people came to see themselves as vulnerable—as caught between their aspirations and ideals and the values and behaviors of the larger system. If the capacity for having shared vision needed to be developed, then what would sustain the change effort during the time needed to develop the capacity for vision?

Dealing with Resistance

Senge et al. have identified ten common challenges to profound change which seem to occur over and over. Did the ten challenges to profound change described in *The Dance of Change* manifest themselves in Iva's story? If so, what was her response?

Iva: I absolutely encountered all of these barriers. I dealt with each one in my typical fashion, a fashion that I think is typical of executive management. For example, when I heard "there is no time," I pushed back. This was too important, I thought, so find the time. Then when I feared that I pushed too hard, I backed off. I teeter-tottered, trying to find the right mix, but I couldn't.

In the early stages, the leader needs to do sufficient work to ensure that both line and staff understand and see the relevance of OL. And, if time is a factor, options must be created. If not, we place people in a "catch-22" where they must either sacrifice results or sacrifice OL. Neither of these issues were successfully resolved during the early stages of the PDC change effort.

Iva: When I started pushing members of my management team hard for more participation it was inconsistent behavior. On the one hand I started with making it really open and free, and suddenly when they became more free they were told, "You've got to give me your best people to do this."

Relevancy: Dialogue as Dichotomy

Iva unwittingly created a vulnerability by the way in which the five learning disciplines were implemented. A key assumption is that all five of the learning disciplines must be engaged for the change effort to bear fruit. However, during the early stages the PDC learning effort tended to focus on dialogue and the building of generative conversational skills using such tools as the ladder of inference and left-hand, right-hand column. The belief was that these skills were particularly needed to enable the relationship building that Iva believed was so key to a collaborative environment. Therefore, some of the five disciplines took root in fertile soil; others did not.

Iva: In thinking about what theory of change I applied, I realized that I did not look at it from that perspective at that time. I did not make absolutely sure that the people who were engaged in this work had a full understanding of proper balance between all the disciplines and that you can't get engaged only in dialogue or only in causal loop diagrams, whichever discipline was dearest to somebody's heart.

Unfortunately, some began to perceive that dialogue was a waste of precious time. The perception was that dialogue leads to reflection and that leads to insight. But the insight was rarely if ever linked to action. Thus, dialogue seemed to be set in opposition to action—rather than as a productive complement to action. The organization was, by its own admission, crisis oriented. Crisis was the engine for action that gets short-term results. Meanwhile, dialogue was seen as a means of suspending action. Unfortunately, the two cycles did not engage each other, as illustrated in Figure 7.1.

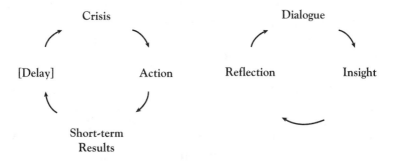

Figure 7.1
Action vs. Reflection

Thus, action and reflection were set up in opposition to each other, whereas there is much agreement that learning is a cycle that involves four dimensions including reflection and action as shown in Figure 7.2.

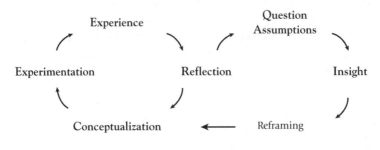

Figure 7.2
The Cycle of Reflection and Learning

Dialogue and other conversational and reflective tools can be seen as being separate from or even opposed to action, but that is an unfortunate misunderstanding. In part this may be due to our reflexive tendency to dichotomize: to think in terms of acting *or* reflecting. Of course, we assume that we only have time for one *or* the other and that reflection takes too much time.

In actuality, reflective observation is part of how we learn, as we also see in Figure 7.2. And, as we have already discussed, there is no learning without taking action. Because our society has somewhat conditioned us to believe that action is all-important, dialogue can be introduced as a means for getting us to appreciate the qualitative change in our thinking that can occur when we are not just acting and reacting without taking time to reflect. The problem is that we can forget to link dialogue and other reflective activities back into action.

From Iva's experience we can learn that OL tools such as Dialogue must be positioned such that people understand their purpose within a larger context. They must also be implemented with the context of Model II, reinforcing the idea that people make a free and informed choice to participate.

Organizational Learning Tools and Cultural Compatibility

Since Dialogue was too foreign to the organization we again wonder if there is yet another challenge, the challenge of compatibility. Research on innovation diffusion tells us that the successful adoption and diffusion of an innovation is generally dependent upon five factors:

1. The perceived **Relative Advantage**—To what degree is the innovation perceived as being better than the idea it supersedes?

2. **Compatibility**—To what degree is the innovation perceived as being consistent with the existing values (and beliefs), past experiences, and needs of potential adopters?

3. **Complexity**—To what degree is the innovation perceived as relatively difficult to understand and use?

4. **Trialability**—To what degree can it be experimented with on a limited basis?

5. **Observability**—To what degree are the results of an innovation visible to others?[4]

Is there a reason to think that OL is immune from meeting the same criteria that seem to predict the success of other innovations? The learning effort at PDC illustrates how OL can be rejected if aspects of it are seen to be too complex to understand or incompatible with the existing culture, or if the relative advantage of OL is not perceived (and embraced) and the results not readily observable.

Despite the fact that these early challenges—relevancy and time—were not resolved, the PDC change effort was able to proceed into the next phase, where it picked up further challenges, like a racehorse picking up handicaps.

The Dilemma of Assessment and Measures

Generally, OL change efforts follow a certain trajectory. First, people are trained in the five disciplines, then a pilot project starts up which applies the disciplines. If the pilot demonstrates some success, then there is a diffusion attempt. While the pilot is ongoing, the three challenges of sustaining usually crop up. The first is the challenge of assessment.

Iva's primary focus was on the long-term viability of the firm but not at the neglect of the short term. She believed that she understood the root causes of the company's current inability to derive a satisfactory return on assets (ROA), and she believed that she was working on the solution.

While she had worked through her strategy with her first boss, that agreement did not carry over to her new boss. De facto, she was proceeding without certainty of his support, but some impediment prevented them from having that necessary conversation. Then, like most corporations in a highly competitive market, there was little to no patience for waiting for long-term results, particularly in the face of short-term drops in profit.

Iva: I was always interested in integrating OL with the business and in producing results. The unfortunate thing was that the larger corporate system and I were viewing the world differently. They had no understanding of interrelatedness and especially no understanding that cause-and-effect are separated in space and time, which makes it very difficult to connect them. Now, of course, that's not unique to Philips.

In the early days of navigation, before there were good, reliable marine charts, sailors operated via a technique they called "dead reckoning," a practice still in use today. They calculated or guessed the course and distance traveled from a previously determined position. Until we have more detailed maps and more sophisticated navigational devices, we will have to dead reckon our way through treacherous organizational waters. We can't do so alone. Both the evaluators and the evaluatees must collaborate in determining how they will be measured. This can sound naïve, for those who measure can often make the rules to suit them. However, if we don't make the effort to predetermine and agree on some measures, we run the risk of getting lost.

For OL to be successful, we must work out ways of assessing and measuring our learning efforts. This is for the benefit of ourselves as well as for those who are evaluating us. Even more important, we must have agreements about our interim and final milestones. We have to know if we are off-course so that we can recorrect as soon as possible. What are the progress indicators that prevent prematurely pulling the plug? Do these progress indicators take into account the fact that things often get worse before better? Do they consider the fact that our results may differ from, and thus violate, our institutional memory?

When Fear Shows Up

The discovery of "two camps" on Iva's management team might illustrate the challenge Senge calls "fear and anxiety." Senge says that challenge tends to show up when some progress has actually been made.[5] So, in a sense, it is a positive sign. The problem is that now the real problems are exposed and people become very insecure. They realize that they are on a very different road from that of the status quo and they want to know how much real commitment they have and how much support they have.

Iva: It was so clear to me that organizational learning made sense that I took it for granted that others on the management team could see this as well. I was driving the learning efforts forward because I had such a strong belief in this work!

If I had known that some on my management team were unclear, that they really didn't see the value of OL, or they really didn't feel ready to make the commitment, I'm certain that I would have slowed down. I would have spent time with them, inquiring and coaching, until they could see it clearly. The problem was that they weren't telling me. They were agreeing with me on the one hand and then saying, "We don't have time" on the other. It was classic left-hand, right-hand column stuff. There was no genuine, shared commitment to profound change. And I failed to see that.

Perhaps I did not want to see. I believed that if this work were to stop, restarting it would be more time consuming and that the chances of success would be diminished. I knew there was no magic formula for making our business more effective. We had to do the hard work of changing our thinking, and changing the way we went about decision making, controlling, commanding, planning, and developing. All of the old rules were not going to work anymore. Of that I was certain.

One interpretation of the discovery of "two camps" on the PDC management team is that they were reaching the point of deep commitment. Some on the team perceived the gulf between the parent company's stance and Iva's vision for PDC. The question had to be raised and the fact that it showed up then was as much a function of how change happens as it was of anything else. It could be interpreted as a sign of health. The system was flexing its might; real change was in the offing. The demarcation between line and staff is currently a weak point in many organizations. The two groups tend to have different priorities and perspectives and, unfortunately, Model I theory-in-use makes it difficult to cross those chasms. So when stress occurs, things tend to break at the weak point.

Holding Strong Belief Lightly

Yet another challenge to learning efforts is the phenomenon that Senge et al. have termed "true-believers vs. non-believers." This, too, was present. The staff people who believed in the merits of organizational learning began to be perceived as a cult by those who felt like outsiders by comparison. The special terms and language of OL became turnoffs. Outside of PDC, Iva's attempts to spread the word resulted first in an apparent opening, and then in a more solidified resistance. Without realizing it, Iva was manifesting the signs of a true believer. Unwittingly, she was threatening the system with the strength of her purpose and her vision—and the system reacted.

Was there a strategy that could have been put in place at that time to keep the change effort going? Rollo May once wrote that there is a curious paradox characteristic of every kind of courage. It is the "seeming contradiction that we must be fully committed, but we must also be aware at the same time that we might possibly be wrong."[6] The antidote to the temptation to be a true believer is to learn to live with this paradox, the paradox of commitment and doubt. If we can stand there, resistance looks different. Resistance must be anticipated ahead of time, ameliorated, but also welcomed as part of the natural course of events. Resistance is our teacher.

Engaging the Larger System

As time went on, management of the interface between the larger system (Philips management) became increasingly problematical. Attempts to diffuse OL tools and techniques were met with some initial openness, and then with almost complete resistance. Iva attempted to seed the governance of Philips with OL concepts, but in fact, she only succeeded in triggering the preexisting tension between autonomy and control. In the end, the OL work was perceived as leading PDC to be out of control. Again, the existing system asserted itself.

Iva: I was perceived as drifting too far from the Mother ship. Everybody else was organized the same except us. My boss wanted to pull me in and I resisted.

In one sense, Iva seems to have had tried to do too much—without sufficient support. Using the metaphor of the proverbial rubber band she seems to have stretched the organization too far toward the vision and too far away from current reality. Rather than trying just to engage the larger system and to gain support for her change effort, she tried to *convert* the larger system as well. The resulting tension—both within the local system (PDC) and between the local system and the larger system—was too great.

Iva: All of this was moving along nicely, but then there was a crisis at Philips. They demanded that we stop all travel, etc., so we stopped sending people to be trained in OL. But sometime later we started again. It was moving in the direction of my vision, which was that you have to give people the skills, you have to give them tools, you have to go slowly.
You have to get the operating people involved because if you only get staff people, nothing's going to happen. But that set up a crucial conundrum: How could I get the factory people involved? They were caught between a rock and a hard place. We had a great position in the market. Our customers wanted more, but the factory didn't have the capacity to meet demand. So we drove people into the ground to make more tubes and then we had a strike. And that's when everything began to fall apart.

Iva was very much invested in stirring the creative energies of the firm through alignment around a purpose The early work in developing a company credo shows her foresight. But, again, thinking "outside the box" seems to have stretched the tolerance of the organization.

Iva: Looking back, I can see that I was always trying to fulfill what I saw as a strategy and vision deficit in Philips. My concern was that Philips was continuously behind in developing a strategy for the business. For example, we were the first to say, "You're going to have to build tubes larger than 27 inches because of this market." But upper management said, "No." Then our competitors did it and took 90 percent of the market in the U.S. Then we came into that market, but five years later. We were too late. Perhaps the European management couldn't accept a vision coming from the U.S.

Unfortunately, in committing herself to the long term, short-term results were not forthcoming in terms the parent company could understand, and Iva was vulnerable. As a consequence, resistance was mounting within and rejection was mounting at European HQ. Without clear results to point to—and some negative impacts apparently in evidence—time ran out. In a sense, the larger system had no "choice" but to respond in a rejecting manner. As Senge reminds us, although these systemic reactions come at us in the form of individuals, these forces are not personal. Despite our tendency to react personally to these perceived "attacks" or strong resistance, there is power in our developing the ability to see these very individual acts as merely the manifestations of the system attempting to preserve itself. And we must also see ourselves as a force attempting to throw the system out of equilibrium.[7] From this perspective we can see that if we are to lead change successfully, we must understand how to work artfully with these systemic forces.

There are several opportunities to reflect, inquire, and learn here: we can reflect upon our own approach to engagement and also upon scope. How much can and should we take on? Are we attempting to "boil the ocean?" Are we too set on convincing people that we know what's best for them? Are we forgetting to manage to the requirements of the old system while trying to drag it, single-handedly, kicking and screaming into the future? Could Iva have negotiated the safety to engage with OL as a corporate-sponsored experiment?

Personal Transformation and Organizational Change: A Crucial Link

In Iva's story, the quest for personal transformation and organizational transformation are much more intertwined than in Bert's story. Iva embraced the notion of personal change. She saw great opportunities for personal growth in the OL techniques and she embraced them wholeheartedly.

Iva: I was very committed to Dialogue, and my involvement with it tended to surface some critical new learnings for me about myself as a person and my leadership style.

Through her work with Dialogue (in particular, with her management team), Iva was beginning to understand the dynamics that led to the fear-based reactions and behaviors that are so intrinsic to Model I. Unfortunately, she was doing this learning without sufficient understanding of, or support for, the transformation required to learn and create Model II.

Iva: Early on when I became president I asked for and got a lot of feedback on my management style. I was listening to that feedback and that's why I started to change the way I acted. I learned that I was perceived as being quite aggressive—but, ironically, that was not how I saw myself. I saw myself as being quite fearful. And when I'm scared I don't run away. I go after what I want even more. This came from the background that I grew up in. In Yugoslavia at that time, if you're scared, you're dead. I learned that nothing good comes out of fear. So I learned to act very aggressively when I was in fear.

While her personal learning deepened, many in PDC were in a watchful and wary mode. Having been sold and having endured several downsizings, as well as being used to command-and-control management, many people in Iva's organization took their cues from their leader. Because they also lacked an understanding of the transformation process, they were often confused by what seemed like contradictory behavior on the part of the leader.

Iva recognized the interdependency between her personal transition and that of the organization. She had had to undertake a "heroic journey" in order to make it to where she was. The success that comes with hero-leadership is a double-edged sword. On the positive side, hero-leaders come to value their ability to forcefully bring about their ideas; they feel masterful. On the negative side, they may become less able to read subtle signals or to work with the intangible forces of systemic change. We believe that most traditional and heroic command-and-control leaders will, by definition, have a hard time making the transition into being a leader of OL efforts.

> **Iva:** I began to realize that in order to build an organization that was capable of learning, I would have to become a different kind of leader. *And I wanted to be a different kind of leader.* I was not happy with how I was perceived. I did not want to be a leader who instilled confidence and fear simultaneously, who was simultaneously loved and feared, but a leader who would enable building of an environment in which people would be able to create what they truly desire.
>
> I was very much a work-in-progress at the time, but I was making a deliberate effort to change and to become a more participatory, enlightened leader. As we all know, it's easy to talk, but much harder to walk the talk, and even more difficult to help others walk their talk. But we started slowly making progress.

Senge's view is that organizational transformation begins with change on the personal level. The one is not possible without the other. Argyris's theoretical framework explains in more detail how and why this link is so critical. As people learn Model II, Argyris believes that they will necessarily create a learning system that then feeds back to reinforce their new Model II theory-in-use. In other words, *the process of individual and organizational transformation occurs simultaneously and it is self-reinforcing.* The transformation of the organization's learning system (from one based in Model I to one based in Model II) cannot occur without the transformation of individuals from Model I to Model II; likewise, individual transformation will be impeded unless the organization's learning system also transforms. The change processes are interdependent.[8]

Iva was deeply convinced of the potential of OL. She was so convinced that she felt it was her duty to try to convince others. Because the organization was taking its clues from Iva, it was very important that she "walk the talk." But for any leader schooled in command-and-control, this style change is not immediately achievable. Even when there was evidence of commitment, Iva tended to be out ahead of the pack, the lonely leader at the top.

The leader who is engaging in this type of change must enlist help. He or she must be willing to ask for and receive immediate feedback on how well their actions are reflecting their espoused beliefs. Iva lacked consistent and sophisticated help in this area. She relied on sporadic feedback, so it wasn't clear to the organization that she was actively seeking feedback and that it was making a difference. But the responsibility does not only lie with the leader. In turn, people in the organization must learn to provide feedback and also allow for a learning curve—but they can't unless they are explicitly asked to do so.

Iva faced particular challenges here in that her personality is charismatic and forceful and because she had learned throughout her life to push through obstacles. Here, finally, was something different. Here was a life lesson of profound portent. Here was the opportunity to understand the true nature of resistance, to see it as a systemic property. Here was a chance for Iva to rethink everything upon which she had built her life. She took that chance, but not without a lot of resistance of her own.

Iva: It's interesting for me to reflect on this now. I see that I was primarily relying on my ability to move things forward because that's what I did all my life. But at the same time I was keenly aware that I couldn't push OL because this is a different kind of work. So I was teeter-tottering between the two positions of taking charge and doing it, and just letting it emerge.

I was able to see the change effort as a system, but I was not able to guide my actions accordingly. I see now that my tendency was to push on the levers on the reinforcing loop—to be even stronger in my vision and my conviction—rather than paying sufficient attention to the balancing loops.

I knew the balancing loops were there, but I had only a conceptual understanding of them, not a practical sense of how to use them. My management training worked against me. I didn't give us a chance to work through the inevitable time delays. I could have also seen that resistance could have been seen as a balancing loop, but instead of inquiring into the reasons for the resistance I continued to try to convince people that this was a good pathway. Rather than exploring or deepening my understanding of the assumptions held by people who resisted, I pushed on.

Building a Bridge Between Two Systems

Iva was, indeed, gifted with a vision of what could be. But vision, like pragmatism, is both a strength and a weakness. Iva was driven to attempt much: she tried to engage deep organizational learning within the context of a Model I learning system without fully understanding the enormity of what she was attempting or anticipating the resistance she was likely to encounter. She tried to build an infrastructure that would support learning while simultaneously trying to get a handle on the basics. She also tried to convert others to her vision more than she tried to inquire into and honor the beliefs and concerns of others.

Iva believed that the future viability of the organization lay in transforming the current conditions to a new set of conditions. These conditions are summarized in Table 7.1.

Table 7.1
Current Reality and Vision

Current Reality	Vision
▪ Hierarchical, command-and-control environment	▪ Participatory climate where we cocreate
▪ Lack of trust	▪ Trusting environment where we support each other's learning and growth
▪ Resentful compliance	▪ Free and informed choice; clarity about what we want to create
▪ Favoring logic at expense of feelings	▪ Balance between logic and feelings
▪ Tendency to conform and be fearful of difference	▪ Appreciation of diversity; people can be authentic and express who they really are

Using Argyris's framework, we believe that Iva saw the possibility—and the perceived necessity—of moving the organization in the direction of Model II. She had a strong implicit commitment to Model II theory-in-use, and her espoused values were in line with it. In essence, Model I values are fear-based and self-protective; they tend to surface in situations of potential threat or embarrassment. This is why we have a tendency to revert to Model I while we are learning Model II.

Argyris has also written that the tendency to operate according to Model I values tends to be universal and is rooted in our upbringing. Therefore, it is difficult to shed or even discern the existence of Model I unless we are taught to do so. We can say, then, that Model I is shaped by a worldview—a worldview that is fearful. Out of the research in physics and other sources, an alternative worldview seems to be arising that challenges the worldview that shaped Model I.

The contrast between the dominant Industrial Age worldview and the alternative worldview that is unfolding is represented in Table 7.2.

Table 7.2
Contrasting Worldiews

Industrial Age Worldview	Emergent Worldview
• Mechanical system	• Living system
• Parts are separate and have only a mechanical relationship to each other	• Parts are intrinsically related to whole and vice versa
• The assumption of linear cause-and-effect relationships	• Non-linear causality
• Reductionistic thinking	• Holistic thinking
• Dichotomous thinking, which makes reconciliation of apparent opposites difficult	• Interconnection and interdependence

If we accept this characterization, then we might see these two learning systems, Model I and Model II, as embedded within two contrasting worldviews. The worldviews are themselves systems, though of a much larger nature. They are equally self-reinforcing.

If we accept this characterization, then yet another challenge emerges. The challenge is for those who believe in the efficacy of Model II and who likewise share a belief in the efficacy of the emerging worldview. The challenge is twofold:

1. To articulate a clear pathway to the new system, while

2. simultaneously honoring the old system.

Because of our tendency to dichotomize (encouraged by our prevailing worldview), our seemingly "natural" tendency will be to set these two worldviews in opposition to one another. This tendency tends to create the true believer and the perception of OL as a cult. What is needed instead of revolutionary thinking is the thoughtful cocreative, skillful creation of a bridge or pathway to the new worldview.

The bridge between Model I and Model II learning systems is relatively well-delineated. This is partly because Argyris does not ask that people abandon their tendencies toward attribution and evaluation; he only asks that they make the reasoning behind those attributions and evaluations transparent so that they can be openly challenged and tested. The same kind of bridge-building needs to occur between these two worldviews. It is possible that the building blocks for the bridge can be found in those things that these two hold in common.

When we focus on the differences between the two spheres (versus the bridging elements) we make it harder to articulate the connections between the two. Ironically, we make the chasm wider and therefore harder for people to walk across.

• • •

Bert's journey spoke to us about values and pragmatism. Iva's journey reminds us of the power of vision and conviction, but reminds us to temper that conviction with flexibility in strategy and tactics. It also emphasizes the importance of inquiry and of gaining consensus around the perceptions of current reality, the possible vision, and the pathway between the two. It also leaves us with some questions about the role of the leader.

In the next chapter, Bert and Iva engage in double-loop learning, reflecting on the assumptions that led them to make the decisions they made in the course of their journeys.

Endnotes

1. Chris Argyris, *On Organizational Learning* (Malden, MA: Blackwell Publishers, 1999), p.181.

2. Stephen Covey, *Principle-Centered Leadership* (New York: Simon & Schuster, 1991).

3. Peter Senge et al., *Dance of Change: The Challenges of Sustaining Momentum in Learning Organizations* (New York: Doubleday, 1999), pp. 42–57

4. Everett Rogers, *Diffusion of Innovations* (New York: Free Press, 1995).

5. Senge et al., 1999, op. cit., pp. 241–247.

6. Rollo May, *The Courage to Create* (New York: W.W. Norton, 1975), p. 20.

7. Senge et al., 1999, op. cit. To further understand these systemic forces and the necessary interplay between them, see Ralph D. Stacey, *Complexity and Creativity in Organizations* (San Francisco: Berrett-Koehler, 1996).

8. Robert Louis Flood, *Rethinking the Fifth Discipline: Learning Within the Unknowable* (London: Rutledge, 1999).

Chapter 8

The Double Loop: What Have We Learned?

In the debriefing chapters we explored and analyzed some of the key aspects of Bert and Iva's strategies. However, an objective analysis is never sufficient for an assessment of a learning effort because such an assessment tends to corroborate Model I theory-in-use. When someone stands outside someone else's experience and evaluates it, they tend to make attributions and judgments. The reasoning behind these evaluations is generally not revealed nor is it open to question. Therefore, this type of assessment does not necessarily engender further learning, particularly on the part of those involved. It is our belief that the most important learning occurs when people can reflect together upon their own and each other's actions, develop insights into their patterns and behaviors, and then make adjustments in their actions based on that reframing, observing and reflecting upon the result. This is double-loop learning and most often it requires some assistance from someone skilled in the reflective learning process.

In this chapter, Bert and Iva attempt to model this double-loop learning process. They will examine the assumptions that they held during their change efforts. Ideally, double-loop learning that happens at an individual and team level would translate into learning at the organizational level, i.e., people in the organization would design their actions based on a revised set of assumptions. This cannot be the case here. Still, we are privileged to listen in, observe what this might be like for us, and imagine how we might do this type of reflection ourselves, in real-time.

Iva: Bert, do you think that your experience with OL was a success or a failure?

Bert: Well, as much as I would like to claim that it was a success, I think that it was something in between. I changed some procedures and changed some people's lives for the better and in that sense, it worked. On a personal level, I think I learned from my mistakes. But at the organizational level, I didn't get people in influential places to adopt organizational learning per se. Nor was I able to find a way to diffuse the learnings that came out of our efforts. I made solid relationships with some unexpected people in the union, but I did not get critical mass at the bottom and I didn't get it at the top either. My motto has always been "leave it better than you found it," and I don't believe I left it better than I found it in any meaningful way.

Iva: Because there was no lasting change?

Bert: There was no lasting change. I don't think that there was a turning point at my company because I did OL.

Iva: I feel similarly. I believe that this work did have a positive impact on many individuals. However, I also think that some people were hurt. Now, of course, there doesn't appear to be a trace of it at PDC and it's not clear how much it permeated the larger system.

Bert: The question is: What can we learn from our experiences that might be useful to others?

Iva: In the spirit of double-loop learning, I'd like us to look at what some of our key assumptions were when we started out. Let's see if they need to change.

Bert: I'll do it, but I'm a little apprehensive. I don't like exposing my misperceptions—which, of course, is exactly what double-loop learning is all about.

Iva: That's precisely why we need to do it. The double-loop learning process is the antithesis of management as we know it. When you're in management you're expected to have all the answers. You have to be ahead of everyone else. You can't be open about your mistakes.

Bert: And, of course, if you know the answers, there's no reason to learn. That's a perfect example of a closed system.

The Road Divides

Iva: I'll start by saying that I have learned a great deal as I progressed on my leadership journey. I developed a deep longing to bring more of my personal values into the leadership of my organization, but I also discovered that that was harder than I thought because, in many ways, I had lost touch with myself. Something had happened on the road to upper management that shifted me away from being aligned at the core of my being.

Bert: Like you, I had these strong values. But I felt that I had to put them on hold for a long time. I believed that I couldn't quite implement them because of the realities of the business, but I always thought, "There's got to be another way." Organizational learning seemed to provide the way to bring those values back into the business.

Iva: For me, too, but that's also where the road divides. You proceeded in a very cautious way whereas I didn't. I was very committed to getting others to experience what I had experienced and to seeing the merit of organizational learning. I think that's because when I got involved with the Organizational Learning Center at MIT we started talking about things that I had been feeling and thinking all my life but had never expressed in the work environment, and I began realizing the importance of them.

So, as president, I tried to transform the organization I led and I also tried to bring these new ideas to the rest of the company. I became the proverbial boss who goes to a course and comes back "talking funny." Then, later, I became the Senior VP of Manufacturing Technology for the American (U.S.) Region. The job was located in U.S. corporate headquarters and that environment seemed as if it came from a previous century. The command-and-control management style permeated the entire environment, from the layout of the executive suites to the furniture, to dress codes, to everything. I tried to proselytize my ideas to the rest of the company. I began talking about organizational learning. Do you think they listened? Hah!

Bert: In the beginning I was also very excited and very gung ho about the potential for organizational learning in my company. I thought I had found the answer to a lot of the problems that the company was facing. I tried to bring that enthusiasm back to my company, but for some reason it didn't translate well and in the early stages I began to worry about why this organizational learning stuff wasn't taking hold. I used to walk around and say to myself, "Why don't they see this?" I began to think that I had done something wrong, or that I wasn't a good enough change agent. I thought the problem was with me.

I found out that you can really drive yourself into an absolute frenzy about your lack of capabilities as a change agent because you think if you've been successful all your life at solving business problems, this is just another one of the problems. I'm an engineer, and engineers are like that, thinking they can solve anything. But being an agent of this kind of change is another thing entirely.

Iva: When I talked about my new view of the world with people in the company I went so far as to say that we will eventually eliminate hierarchies as they are seen today. I had a metaphor that I used: an organization is like a slinky. It moves very rapidly in different directions. It has a continuously changing and evolving shape with tremendous flexibility. And then I talked about the organization as being a spiral instead of a pyramid. You can be on the same side of the spiral and have more influence, depending on what side you're going to. I could see it so clearly!

But I learned that others weren't able to see it. Or they were afraid of it. Or I just wasn't clear. Later, I learned that as a leader of organizational learning I have to take more responsibility for my communication. I need to ensure that people understand the intention behind my communications because it appears that many times they misunderstood and I was unaware of it.

Bert: The failure of that first project told me that my approach to changing the organization wasn't working. That caused me to rethink my strategy. After that, I switched gears and I got very pragmatic. I knew I needed a very practical platform from which to introduce new ideas because when we tried to introduce quality into our organization people didn't have time for it because they didn't perceive it as real work. They had their "real job" to do so they couldn't go to the Quality Improvement meetings. I always found this very exasperating, but that's the way it was perceived.

I began to think that those of us running the Quality meetings had created those perceptions ourselves because the kinds of problems we gave people to solve were affectionately known as "moving the water cooler around." Basically, they were meaningless in terms of people's real day-to-day jobs. So TQM got a bad rap. I tried to use my learning from that and not make the same mistake when I began introducing systems thinking. So I made *other* mistakes instead.

Working with Culture

Iva: One of the things I did was underestimate the importance of culture. Looking back I can see that I didn't really understand how to work within the culture of my organization. I tried to change the culture and create a new culture.

I believed that I understood the culture of the factory, but I did not do a formal cultural assessment. Then I tried to change the factory culture and make it more like the culture in the headquarters by bringing in organizational learning, but I failed to understand that the employees in the factory really did not appreciate things that came from outside.

Bert: So you had two assumptions: You assumed that you understood the factory culture and you also assumed that you knew how to change it.

Iva: Not only that, I assumed that the culture needed to change and that it needed to be homogenous. Those were critical assumptions and I did not inquire into them at all.[1]

Bert: One of the things I assumed from the beginning is that the culture of a company is like a slingshot. It can only stretch so far before it snaps back—and when it snaps back you can really get hurt. To go into it with the idea that you're going to change the culture is to encourage what I call the "biological rejection phenomenon." Like a slingshot, if you create too much tension in trying to change it, the culture will try to restore itself. Therefore, *you have to use the culture in order to change the culture.*[2] In other words, you have to use what people in the culture currently value, like results, as a platform for initiating new ideas and in this way pull them along to a new approach.

Iva: I see what you're saying, but I wonder about it. You can't pull anyone along. A change in culture happens only through learning so I agree that you have to start with understanding the culture to see what people value and are willing and capable to change—but then you have to help them learn.

Bert: My belief is that you have to move incrementally, by staying below the "alert" level. Ideally you work with people in such a way that they get an "Aha!" and they think it's their idea. That's what I tried to do, whereas I think you were too visionary in your approach. The role of the leader is to create the path between the vision and the current reality. The leader has to create the mechanisms that enable the organization to adapt to change while not foregoing the issue of management. The role of the leader is not to be a revolutionary but to reform. You were more on the revolutionary path.

Iva: So the answer is to be more pragmatic?

Bert: Yes. The more we believe in something the closer we get to being zealots, and therefore we are less likely to see the pitfalls. I think that happened in your case. I proceeded more cautiously than you did— but maybe too cautiously, as I think back. Our biggest strength is frequently our biggest weakness. The one thing I'm still sure of was that I had to play the financial game. I knew I had to deliver my financial results while making these changes happen.

Iva: I was very conscious of financial results, also, but I believed that there were systemic reasons why our results were lagging behind, such as lack of capital, outdated processes, and a culture that was resistant to change. I was trying to work on those systemic reasons but I failed to create the conditions with my new boss so that he was in support of my efforts. Without that, we were at risk. Instead, I assumed that I could hold him off until I created the results, then he would see that I was right. That was a huge assumption on my part. I see now that I should have inquired into his reasoning and tried to see the situation from his point of view but at the time I was not far enough along in developing my capacity to act in accordance with Model II.

Bert: We both struggled with the fine points of strategy. I found that I was lacking in strategizing skills. I believed in using the culture to change the culture, but I didn't know much more about how to go from A to B—I sort of went by gut. Sometimes it would just click. I would do things sometimes on the spur of the moment. I had a catch phrase that I always used, "I'll make the decisions and deal with the consequences."

Iva: What do you think about that now?

Bert: I don't think it was the most effective way. Although I made a lot of friends with this approach, I also made a lot of enemies.

Iva: So maybe you had an underlying assumption that got in the way?

Bert: I was a hands-on person, a construction guy. Everybody knew I was a technician from construction. That was an advantage in our culture. If I stood up and said something in a meeting everybody listened because they believed that I knew what I was talking about. Me, too. I used to think, "I came from the ranks so I know what's what." As long as I was in my element, I knew my element. After my first project attempt failed I found out very quickly that I had better learn more about what works and what doesn't work in terms of a change strategy. Now suddenly I was not so much the expert. I was also very concerned about dealing with people who had power and who also had different opinions. That was a big challenge for me and, as a result, I started going on a learning journey.

Iva: This is the exact same experience I had. I knew picture tubes in-and-out. I was the expert. I sat on a global management team with a whole bunch of guys who knew less than I did about picture tubes so when I spoke about picture tubes and processes, everyone listened. But then, when I started talking about organizational learning, that was the end of my influence.

Bert: How do you speak with expertise about something that by definition you're just learning about? You're on a journey and you don't have definitive answers—

Iva: In most business environments your position is based on your expertise. You have to know the answers. If your answers are right, then you deserve to be where you are. But if you suddenly start talking about learning, everyone starts to ask, "What happened to you? Who needs you if you have to learn?"

Bert: So, I was no longer the expert. Then I realized that I had to learn how to anticipate things more. My natural tendency was to react and to make the decisions and then deal with the consequences. I needed to be much more of a reflective person. It was devastating to me when my first project failed. It just blew me out of the water. I couldn't deal with the consequences. It hit me harder than I thought it would.

Iva: So, you were in this cycle of making a decision and dealing with the consequences later. Was there an underlying assumption?

Bert: The assumption was that I wouldn't make mistakes very often! That comes out of a little bit of cockiness and self-assuredness. But I was doing OL and slowly realizing that I don't have a very efficient way of learning myself. I didn't do much double-loop learning while I was in the middle of things.

Iva: Well, I can relate to that. I, too, am very action-oriented. I can push very well for what I want. And instead of reflecting when I come up against an obstacle, I tend to push harder.

Therefore, my number one learning with regard to strategy is: Understand the origin and construction of the balancing loops. This is especially important for leaders, like myself, who have been successful by pushing on the reinforcing loop. Most leaders know how to do that very well, particularly leaders in my age group.

Bert: Is there a double-loop learning for you?

Iva: All through my life my deepest assumption has always been that success comes through effort. I have always had to push for what I want. That has been a very successful strategy, but now I have learned that that strategy can sometimes backfire.

The skill I need to develop is to be able to see the systemic structure that is operating in the moment. If I can stop myself from jumping into my old pattern and see the situation from a systemic point of view, then I will know when it is time to stop pushing and deal with the balancing process by removing barriers. I know intellectually that if you minimize the effects of the balancing process, the total result would go up probably more than if you continue pushing on the reinforcing loop, but it is hard for me to think that way in the moment. It's much easier for me to jump into pushing.

Bert: I also feel that I didn't do a good job of anticipating consequences and barriers. I let the ten challenges Senge describes come up and then walked right into them.[3] I would almost call that incomplete thinking.

Iva: I did the same. Often, I didn't even recognize that the challenges had come up. What is the assumption operating there?

Bert: I was working in a just-in-time mode. I assumed that I didn't have to think about these things ahead of time and I also assumed that I'd be able to deal with whatever showed up. But I found that I failed to apply some of the things I know. I mean, I knew them but I didn't apply them when I needed to.

Iva: You had the knowledge and you had the experience. I just wondered what got in the way of putting them together?

Bert: Oh, I think I know exactly: a personal deficiency when it comes to rejection. I felt rejected.

Iva: So you saw it as rejection—instead of, of course, here's the barrier, here it comes—

Bert: I see those things as fiascoes. I use that word because I blew it. Failure is one thing. Failure is when something doesn't go the way you planned. A fiasco is much worse.

Iva: So you don't like to fail.

Bert: Not at all. I evolved to having patience with both myself and the change process, but I didn't start there—I learned it through pain. My first inclination was to beat myself up. I kept saying to myself, "Why don't they see it?" Oh, I was very frustrated. I just couldn't put the two ends together. I was stuck because I have these strong opinions about the bottom line and the financial aspect of things. I am almost married to that. And then I see the other side and I recognize that the two of them could actually be very harmonious, but I don't know how to put them together easily because it takes time and I'm a Type A personality.[4] I get very frustrated.

Later on I evolved to the "field of dreams" idea. I wanted to get acceptance for what I was trying to institute. So in order to speed up the timing my tendency was to move the tension the other way, move it closer to current reality—

Iva: Whereas I kept creating more tension both for myself and for everyone else by emphasizing the gap between current reality and the vision, and constantly stretching toward the vision.

Bert: In contrast, I thought I was pretty astute to negotiate for air cover. My air cover would be like the proverbial "canary in the mine" and that feedback would help me modulate my pacing and timing. I didn't trust myself to be sensitive enough to perceive how the organization was responding so I was going to use my air cover to help me. In that way I thought I could balance action and nonaction.

Iva: You found an external monitor since you couldn't do it yourself. I didn't even seek air cover because I was a heroic leader. I had to be in front of the troops. I had to take the bullets. I had to be up in front and I had to protect them. I created the air cover for other people.

Bert: Well, I am still very much into the hero thing. I think OL takes a leader who provides the environment that's necessary, who's associated with it, who's in the right position. Absent that, upper management could stop it in an instant.

Iva: I think that the sustainability of a learning effort requires more than heroic leadership; it requires critical mass. It's tough to sustain organizational learning if the interest is just at the top or just at the bottom. The critical factor isn't necessarily the percentage of people involved, but rather the importance of the projects where OL is used. It has to be strategically placed within the organization and that's going to be different for every organization.

And then, of course, it requires the leader to manage upwards. I didn't do that well enough. Do you think that maybe you could have gotten your upper management to buy in?

Bert: Oh, absolutely. My problem was that I didn't do a lot of missionary work. I didn't do anything to reconcile, mitigate, or include resistance. When I met with resistance I would stop and evaluate whether it was absolutely essential for me to deal with it. But the truth of the matter is that I did not spend a lot of time and effort trying to engage people or trying to understand the rhythm of things. I just said, "Well OK, under condition A, go to solution B."

Iva: Very linear thinking.

Bert: Oh, very linear. I justified it in my own mind by saying I just wasn't going to play the political games. In retrospect, I should have spent a lot more time in conversation. For a long time, I did not value Dialogue very much.

Iva: And by extension, conversation?

Bert: Well, hopefully not that far, but I didn't have a lot of patience with conversations that didn't have an intended outcome. If a conversation looked real open-ended, I called that "fluff and stuff."

Iva: I wonder if you feel that way because we in management have a tendency to overcorrect? For example, we spend the majority of our time in meetings trying to define outcomes that get us the results we want. Then we take some time out and go get some management training. Through that training we realize that we might not be getting the results we want because we don't know how to really talk with each other any more. So we start to practice holding conversations where we don't look for immediate outcomes. Maybe we do this in such a way that it becomes an overcorrection—and, as a result, people like you don't see the value and they get turned off.

Learning and Leadership

Iva: I've come to the conclusion that the sustainability of a learning effort also has a lot to do with the leader's capacity for learning. The leader has to continuously learn. That means you have to continuously reflect, which says you have to be open to the fact that you don't always know what to do. You have to be willing to admit to your own mistakes. Once you recognize and reflect on them you will learn.

Bert: That's a good point. And tough for me because I'm not a reflective person by nature. I didn't do a lot of double-loop learning along the way.

Iva: That connects to my second key learning, which is that to be able to do all of the above, leaders need to have personal mastery (one of Senge's five disciplines). It's very nice to say, "We're going to do all this. We're going to learn to trust," and use all these beautiful words, but as leaders we have to be able to live according to our words. Leaders need to have the capacity for reflection and they need to be able to attend to feedback of all kinds.

Very often I didn't see the assumptions that underlay my thinking. In fact, I did the typical thing that so many managers do. I saw only those things that I wanted to see, the things that affirmed my beliefs. It goes without saying that I did not have this insight while I was in the midst of things. That realization only occurred upon reflection, and much later. Eventually I discovered that my approach—this evangelistic approach—was not successful. But it took me a long time to realize that.

Bert: In the beginning I did not put a lot of value on personal mastery. I thought that the concept of "situational leadership" was more important. I thought it was sufficient to describe the kind of leader that was needed. To me situational leadership meant that the leader had the ability to be the right person at the right time. It's not only about having the knowledge, it's also having the ability to be attuned to the specifics of the situation: to do the right thing at the right time at the right place. Doing the right thing but not at the right time and place is bad. Being in the right time and the right place but not knowing what to do—that's not so useful either.

Iva: I don't think the term "situational leadership" is sufficient to capture all of what's needed in an OL leader.

Bert: In the last couple of months my thinking has shifted. I still believe that you need to attune your leadership to the situation, but I don't think you can be a good situational leader unless you know what to draw upon. For example, I need to learn how to be more sensitive to pacing and timing. I was very good at pacing and timing in the old world, but in the new world, different rules apply. The signals you get mean different things.

Living in and Between Two Worlds

Iva: It almost seems as if in order to be leaders who will lead organizations with OL in mind, we have to live in two worlds—two systems—simultaneously. We have to live in the system that we have emerged from—command-and-control, mechanical, hierarchical—and the one we are being led into which is based on the principles of OL. We have to live in the business world of today. We also have to live in a new reality at the same time that we are trying to create it.

Bert: That's the way it seems, but I have never experienced two systems living harmoniously. When I met the Japanese guy at MIT he talked a lot about harmony whereas I often said, "I just don't see *how* it's possible."

Iva: So you have an underlying assumption that harmony is not possible. Maybe you have to change your view of what "harmony" means. Being in harmony does not mean coming to peace with something and putting it behind you. Harmony is dynamic. Believing that harmony is possible gives us the courage to find out more.

Bert: I did a much better job networking downwards than I ever did upwards or sideways. The reason was that, at the time, I did not really believe that having harmony between systems of traditional command-and-control and an organization based on learning was possible. That was my assumption. I can see now that that was a powerful assumption because I also believe that OL leaders have to have the strength of their convictions. The skill is to articulate the value of OL and link it to what the people in the corporation value. The other skill is being able to talk passionately and effectively about the value of organizational learning without coming across as being phony or mushy—and to do that equally well with both employees and higher management.

Iva: But for me, understanding what's needed to be a leader of learning is less a matter of defining the skills—though I think they are important—than of delineating some sort of transition path from traditional command-and-control leader to this new way of being.

For example, I know that I was trying very, very hard to model this new way of being, but I had a hell of a time. I was the consummate CEO-type who turned the company around. Remember there was a *Businessweek* article that talked about me slashing this and slashing that, and what a great "slasher" I was.[5] Then I realized that there was another part of me that was much more important. I was dedicated to creating a better workplace, but that was out of line with the expectations and the vision of those above me! Even those below me couldn't believe at first that I was trying to change.

There were quite a few times when I slipped back into my old command-and-control behaviors. I know this confused people in my organization. When you as the leader try to do things very differently, sometimes people don't observe it. Sometimes they don't believe what they are seeing. They are confused at first and they don't trust you because they don't trust their own observations. They think, "It can't be! She was a command-and-control leader yesterday and now she's this servant leader?" That was very hard. They had a picture of what the president ought to be. They might not like it, but that was what they expected. Yet, the way I was characterized was not the way I wanted to be characterized anymore. That was not who I was—even though I had to be that way to get to where I was. And that old picture of me that the people in the organization had—that old mental model of what they expected their leader to be—that turned out to be a tremendous obstacle. More so than I had ever expected.

Bert: That was a challenge for me, too. I've since learned that people thought of me as a "Theory X manager trying to be Theory Y."[6] That really stuck with me because I think it's true. Then I think that I tended to overcompensate for my Theory X tendencies by staying with people too long when perhaps I should have told them that they were not performing up to my expectations. My decision making sometimes wasn't consistent.

Iva: There were times when the management above me expected—and wanted—me to exhibit those old command-and-control behaviors. When I didn't they were also confused.

Bert: So why is it that we struggled so much with the transition?

Iva: I think that many of our readers will also struggle with this transition. We may only have a vague, intellectual understanding of what OL leadership entails. Also, we have been so conditioned by the business culture to behave in certain ways. Just as we ourselves have had to unlearn some of these conditioned responses, so will others.

Bert: So the unlearning is as important as the learning.

Iva: Yes, and to engage in that dual process of learning and unlearning we must continually strive for clarity about our assumptions.

Key Similarities and Differences

There were key similarities between Iva's and Bert's situations:

- Both were senior line managers who reported to others higher up within a much larger system;

- Both faced enormous external, competitive pressures but were hampered in their ability to implement strategies to respond to those competitive pressures;

- Both inherited relationships with other divisions within the system that were problematic and/or strained;

- Both had to manage around unforeseen discontinuities, such as a strike or a reorganization or downsizing.

- Both had to manage to today's performance expectations while trying to lead their respective organizations into the future—without sufficient support or the auspices of top management.

Iva and Bert responded in different ways to that similar set of constraints.

Two Approaches: Pragmatic and Visionary

Both Iva and Bert embarked on their learning journeys and faced these challenges without sufficient support or sanction. Without upper level management support, neither Bert nor Iva could make sustainable headway. Also, without very attuned coaching support they also were not able to fully understand the limitations they were facing nor make lasting breakthroughs in their own personal development.

For the purposes of learning, we have characterized Bert as a pragmatic leader who continuously responded to and adapted to constraints. Using the proverbial metaphor of the elastic band to represent the tension created when we consider both current reality and vision, we might say that Bert's tendency was to reduce the creative tension by moving the vision closer to current reality.

Iva, on the other hand, represents our visionary tendencies. She was on fire with the possibility of transforming the entire corporate culture from Model I to Model II. She attempted to "engineer" that transformation without knowing or understanding exactly how she was enlisting the existing organizational learning system (which was most likely based in Model I) in resisting her efforts. Her goal was to build a learning infrastructure. Her methods included stretching the organization toward the vision, superceding constraints, and delaying attention to feedback and resistance.

Despite these differences, there were also key similarities in the assumptions that underlay their strategies. In their double-loop exchange they surfaced some of these key assumptions, which are summarized in Table 8.1.

Table 8.1
Bert and Iva's Key Assumptions

Bert's Key Assumptions	Iva's Key Assumptions
I have to be the heroic leader. I'll do the learning for the organization.	I have to be the heroic leader. I'll show them I'm right. I'll protect others.
I understand the culture of my organization. I'll use my organization's culture to change my organization's culture.	I understand the culture of my organization. The culture needs to change. I know in what ways it needs to change and I know how to change it.
Personal values can be aligned with organizational values.	Personal values can be aligned with organizational values.
I know what works in this organization.	I know what works in this organization.
I can't create too much tension in the organization or I'll be rejected.	If I don't create enough tension, people won't change.
I can do this the same way I've always done things—by trial-and-error—and I'll succeed. I always do.	I can do this the same way I've always done things—by pushing hard—and I'll succeed. I always do.
If I get the results, they'll see the value.	If I get the results, they'll see the value.
I have to be the expert; failure is intolerable.	I have to be the expert; failure is intolerable.
I can't engage the whole organization. (I don't know how so I won't try.)	I can't engage my boss. (I don't know how so I won't try.)

What is the source of these assumptions? To varying extents, the mental models of leadership that we hold are shaped by our personality, our experiences and the culture of our organizations, but they are also shaped by a higher level of assumptions embedded in the larger context.

In *The Fifth Discipline,* Ray Strata, President and CEO of Analog Devices, Inc., makes the following observation:

> **Strata:** (T)he "pragmatists" of modern philosophy take the view that there is no point in worrying about general theory. You should do what works, and whatever works today may not work tomorrow. This view is strongly reinforced in contemporary management with its emphasis on solving problems. It's so easy to just go from one problem to the next, "from pillar to post," without ever seeing a larger pattern. Pragmatism denies any ability of the human mind to synthesize, to see a bigger picture.
>
> Pragmatism has become dominant, in part, because of the previous dominance of elaborate theoretical systems that had no real correspondence to reality. The nineteenth century was a great time for this; and the obvious failure of these great systems of thought like Marx's world system has been one of the justifications for pragmatism.

Strata's quote underscores the need for practitioners of OL to recognize that pragmatism and vision are not opposites so much as complements. Good strategies should have elements of both.

> **Strata:** I think, to some extent, we jump back and forth between these two extremes of overconceptualization and pure pragmatism because we don't have the tools to connect them. The core challenge faced by the aspiring learning organization is to develop tools and processes for conceptualizing the big picture and testing ideas in practice. All in the organization must master the cycle of thinking, doing, evaluating, and reflecting. Without that, there is no valid learning.[7]

A Developmental Perspective

Rooke and Torbert (1999) have developed a framework that may help us to understand Bert's and Iva's behaviors. They describe five levels of managerial "action-logics" (see Table 8.2) that represent certain clusters of observable behaviors. Because these behaviors can be observed to cluster together, we can assume that there is an underlying "logic" or mental model (or theory-in-use) that holds them together. Rooke and Torbert believe that these action-logics also represent a developmental continuum. In other words, the belief is that people can, and perhaps ought to, evolve from one category to another as they develop, i.e., mature and change over time.[8]

Table 8.2
Managerial Action-Logics

Opportunist	Seeks short-term concrete advantage for self; rejects feedback; externalizes blame; manipulates others.
Diplomat	Seeks acceptance by colleagues; observes protocol; avoids conflict to save own and other's face.
Expert	Seeks causes and perfect, efficient solutions; accepts feedback only from master of the particular craft.
Achiever	Seeks effective results by teamwork; welcomes goal-related, single-loop feedback.
Strategist	Seeks to construct shared vision, transformational conflict resolution, and timely performance through creative, witty, double-loop, reframing feedback.
Magician/Witch/Clown	Seeks triple-loop transformation "systems experiencing" that creates positive-sum, mythical events and games by blending opposites (e.g., civil disobedience, feminist politics, social investing).

Reprinted by permission from *The Systems Thinker* (Pegasus Communications, 1999).

As Bert and Iva describe their struggles with their organizations, we can hear echoes of these action-logics. They talk about their being valued and rewarded as experts. As a general rule, organizations tend to value and reward "expert" behaviors.

Rooke and Torbert maintain, however, that the cluster of behaviors they call "the strategist" best represents the capabilities needed for leading a deep OL effort. The strategist is the "true learning leader." The strategist is concerned with creating shared vision. The strategist manifests "vulnerable power" and models vulnerability to personal transformation—without, somehow, making him- or herself too vulnerable.

Executives who find a connection with OL often want to evolve their leadership style to mesh with their evolving beliefs, values, and what they now aspire to. Yet, the work of evolving one's leadership style is difficult because there are many factors—both internal and external—that contrive to keep managers and leaders in their old, familiar grooves. Bert and Iva both struggled with how to evolve their leadership styles. In both cases people in the organization noticed the attempt, but were also confused by the inconsistencies and questioned the authenticity of the change.

How does a leadership style evolve? Argyris believes it requires engaging in a deliberate dialectical process to learn to act in accordance with Model II theory-in-use. Brian Hall has written that personal transformation and development is facilitated by learning interpersonal and imaginal skills and by learning how to think systemically.[9] With this view in mind it seems that developing one's skills in the organizational learning disciplines of systems thinking, shared vision, personal mastery as well as generative conversation can facilitate the developmental process of managers.

What are the critical qualities that define a leader of learning? In the following section we will hear from other leaders of OL efforts about what they have learned about leadership.

Endnotes

1. Ralph Stacey, *Managing the Unknowable: Strategic Boundaries Between Order and Chaos in Organizations* (San Francisco: Jossey-Bass, 1992), pp. 2, 4, 14, 197–198.

2. Edgar H. Schein, "Organizational Learning: What is New?," in M. A. Rahim et al. (eds.), *Current Topics in Management*, Vol. 2 (JAI Press, Inc., 1997).

3. Peter Senge et al., *Dance of Change: The Challenges of Sustaining Momentum in Learning Organizations* (New York: Doubleday, 1999), pp. 26–30.

4. For more on "Type A," see Meyer Friedman and Ray H. Rosenman, *Type A Behavior and Your Heart* (New York: Alfred A. Knopf, Inc., 1974).

5. Emily T. Smith, et al., "The Women Who Are Scaling High Tech Heights," *BusinessWeek*, August 28, 1989, pp. 86–88.

6. Warren G. Bennis and Edgar H. Schein (eds.), with the collaboration of Caroline McGregor, *Leadership and Motivation, Essays of Douglas McGregor* (Cambridge, MA: MIT Press, 1966).

7. Peter Senge, *The Fifth Discipline: The Art and Practice of the Learning Organization* (New York: Doubleday, 1990), pp. 350–351.

8. Excerpted from THE SYSTEMS THINKER Newsletter article *The CEO's Role in Organizational Transformation* by David Rooke and William R. Torbert. (Waltham, MA: Published by Pegasus Communications, Inc., 1999).

9. *Brian P. Hall*, The Genesis Effect: Personal and Organizational Transformation (New York: Paulist Press, 1986).

Part 3
Leadership

A great deal has been written about leadership *per se*. Much has also been written about the role of the leader in organizational change. Without diminishing those contributions to the field of leadership, we offer a contribution because we believe that there is a need to deepen our understanding of learning leadership as lived and experienced by leaders.

There is vision and there is current reality—and then there is the gap between the two. So, too, with leadership we have a current reality: leaders who have been shaped and rewarded by traditional organizations yet who are also reaching out for a new paradigm of leadership. We have a vision: abundant concepts of effective, transformed leadership. And we have the gap in between. What is still missing, we believe, is the bridge between the two: a specific sense of the pathway of transition.

To that end we set about on a search for a *practical* model of leadership. We wanted to investigate how other leaders of OL efforts trod that path and what they encountered along the way. What did they think? What did they do? What did they learn as they evolved their leadership? It is our hope that these learnings about leadership might help leaders to transition successfully from their current styles—which may include a heavy reliance on command-and-control—to a new leadership model which contributes to organizational learning.

In the previous chapters we focused on Iva and Bert's journeys. In the following chapters we share what we have learned from our interviews with four other leaders of change who were also pioneers in OL. They are:

- **Phil Carroll**—former CEO of Shell Oil and current chairman and CEO of Fluor Corporation;

- **Dave Marsing**—former Vice President, General Manager of Assembly Test Manufacturing for Intel, and now COO of Intel's new Network Communications Group;

- **Bill O'Brien**—former CEO of the Hanover Insurance Company and founding partner of the Centre for Generative Leadership, a consulting firm; and

- **Rich Teerlink**—former chairman of Harley Davidson.

Each of these leaders brings a unique perspective to the table. And yet, there are common threads which, if woven together, may help us all to evolve our collective wisdom about leaders, leadership, and profound change. In the following chapters we have tried to weave their perspectives and reflections on leadership together with our own.

Chapter 9

Leadership: An Inquiry

Mind Images of the Organizational Learning Leader

In this chapter we attempt to identify some of the distinctive characteristics of OL leaders. We believe that such leaders are *leaders of a transition:* the transition from one kind of business organization to another, the shape of which is still being formed. For this reason we don't think of the profile of these leaders as being either uniform or fixed; rather, we think this type of leadership is still evolving.

All of the leaders we spoke with are foresighted; yet they don't all see the world exactly the same way. There are individual variations. Likewise, none of the leaders lead in exactly the same way. Each leader is shaped by his own personal experiences and his own perspectives on reality. Yet there seems to be some convergence, and we think that convergence is illuminating.

So, while there is no formula, no course of instruction for becoming this type of leader, we think that there are some characteristics that mark OL leadership. In this chapter we try to identify some of those critical attributes.

Whither the Heroic Leader?

Iva: I'd like to frame our discussion of leadership by referencing the discussion of leadership in *The Dance of Change*.[1] The authors talk about the tendency in our business cultures to continuously reinforce the notion of heroic leaders. Instead, they see leadership as a systems phenomenon. Now we're about to share the results of our interviews with several executive change leaders and I wonder, are we about to reinforce the concept of the hero leader?

Bert: I'm not ready to throw out the notion of the heroic leader just yet. In fact, OL needs heroic leadership—particularly heroic executive leadership. While leadership is important at all levels, we are still in corporate environments where executive leaders set the tone for an organization. They can change the direction of organization. They create the environment where change can occur. They can also provide an environment where change will be killed.

But at the same time, I don't believe that the success of a change effort should be invested in one person or that one person creates monumental change.

Iva: But if we focus on the individual executive leader, that'll tend to reinforce the importance of those leaders to the change process—

Bert: No. That's not our message. If the culture of a company is such that everybody believes that everything is up to the people on the so-called "top," then there's a problem. Even though the company may be very successful financially.

At the same time, I do think you need executive leaders to catalyze change. I believe they can do it in a variety of ways, depending upon the culture and the leader. In our interviews we saw several different models. If that's not heroic, then it is at least insightful and creative. And it's certainly leadership.

Iva: It's heroic because most of today's leaders were brought up in the command-and-control environment. They are now trying to change that. They're willing to move away from the system that brought them to power and they're willing to try to build a bridge to the new model of management.

Bert: They're heroic because taking that on is in defiance of the dominant management paradigm of command-and-control. So there *are* heroic leaders in OL, but they are heroes of a different kind.

Iva: They are the heroes of the transition. And in this chapter we honor what we have learned from some of them.

First Learning: Organizational Learning Leaders Are Pragmatic Visionaries

Iva: One of the first things we learned in our investigation was that leaders who have embraced organizational learning tend to see their work in a larger context. Their lenses are sensitized. They believe that there are significant events that are affecting the reality external to the organization. They have an *inner knowing* about how those forces are shaping up and how they will affect the future. In this sense, they are visionaries.

Bert: At the same time, OL leaders also seem to blend that strong sense of vision with a strong sense of current reality. They can see the practical implications of that vision for the firm's success. They are able to craft a link between their sense of changing external reality and pragmatic results. They can effectively translate their vision into strategies and tactics that have meaning for the firm and engage in the process of educating the firm so people understand how the strategy links up with results.

Bill O'Brien is in many ways the founding father of organizational learning. He presents his interest in OL as extremely practical.

Bill: In the beginning I certainly didn't conceive of myself as leading a movement. I just recognized in my corporation a basic sickness. Then I met Peter Senge and I thought, "Here's this whole body of knowledge and practice called organizational learning. Wouldn't it be great if we could apply this knowledge?"

Let me give you an example. When I came into the business I was pretty shocked to discover that "spin" is a professional activity in a corporation! And it's worse now than it ever was. We would have a meeting and decide what we're going to do. Then somebody will say, "We need to have a meeting tomorrow to decide how we're going to tell people what we're going to do." Well, if there's integrity in what we're doing, why do we need a separate meeting? Why don't we just go out and tell everybody what happened.

I wasn't smart enough to figure out what all this spin was doing, but I believe that if you tinker around with the truth, there are bad consequences. Oh, of course, we might fool somebody into buying stock because we put a little spin on how well our company's doing—but the ultimate consequences are that nobody trusts each other any more. If spin works with outsiders then pretty soon there's spin *inside* the company as well. Everybody's spinning everything and suddenly the whole corporation is built on distrust.

I felt the same way when I saw how we hoarded power. First of all, it's unhealthy for the hoarder. It's not congruent with human nature. And what does it do to the enterprise? It makes everybody get in a lackey mentality so they're checking their imagination and their creativity at the front door. They just want to be told what to do. What does that do with relationships between people? We say to ourselves, "Oh, there's no sense talking to this guy, he just goes by the book." This human frailty of hoarding power is causing dysfunction.

I saw all this dysfunction in my company, and I thought, "If we could eliminate all that, what would happen? How much more productive would we be!" And I believed to the bottom of my boots that if we did this we'd make more money. I looked at the other hundreds of insurance companies who were plagued with the same diseases and I thought, "If we only get 20 percent better, we could run circles around them." And we did!

Iva: While Bill insists that his aims were modest and very grounded, he is also acutely aware of the thrust of history and its impact on business organizations.

Bill: The way I look at it is: For 300 years the family business was the way commerce was conducted in this country. It was during the 1920s, or maybe a little earlier, that the large corporations, General Motors, Ford, Dupont, began to ascend. And obviously in the 1970s at the thrust of the Japanese invasion of electronics and automobiles, they began to dysfunction. The dysfunction was all the things we just talked about, the hoarding of power, the spin, the alienation of the worker.

Out of that crisis is born a new form of governance that's going to succeed command-and-control. I don't think there's any question that the basic governing theories that took us from 1920 to 1990 are being seriously renovated. We're going to have a new architecture and this new generation of management has got the rare privilege of participating in the design of the architecture—while at the same time they have to run the ship.

Bert: I concur with what Bill said. I also see OL in the context of historical evolution, but I see it somewhat differently. Early on when we were trying to organize work we adopted Frederick Taylor's model.[2] We designed work by breaking tasks down into their smallest components and then measured how long it took people to perform them. That became our management model. Eventually we became so focused on breaking down and measuring tasks that people didn't count at all. For many years this Taylor principle dominated management thought until the classic experiment at Western Electric where scientists tried to measure the effect of improved lighting on productivity. The scientists discovered that it wasn't the lighting but the fact that the scientists were paying attention to people that actually led to improvements in productivity. They called that the "Hawthorne Effect." So the business world began to pay attention to people. But then that was followed by a focus on statistical quality control and we started breaking tasks down again.[3] Then came reengineering.

Now it seems that we're going back to paying attention to people again. We're beginning to see that people are our most competitive advantage. We're beginning to understand that there are a few key factors that will differentiate one company from another. Those factors are creativity and the ability to innovate and solve problems. All of those things involve people and that's where OL comes in. Competitiveness is directly linked to the capacity of individuals and organizations to learn. Success is a function of who learns faster and better about what the marketplace is saying—and who is better able to put in place strategies that attune the organization so that they are better able to learn and respond.

Iva: You see a kind of oscillation whereas Bill observes a sea change. Nevertheless, your points of view converge.

Bert: As CEO of Harley Davidson, Rich Teerlink saw some tough times. Harley went through a make-or-break survival period that lasted five long years (from 1981–86). Rich seems to have come out of that period with new insights.

> **Rich:** Essentially, a business does three things on an ongoing basis: it creates demand (marketing), it produces product (manufacturing), and it helps, i.e., it provides support or service. One of the things we learned, I think, during our "survival period" was that all parts of the business must function well and together. We learned that if it's not together, you're in trouble. For example, we always had strong marketing, but when our manufacturing was inferior, our market share was down to 13 percent.
>
> As we looked at what was going on in our company, I kept saying, "We've got to realize our interdependence upon one another." Whenever things went wrong it was because we weren't recognizing that interdependence enough. People weren't talking to one another.

Iva: When Phil Carroll was the president and CEO of Shell Oil he also saw a great need for change. He evaluated his organization in light of the larger context and saw a serious mismatch.

> **Phil:** At the time I took over Shell Oil it was operating as an independent entity. I believed that was becoming an anachronism. The organization of Shell was based on the nation-state; every country had its own Shell company, with its own chief executive.
>
> That was the manner and form of the management philosophy. It was the right model for the post-war world, but with what's happening today in the world, both technologically and in the process of globalization with the intensification of competition, you can't do that anymore. You've got to globalize,

you've got to make central decisions, you've got to have better access to true market data at a global level.

Bert: I saw some similarities between the challenges Phil had at Shell and those Dave Marsing faced at Intel. Dave had the formidable challenge of continuously retooling manufacturing capability in order to keep up with market demand.

Dave: One of the dynamics at work within Intel is to reduce both the overhead and the cost of what we make. Furthermore, as the market demand shifts toward more generic products with perhaps less high performance, we've got to respond. So we've got to be able to introduce new products very quickly. That means that our manufacturing has to have a tactic that enables us to retool very fast. We have to be able to develop a prototype, develop the product, do initial qualification of the product, and then ramp it to maximum volume as quickly as possible.

Now to accomplish all that, we've had to ask people on the factory floor to take on decision-making responsibilities the like of which they've never had before. We can't afford to populate the factories with Ph.D.s in electrical engineering, but we really need people who can make decisions with the minimal direction. If they need help, they need to be able to get it from anywhere in the world. That's no small challenge.

Iva: Again, this practical view of the here-and-now is tempered with a sensitivity to changes in the world outside the factory.

Dave: Our work is really taking place in a global setting now, and one of the things that concerns me is the three decades of training that people have had in how to be very autonomous in their own particular physical site. Until about three years ago, the sites didn't have to interact. Nor was there any formal inter-dependence between any of the sites. There was no connection between what one site did with another factory anywhere else in the world, other than the traditional linear supply line.

But that has changed. Now the environment is such that the factories depend upon each other and one factory cannot really make a decision unilaterally.

That presents us with a significant challenge. We've got to change behaviors. Part of the challenge is getting people at each site to shift their priorities away from optimizing their local site and shift it toward trying to figure out the right thing to do for a whole network of factories.

Iva: In all of these cases it seems that it's an awareness of pragmatic issues, and the larger forces that create those issues, that gives rise to vision.

Second Learning: The Centrality of Values

Bert: I believe that the source of OL leadership is the strength of your conviction. At the heart are values. Again and again, our leaders emphasized the importance of a core set of values. For example, according to Dave Marsing, leadership begins with a focus on people.

Dave: To be an effective leader in the kinds of domains and contexts that we've been talking about is impossible without having an appreciation for the richness and the diversity of the people in your organization. That's a prerequisite. Then, leadership itself is merely opening the opportunities for people to see who they are and to achieve their potential.

Iva: Yes, Dave really has a focus on people. And it isn't just a simplistic notion about how people are a competitive advantage—it isn't the kind of idea that falls apart the minute priorities shift. It's a sophisticated understanding of people that includes an ability to esteem and deal effectively with the varying traits, skills, and capacities that people bring to work. Dave Marsing's OL work focuses on Human Dynamics™. Human Dynamics is a body of work that identifies fundamental distinctions in how human beings function as whole systems and helps people to recognize, value, and develop their own diverse capabilities and those of others.[4]

Dave: Our selection process at the factory was certainly influenced by what we learned about and our commitment to the principles of Human Dynamics. We looked for and hired people who valued the capabilities of others and who saw developing the potential of both the people under them and those around them as an important aspect of their work. The message we gave them when we brought them in was: Develop the capacity of your organization. The message was not: Go in and be technologists.

Bert: Dave's work with Human Dynamics seems to spring out of a deep commitment to the value of people's strengths and gifts. Values were also at the center of Rich Teerlink's work at Harley.

Rich: Values have always been important to me. Very important. I once had a very prestigious job but I quit because I disagreed with the values of the company. I felt that senior management was more interested in senior management rather than the whole business.

So when senior management at Harley was considering its vision we started with discussion of our values. Only after that did we discuss the issues and the stakeholders, and then we talked about the vision statement. That's a little different because most people start with the vision first. Instead, we started asking, How do we want to behave towards one another? What's important to us? And, who do we serve?

Bert: I see values as the source of commitment. Phil Carroll's strategy at Shell was about creating an alignment between personal and organizational values, which I believe is critical.

Phil: Commitment comes only when people perceive that their life and their priorities are consistent with and tied to the priorities and direction of the company. I mean, they can be a little off, but if those are not basically lined up, then you have an uncommitted workforce. In the long term, that's a formula for going out of business in these competitive times.

Bert: If there ever was an important point, that's it. It's so important to have articulated, shared values up front. This is the linchpin.

The only argument against it is that sometimes values come out as platitudes. Most companies have values, but does the leadership walk the talk? Do the people in the organization walk the talk? The next question is: Do the corporate values align with employees' values?

Iva: I understand that Rich Teerlink's organization had a process for aligning personal and organizational values. It's a process that asks you to define what it is that you value and also determine whether you have in place any practices that contradict those values. For example, one of the things that drive organizations today is fear. OL leaders don't exploit fear as a source of motivation.

Phil: The most prevalent dysfunctional emotion that is present in corporate life is fear. And to say that you're going to deal with effective functioning of corporations without having the ability to deal intelligently with fear is very shortsighted. Most people say, "Yeah, well, fear is a weapon. It's a tool of management to scare people into behaving in certain ways."

Fear is a very debilitating thing in terms of individual and collective performance. If you don't know how to deal with that one emotion—if nothing else—you're in trouble. Particularly if you're trying to produce the right kind of alignment—the true alignment of individual and corporate values that produces real commitment on the part of individuals.

Bert: If there's fear in the organization, then the values are just platitudes. The leadership doesn't know how to live up to them and everybody knows it. A leader should make an objective assessment of what they are doing and how it relates to their values. The whole leadership team should do that.

Iva: If leaders draw their conviction from values, what is the source of these core values?

Bert: Bill O'Brien theorizes that those values come from an underlying belief system.

Bill: Leaders must have a philosophical worldview into which they integrate what they learn from Senge or Argyris or somebody else. You cannot lead an organization if you are dependent upon the thinking of any management guru. You cannot lead an organization without having a belief system of your own.

That belief system has to be more holistic than what they teach you in Wharton about financial models or what they teach at Babson about accounting or what you learn in engineering schools. We promote all of our leaders because of their credentials in these physical belief systems, but to really get people to rise above the ordinary, you've got to have a metaphysical belief system—a set of core beliefs that transcend the merely physical. That's important and we don't pay enough attention to it.

I don't think that people need to get this metaphysical belief system from some special school, but they've got to get one. They've got to give thought to human nature, human purpose, the role of the corporation in society, the role of work in happiness, in life. They've got to have some kind of a metaphysical belief system in which to integrate all of this other knowledge. I mean, I got excited about systems thinking, for example, but it was not my core belief. It was integrated into an already-existing set of core beliefs.

Bert: Bill is saying that OL should not take the place of a more fundamental belief system. I agree with that and I think that has happened to some people. That's partly why there is some danger of OL being perceived as a cult. People have to be careful about losing their footing and becoming too carried away.

Iva: I agree, but the notion of a belief system—particularly a metaphysical belief system—is controversial.

Bert: Granted, but if you're going to be a leader, you've got to have a leadership philosophy. It may not be a metaphysical philosophy, but you've got to have a philosophy of business and that philosophy needs to include ethics. You've got to have a philosophy of right and wrong. You've got to have a practical philosophy. Organizational learning can't be a substitute for that philosophy.

Iva: No, but OL can certainly contribute to it.

Third Learning: Organizational Learning Leaders Are Master Strategists and Tacticians

Bert: These leaders seem to have an inner knowing about how external forces are shaping the business world and, perhaps, the course of history.

Iva: And, as a consequence, they've been able to articulate a travelable path to the future. They know the steps to take that will guide their organizations into that future. They are expert navigators because they can read the stars and they also have a sense of the currents and the shoals, the tides, and the eddies.

For example, Rich recognized that the traditional functional stovepipe method of organizing had created unacceptable blocks to communication. With assistance from an organizational consultant, Lee Ozley, he began to envision a new form of governance.

Rich: We started by viewing the business as having three primary activities—producing products, creating demand, and providing support. We visualized each of these as a circle. Each circle had 5–8 key people so we had a total of about 20 key people in all. We named them the Functional Leadership Group.

Then we put those three circles together in a Venn diagram. Interesting thing! Now, they overlap. That implies interdepen-

dence. Then we drew a big circle around it and we put our stakeholders outside the circles and we had arrows going out from
each one of the circles which illustrated that we all served the
stakeholders but we were interdependent inside.

Where the three circles overlapped we established the
Leadership and Strategy Council which included the division
president and six peer-elected representatives from the
Functional Leadership Groups. All of a sudden we've got natural
work groups of 5–8 people. We couldn't call them that, of
course. We called them "circles" because if we called them natural work groups people would have said, "We're vice presidents,
we're not work groups." But it turned out to be natural work
groups.

Bert: Rich and Phil destroyed the structure that was supporting
command-and-control by creating a structure that supported interdependence. That was extremely insightful and very courageous given the
fact that this company had come from a situation where it had been in
financial trouble. They did it when the company was financially sound,
but it was a risk because it could have set them back.

Iva: Rich led the way to the future by creating a new structure and
he did so in a way that didn't threaten people too much.

Bert: Phil Carroll also envisaged a structure that would bring about
a new way of working.

Phil: In 1997 Shell initiated the process of globalizing its
business worldwide. Let me define what I mean by "globalization." The concept was that you set up global organizations with
worldwide coordination and a certain amount of decision making, but under that layer you have a whole series of connected
nodes where people and strategic business units can operate
with relative autonomy.

The only thing required is that while you pursue your independent goals in whatever node, you also have to think about
the network. You also have to be linked financially because the
financial strength of the whole is vastly superior to the individual elements. Additionally, you have to be linked with information. That is, your knowledge, skill, and commercial intelligence
has to be available to all others. Finally, you also need to have,
within limits, the ability and necessity of moving key people
among those nodes.

We began to evolve toward this networked organizational
structure. Below the general structure there are now a whole

host of relatively independent but highly connected business entities. So, instead of being geographically-based, they're now globalized and networked.

Iva: Along with changing the structure, Phil took some brave steps toward reviving the human element in his organization.

Phil: Along with the rest of our Leadership Council, I embarked on a journey of what I call "personal integration." This was a major journey for me. My fundamental belief with regard to business was, "Look, this is all about logic. This is all about factual data and information." We did not deal with the emotional side of ourselves because it wasn't relevant. That belief was very strongly ingrained and I was very protective of it, but with help from some consultants I began to see that everything that happens to us has an emotional element and that to ignore the emotional aspect of things completely is not healthy.

We began to practice integrating emotion and logic. I believe that these skills are essential if you're going to do anything akin to really building coherence and cohesion at top management levels. People have to be able to have those kinds of conversations.

Bert: Dave Marsing's strategy also involved a blend of technological improvements and the development of specific people skills.

Iva: Yes, but their approaches had to be different. As executive leader, Phil Carroll assumed a great deal of responsibility for the overall approach to organizational change. Marsing's strategy was to seed the organization, to open minds and set a learning process in place, and then to shepherd people along as they went on a learning journey with him.

Dave: How did we respond to those kinds of needs at Intel? Number one, we've made pretty significant investments in information technology systems that allow access to those resources around the world. Secondly, we've built the capacity in our people to make the decisions that get the kind of results that keeps the momentum of improvement going without major setbacks.

So, as the demands on the people who are working on the floor increase, we continuously reengineer their jobs on two fronts. We provide more automated solutions to help them run their areas and we also leverage their problem-solving skills. We enable them to work better together, both with people in the same factory and with people who are running similar modules in another factory somewhere else in the world.

A primary tool for accomplishing that later challenge has been the use of Human Dynamics.

Iva: Dave's work with Human Dynamics is good business strategy but it's also more than that. You can really perceive the value he puts on human potential by listening to the way he talks about it.

Dave: From my perspective, the Human Dynamics work gives you the opportunity to affirm your sense of yourself in a very positive way. You begin to see your strengths, idiosyncrasies, and attributes as part of a whole spectrum of human talents rather than comparing yourself—perhaps negatively—to the dominant norm of your family, community, work organization, or culture.

At the organization level, this gives a tremendous foundation for doing work around the appreciation of diversity in an organization. You find that you actually go out and seek out the diversity to get better answers.

Bert: Dave has also found a way to strategize about these larger issues by leveraging organizational learning tools and techniques including Human Dynamics.

Dave: Our strategy for getting there involves the use of OL tools like causal loop diagrams. But it also involves having what Senge calls generative conversations, having genuine dialogue around these issues.

Now, let me lay some context. In the past, in some cultures, people have not been comfortable being a part of the dialogue. And the reason behind that is twofold: First, they don't really want to talk. They'd just as soon take an order and go execute and meet whatever they think the expectations were. If they hit the objective they think, "Great, we'll be left alone." So they marshal the resources to make sure they'll get that accomplished and then behind that, they do whatever they want to do.

The second reason that they're uncomfortable is that very often English is not their primary language. So their involvement in a very in-depth and abstract dialogue is very difficult. This is far from a done deal, but Human Dynamics has enabled us to begin to surmount those barriers by helping us develop a language that was common among all the people from all the different cultures.

At an international and global level, it has really amazing capabilities. People begin to realize that some of the issues that they encounter aren't so much cultural differences as they are running up against clashes between dominant dynamic norms—between, say, Santa Clara, CA and Penang, Malaysia, or Shanghai. *Human Dynamics has given us the capacity to recognize how different people process information.* When you establish a foundation like that across an organization, the quality of conversation, and the creativity and contribution of coming up with new ideas and new innovative approaches to problems goes up significantly. It's an exciting place to be.

It's also very freeing both at the organizational level and the individual level. Watching people in Asia who have had exposure in the last three years to this kind of training is like watching a person evolve out of a shell. I mean, all of a sudden you see people who have passion and life and feel good about themselves, as opposed to feeling that they're cogs in a huge machine.

Another result is that they begin to get a voice. In their culture, perhaps, they have been almost suppressed or oppressed in a very hierarchical system. They expect that and they demand that of the people who are above them. And they fall into these roles. The Human Dynamics work, however, gives them a language, it gives them a thought process, and it opens up tremendous capability for them to begin to really explore potential, both their own and that of the people that they work with.

Iva: It seems that Phil, Rich, and Dave all developed strategies that had a structural element—

Bert: And also placed value on human beings and on developing the capacity of human beings. That's a common denominator.

Iva: It's also very different from the way in which we've traditionally brought about restructuring. Generally we've thought about structures *or* we've thought about people. Here, those two concerns are brought together.

Fourth Learning: The Essence of Organizational Learning Leadership Is the Skillful Devolution of Power

Iva: Underneath Phil Carroll's drive to create a different structure was a philosophy.

Phil: I was interested in decentralization and atomization of organizational structures. That idea was basically built on a political philosophy regarding individual freedom within those structures. The action that comes out of that philosophy is that you have to devolve power.

Iva: To my mind it seems that the essence of the work of OL leaders is to find how to intelligently give power away.

Bert: That may be too strong.

Iva: Maybe not. I believe that we're saying that it will benefit the organization for power to become more distributed, and there are implications for leadership, as Phil said.

Phil: Everyone has positions or moments in the course of a day when you defer to someone else. That's my concept or mental model of distributed leadership.

Bert: If power is distributed it means that the person—or team of people—who have the needed knowledge or expertise take the lead at that moment. Now the question is, Do we have the capacity within organizations to do that? Phil gave a good summary of current reality.

Phil: Number one, a big problem in most companies is developing and maintaining sufficient leadership capacity within the organization. That is a big issue for all companies.

Iva: But Phil also said that people in organizations have latent capacity for leadership.

Phil: The good news, I believe very firmly, is that all of us are at times leaders. Likewise, all of us are at times followers. That certainly goes for me. There are many times during the course of a day when I properly function as a follower. My secretary, for instance, will take on roles of leadership with respect to our working relationship. She says, "Look, we're going to do this, that, and the other." I accept or defer to her judgment because if I didn't want to do that I'd keep my schedule myself.

Bert: There's another aspect to leadership, which is that it has to also be situational.

Phil: Leadership is not the same in all situations. When there's a fire in a chemical plant, for example, you don't want any participative leadership. Instead you better have General Patton there saying, "Do this. Do that." Conversely, when you're up against complex problems that are not given to straightforward, known solutions, that requires a very different kind of leadership.

Because leadership is now becoming situational, individuals have to learn to take on the responsibility of acting differently depending upon where they are at each moment of the day. At any time you may have to make a judgment. Leaders may have to ask themselves, "Hey, wait a second. Am I sitting here trying to get consensus about how to install something?" That's not the right leadership model for that situation. If there's a way to do something you can be very direct about it

Bert: So everyone who intends to lead has to develop a kind of situational acuity, the ability to read and respond appropriately to different situations.

Iva: There's more to it than that. All leaders—positional or distributed alike—will have to call upon others for help.

Phil: Many times the leader has to stand up and say, "I don't have the answers folks. How are we going to do this and how can we together work with or cope with or deal with this situation?" Now, that requires a very different leadership.

Bert: So, to summarize: Positional leaders must recognize that there is a need for greater dispersion of power.

Iva: And for a more collaborative form of leadership.

Bert: The implication is that there is also great potential for the dispersion of leadership within any organization. All of us are potentially leaders at any time; likewise, all of us are potentially followers at any time as well.

Iva: We're also saying that as part of this new model of leadership we have to recognize that there is no one best way to lead. Hence, everyone who would be a leader has to develop an almost instinctive ability to recognize what type of leadership is appropriate to the circumstance they're in.

Bert: Yes. And that also means that we don't invalidate command-style leadership. If it's appropriate at the time, use it!

Iva: I *think* I agree. So if leadership is distributed and situational, it will also need to be far more collaborative.

Bert: Of course, there have always been leadership teams—

Iva: But I sense that collaborative leadership is a qualitatively different kind of leadership than most of the leadership teams that are currently in place. By "collaborative" I mean that we recognize that leadership can really benefit from taking into consideration much more diversity. I am aligning here with Dave's perspective. If we can create environments conducive to a more collaborative form of leadership then individuals will come into leadership as their strengths and abilities are required. Ideally, this would be a very organic process. We need to learn how to do that. There's great untapped potential sitting in organizations already but we've relied on the hero leader for so long that this movement toward greater collaboration can't happen spontaneously. Positional leaders need to do a lot of learning and soul-searching. Likewise, people who aren't in formal leadership positions now need to be effectively skilled and nurtured so that they are ready to take on more leadership responsibilities.

Bert: That goes to Phil's point about why most "empowerment" programs fail. We seem to inadvertently set them up to fail.

Phil: You do someone an enormous disservice if you "empower" people in an arena where they do not have the skill to operate. That's what happens most of the time. Then people say, "See, empowerment doesn't work." Well, sure, it doesn't work if you give someone with four years of experience the responsibility for a huge billion-dollar project. That's dumb. *The workers* weren't dumb. *Management* was dumb. You really have go through a careful process of inventorying skill levels so that when you do empower people you're giving the responsibility to people that you believe have the capability, the talent, and the experience to carry it out—and you won't always be right.

Bert: It's unethical to measure people on their results but not give them the tools and skills to prepare them. That's a perfect example of when the reason for failure is the system rather than the individual. The reason for failure is our policy of cutting back on training and not giving employees the tools they need. It's a setup, plain and simple. Phil Carroll has done a lot of thinking about how to develop leadership capacity within an organization. He talks extensively about the principles that underlie his strategy for developing leadership capacity.

Phil: There are, for me, three absolutely necessary conditions that have to preexist in order to carry out the exercise of devolution of power or the production of more freedom in an organization.

First, there has to be truly a deep clarity about what is wanted such that every employee knows what is expected and what we're trying to do in the company with respect to strategy, methodology, approach, etc. Quite often that's not the case. Often leadership only provides very simplistic directions such as, "We want to grow the company very rapidly." That is not a sufficient articulation of what is wanted in a business.

Clearly, if leadership cannot make a convincing case for where it wants to go, it will fail in its leadership. I believe that it is leadership's general responsibility to shape that direction and to articulate it. They also have the responsibility to change the direction, if necessary, based on the input of the people in the organization. So clarity is a very important element that requires an almost constant conversation and engagement with people throughout the company.

That demand puts intense pressure on leadership to be constantly in communication, repeating statements over and over, answering questions, and discussing. The process has to be very deliberate so that the result is a very clear understanding of the company's direction.

The second thing if you have a very clear message of where you're going is that you have to be sure that the people have the skills and capabilities to go there. It doesn't make any difference if someone says, "Phil, we're going to take you to the top of Mt. Everest"—I'm not going to make it. I don't have the capability or the physical strength to climb Mt. Everest. For people who empower individuals and say, "It's all yours. Here, son, are the keys to the car. I'm sorry we didn't have time for driving lessons, but take it out and I'm sure you'll do fine." Well, there's a wreck in your future. And that's very clear.

The third element is that you have to have a just and clear system of accountability. There have to be consequences. It's OK to make mistakes. That's an important distinction. But if someone constantly doesn't execute, either by lack of commitment or demonstration that he or she doesn't have the skill, and there are no clear and visible consequences, then people lose confidence in the system.

Iva: Command-and-control environments create heroic leaders because everyone looks to the leader to find out what they should do next. Conversely, OL involves the process of skillfully devolving power, shifting power away from the leader. Therefore, OL leaders are engaged in developing the capability of the organization so they can give more power to the people in the organization. That is heroic. Giving away power is heroic. So it's a little paradoxical.

Fifth Learning: Organizational Learning
Leaders Are Stewards of Learning

Iva: It's clear that OL leaders encourage others to learn. The focus of the learning may vary, but this is their distinguishing characteristic.

Bert: If your focus is on learning, you'll be a different kind of leader, as Dave pointed out.

> **Dave:** OL leadership is not like our traditional view of leadership. In the traditional view, the leader comes across as saying: "I am going to take you somewhere and show you how to do this." That kind of leadership does happen, but in a way, OL leadership is more like "husbandry." It's the practice of cultivation. To me an effective leader is a kind of master teacher—but in a way that is very soft, that is very gentle, but also very deliberate.
>
> The role of a leader is to give people freedom, and enable them to think, contribute, and participate. If you take that away from people, you might as well throw them in an institution, into a prison, because the gratification of doing a job and contributing disappears immediately. Therefore, the performance, the overall long-term capability of the organization is crippled.

Iva: I'm really struck by the idea of giving people freedom because that has been such a strong idea in my life. Yet I also know that it's not simple. Many of us have to learn how to be free.

Bert: Many of us managers have also spent our lives thinking of people as resources from which we extract value, but Rich redefines our job.

> **Rich:** I've always had a bias toward believing that if the environment is right, leaders are almost unnecessary. So what we've got to do is create the right kind of environment. My fundamental premise is people are my long-term competitive advantage. If that's the case then the job of the leader is to create an operating environment where people can do great things. That means that you have to invest capital and expense to support the efforts of people.

Iva: So leadership means creating opportunities for others to experience deep learning.

Bert: Yes, and they also have to operate on their gut sense of what will enable others to grow. They have to trust in that process and they can't back down. That's what I got from Rich Teerlink's story.

Rich: There were some problems in the plant that weren't getting solved. It was my sense that one person could not solve the problem. So I decided to use two people with different backgrounds.

Well, each of them came to me individually and said, "You know we can divide this job up. I could take this part and he could take that part." I called them both in together said, "No. You've got to understand. You are going out there together. You're going to work together to get this thing fixed."

Now it was clear to them that they had to work collegially—which was a whole different approach for them. Not only that, but the situation was set up differently. We usually sent people out on missions like that on white chargers. We usually gave them all sorts of formal authority, like giving them a big saber to go and slash through everything. But this time we just said that they're temporarily being assigned to help. It was a whole different thing. It forced the two of them to operate completely differently.

The problem was bigger than either one of them, and they knew it. And they couldn't divide it up because I wouldn't let them. So they each had to go through the process of learning to value the other's perspective. Well, you know, it worked. And they've both thanked me for that assignment.

Sixth Learning: Organizational Learning
Leaders Are Learners Themselves

Iva: I was struck by how open these leaders were to new learning themselves, despite their extraordinary gifts for vision and strategy.

Bert: That's not easy for many of us who have been known as experts. It's not easy to let go of that recognition and credibility, but Dave is very convincing.

Dave: I believe to be a leader requires the hunger and the desire to continue to learn. Without that, I don't think a person has the generative capacity to continue to bring more resources, more ideas, and more creativity into the kinds of evolving or very fast-changing situations we have in business today.

I believe that because of my own personal experience. I have been very fortunate to be a student of some very old, structured, orthodox disciplines in the martial arts. Once you make a commitment to go down these paths, you make a commitment to do it for life.

Leadership is the same. You have to be willing to be a student forever. When I was 13, I had a martial arts teacher who was 82 years old. His belief was that you really didn't know something until you had done it 10,000 times. Correctly. Not only that, he said it might take you 200,000 tries before you do it once correctly. And that's only if you have a really good attitude and a strong work ethic!

For these reasons I believe that there is a relationship between the capacity to be a good student and the potential of developing the characteristics and the discipline of being an effective and an effectual leader.

Bert: So leaders must be learners. At the very least, leaders will have to learn some new skills, as Phil said.

Phil: You have to learn techniques, because OL involves a lot of actual tools and techniques. There are concepts to learn like the Ladder of Inference and suspension of judgment. Those things are very important. Yet, most of us in the corporate world never heard of things like that. We don't know about them.

Iva: It's not only that. Most of us were pretty good learners, in the traditional sense. We mastered all kinds of knowledge to get us where we are today.

Bert: But this is different. Can you say how?

Iva: Many leaders are not used to being learners because they are used to being *knowers*—so they might experience a profound sense of discomfort. Some of us will resist learning OL tools and concepts and instead we'll delegate those responsibilities to others. But once we get over the fear of appearing not to know, leaders can tap into the exhilaration that Dave found in his learning experience.

Dave: When you go through the process of learning about yourself and others in the context of a Human Dynamics seminar with 30 other people it's very uplifting.[5] You finally have a language that enables you to talk about things as they pertain to your own development as an individual. You can articulate what your specific learning approaches and communication styles are. This allows you to function very effectively—and objectively—within a team or organization. And you get the opportunity to do that with people whose emerging awareness of themselves and the people around them is happening at the same time.

Iva: OL leaders need to be deeply engaged with the process of learning. If not, they will not be capable of sustaining the journey. I agree with Rich.

Rich: Leaders have got to be more willing learners. And not learners for the sake of control but learners for the sake of being able to present different concepts to people for them to think about. Not necessarily to say, "We're going to do this," but instead to help enlarge the sense of possibilities.

Seventh Learning: No Single Path

Bert: I was struck by the fact that in our interviews we saw such different approaches to OL. There wasn't a single path. Phil Carroll's OL work was done within the context of people developing an understanding of their business model. Rich Teerlink was using OL as a means for truly letting the people learn. He didn't know where that learning would lead, whereas Phil knew exactly where he believed the organization needed to go. Two different leaders with two different approaches.

Iva: There are multiple pathways for bringing learning into your organization. The choice depends on what the best fit is with your organization, your culture, your burning platform.

Bert: It's also interesting to think about how each of the four leaders came to organizational learning from such different directions. Dave links it to his martial arts practice.

Iva: Bill goes back into ancient philosophy and his metaphysical beliefs.

Bert: Rich, I think, was a "natural."

Rich: Every place I've been, every job I've had, I've always been a changer. I've been a CFO, but I was never a typical CFO. I've been a member of a union and actually lost a union election by three votes. I've been a manufacturing plant manager. I've been a strategic planner. I've been in a division level, corporate level, big company, small company, public company, private company. I just couldn't keep a job!

But always, I've just had a sixth sense that told me, "You know, things could always be better." When you stop thinking about things differently, when you stop thinking about how they could be better, and you say, "Hey, we're here, we're pretty good"—that to me is death. I honestly believe you're never as good as you could be. That's in my bones.

Iva: And Phil was willing to let go of his belief in the primacy of logic. Yet, there are these very significant similarities in the way these leaders think.

Bert: All of them have a capacity to see a bigger picture. They try to bring their organization in alignment with what they see, encouraging everyone to help build a bridge between vision and current reality. Often they make structural changes that focus their organizations on interdependence.

Iva: They're also building that bridge by developing the capacity of the people in their organization to share power and lead.

Bert: They value human beings and they show that explicitly by their actions. They're willing to challenge people to learn and also help people to learn.

Iva: They're willing to learn themselves, even though that may require exposing their vulnerabilities and letting go of old assumptions.

Bert: I'm also thinking that, with the exception of Dave Marsing, these leaders were all CEOs.

Yet, the fundamental approach that each of these people exhibited is applicable at all levels of leadership. I don't want people to give up if they're not a CEO. If you believe this is important, then you can go forward.

Iva: I very much agree, but I have a lingering question, Can anyone become this type of leader? How do you know if you have the capacity? I'm thinking of what Dave Marsing said.

> **Dave:** Unfortunately, not all managers can be learning leaders. Some managers are so sensitive and so fragile in their egos that they can really wound and hurt a very capable organization. The pairing of the motives of both the teacher and the student is also very, very important. Not all people want to be led and not all leaders want to take responsibility and accountability for the health and integrity of an organization and its people. Nor do they have the compassion or the ability to be attentive to them.

The OL leaders of today are leaders of a transition. They are willing to go where the path leads them, never rejecting the possibility of learning no matter what the source. They are passionate about and committed to a vision that they think is infinitely practical *and* attainable if we are willing to learn—and unlearn—all along the way. But where will these much-needed transition leaders come from? Can they be produced by our customary management education? Bill O'Brien thinks not.

Bill: We spend a great deal of money and time in this country talking about leadership and designing leadership education, but I don't think we have any idea what we're talking about.

There was a time in my life when I was awed by the Harvard Business School. There was a time when the Fortune 500 were all Harvard B-School graduates. But now I believe that those business world giants were really molded in the combat of WW II, not at Harvard. Today I'm afraid that we're not producing great leaders in our graduate schools. We may even be producing great plunderers—people who know how to siphon off wealth that others have created.

If you look around at the real leaders in the world today you see people like Nelson Mandela, who spent 27 years in prison. You see Vaclav Havel in Czechoslovakia, who spent seven or eight years in jail. Pope John Paul II was once in a forced labor situation. The conclusion that I've come to is that the people who are going to do the leading ought to emerge out of the suffering of the organization. "Suffering" could be too strong a word, but certainly leaders need to have experienced firsthand the frustrations of dealing with the politics, the bureaucracy, the inconsistencies of today's business organizations. And then, the miracle is that rather than becoming cynical or defeated, through some kind of internal alchemy they've turned that frustration and pain into a *constructive* frustration.

That's the transforming energy that's going to help us make profound change in our organizations. It's generative energy and it's informed by both experience and compassion.

We agree with Bill that it does not seem likely that traditional management education can create these learning leaders, these leaders of the transition. Rather, these leaders may need to be forged by life experience. The way in which each leader arrives at this point seems to vary. Bill O'Brien's own story provides a good example.

Bill: I would say that the reason why Peter Senge and I have had such a fruitful relationship is because we both are heading in the same direction. He's going by way of knowledge and learning and I go there more by way of virtue and ethics.

Back in 1980, I was working with the president on a strategy for the company and we hit some snags. We knew we hit these snags because we were basing our strategy on linear cause and effect thinking. So one day we brought in an iconoclastic, brilliant professor from the University of New Hampshire who had developed a course he called "Thinking about Thinking," subtitled "Sandpaper on the Brain." He took us all the way through the evolution of Western thinking, including Descartes, Galileo, and Edison, all the big ideas and inventions. We all just sat there and said, "My God we should have paid more attention when we went to school! The stuff wasn't as useless as we thought it was!"

Then he took us through Eastern thinking and discussed how they looked at the world as a process or a flow versus a snapshot, which is the way we tend to look at it. Then he explained the concept of "unintended consequences" to us. We began talking about breaking down the walls that we'd built up around our thought processes and how these walls were keeping us from using all of our brainpower. This was almost 20 years ago, long before these ideas were in vogue.

There are many paths that can lead to a commitment to organizational learning. The leaders of the transition may begin by discovering that their current thinking is inadequate to guide their actions, so they go spelunking, in search of new ideas. As they go on their learning journeys they may find wisdom in unlikely places, perhaps discovering the roots of knowledge and integrity in ancient traditions. One might also proceed by way of logic, seeing organizational learning as the next evolutionary step. Others might show up through a process of reflection on the meaning of their lives and their potential legacy; others may come reluctantly, forced to seek new answers because of crisis. Others may be called by a sense of mission. They may have awakened anew to this calling, or perhaps it has always been their way of being. Whatever the reason or the path, they arrive at an appreciation for learning and an awareness that leadership must become more collaborative.

But how do people who have been conditioned all their lives to be command-and-control leaders make the transformation to being a learning leader? What does that transformation actually involve? In the next chapter we explore those questions.

Endnotes

1. Peter Senge et al., *Dance of Change: The Challenges of Sustaining Momentum in Learning Organizations* (New York: Doubleday, 1999), pp. 19–20.

2. F. W. Taylor, *Scientific Management* (New York: Harper and Row, 1911).

3. Edgar F. Huse and James L. Bowditch, *Behavior in Organizations: A Systems Approach to Managing*, 2nd ed. (Reading, MA: Addison-Wesley, 1997), pp. 22–24.

4. For more on Human Dynamics, please see Sandra Seagal and David Horne, *Human Dynamics* (Waltham, MA: Pegasus Communications, 1997).

5. The Human Dynamics™ body of work identifies fundamental distinctions in how people function as whole systems. These distinct human systems, termed "personality dynamics," cross culture, race, age, and gender. Five personality dynamics have been found to be by far the most numerous, and they are the focus of Human Dynamics seminars. In those seminars the participants, through a unique process, identify their own personality dynamic group. They also begin to understand the ways in which the other personality dynamics function so differently from themselves. In the flow of the seminar, participants gain the understanding of their own dynamics and the appreciation of other dynamics in the context of learning about teamwork.

Chapter 10

Reflections on Leadership

Iva: I'm reflecting upon the fact that all of the leaders we interviewed seemed to believe that a key aspect of learning leadership is the devolution of power.

Bert: OL leaders tend to believe—and I agree—that in order to meet the demands of the changing environment business organizations must evolve in the direction of more collaborative leadership. Decision-making power has to reside with the people who are in the best position to learn from the feedback and adjust their actions accordingly.

Iva: Each of the leaders had a different approach to building that capacity. Bill O'Brien's way of building capacity at the Hanover Insurance Company was to get away from the hoarding of power and focus on the integration of more meaningful core values into the workplace. This wasn't about values for their own sake. His idea was that business results would be improved by giving life to these values.

Bert: At Shell, Phil Carroll's focus was on developing people's basic understanding of the business and related fundamental business skills.

Iva: At Intel, Dave Marsing used human dynamics training to develop people's understanding of their own inherent strengths and abilities as well as those of others in their organization. As a result, they had a greater sense of how to draw on and benefit from each other's leadership capacities.

Bert: Rich Teerlink at Harley also built capacity, but he did it more by virtue of the way in which he challenged the organization to lead itself rather than by any kind of formal training. He seemed to know rather instinctively how to lead without leading and how to act so that he could bring forth the leadership already inherent in people. For example, remember what he said when we spoke to him about the beginning of their learning effort?

Rich: I said, "Look, we need a revolution around here and *I'm not going to lead it.*" That's always been my philosophy. *I'm not going to lead a revolution.* I'm not jamming it down the organization. I'm waiting for it to catch fire.

Iva: So in order for leadership to become more collaborative, two things need to happen: One, people in the organization may need to develop their capacity for leadership. That means that the devolution of power isn't just about deploying an "empowerment" program. Positional leaders have to design robust strategies that devolve power and create greater capacity for distributed leadership—not an easy task, as Phil pointed out:

Phil: You have to believe very strongly that that's the right thing to do. Then you have to have a sensible strategy, but one that's also extremely flexible because you're going to have to learn your way through this. There is no map, no set of steps. That's why so many attempts at so-called "empowerment" fail miserably. They are just too simplistic.

Iva: So the positional leader must catalyze a profound, systemwide organizational shift to more collaborative leadership and then both positional and potential leaders must learn their way through the process. There's a paradox built into that. As a positional leader, you must set that clear direction. So, at least at the beginning, you must act very much like a "heroic" leader.

But then you have to skillfully devolve power in such a way that people are no longer looking only to you for that direction. And—again, paradoxically—that requires heroism. The real heroism comes in the act of giving power away. It comes in giving up the role of hero.

Bert: There must be an art to making that transition away from heroic leader so that it's seamless and doesn't create confusion for others.

Iva: Given what we just described, it seems that OL requires a unique kind of leader. Dave Marsing had a perspective on that.

Dave: The maturity of the leaders of the organization is very important. They have to be mature in two senses. First, they have to have a pretty sophisticated way of looking at the organization and seeing its potential. Then, management has to be willing to surrender control. If a manager is not willing to surrender control—or their ego isn't developed enough to be able to surrender control—organizational learning will never happen. There are more ways to kill this than there are ways to cultivate it. For example, if the leader is a really good technologist who isn't very well developed as an individual, it doesn't stand a chance.

Iva: I agree with what Dave said and so I do not see clearly how we go from where we are today, where we have many hierarchical, command-and-control organizations led by heroic, even charismatic leaders, to organizations where leadership is more collaborative.

My sense is that there will be leaders who see the value in OL, and who will want to pursue it, but they'll get stuck because they will have a difficult time surrendering control. For example, I know that I was trying very, very hard to model this new kind of leadership, but I know that there were quite a few times when I slipped back into my old command-and-control behaviors. I know this confused people in my organization.

Bert: I can't argue with that. I was a Theory X manager trying to be Theory Y, and sometimes I'd overcorrect by going too far toward Theory Y when I shouldn't have.

Iva: So I wonder, what can we learn about how to make this transition? It would seem that most leaders—leaders like us who have been conditioned to exercise command-and-control but who see the value in OL—would have to undergo some kind of major transformation in order to participate in OL. Remember what Phil Carroll at Shell said.

> **Phil:** The executive leader has to start with him- or herself. I think executive leaders *can* make that transition, but it is a process and it takes time. I don't think any of us make a transition from being a dictator today to being Mahatma Gandhi in five years' time. It's more like a journey in which you have a general direction, which is the desire to devolve power and decision making down into the organization.

Bert: Phil would agree with you, but I'm not so sure. I agree wholeheartedly with the need to devolve power. It's a matter of degree. Regarding the need for personal transformation, it's a question of how it happens. I thought Peter Senge's view was you had to go through personal change—then you could lead. I understood that to be a sequential process. Now I see that it isn't sequential but concurrent. Both the leader and the organization transform incrementally as the journey progresses.

Iva: In my view the process is both sequential and concurrent. It begins with an awakening. Whether it comes by way of discovery or disaster, something sets you on the path. So we are not in total agreement on this point. Is there a way we can talk about this transition in a way that would be helpful to others?

Bert: We should try.

Learning Leadership: A Debate

Iva: Let's review the argument. We agree that there are two major challenges facing leadership. The first is the challenge of transforming our organizations, which involves developing appropriate leadership capacity within our organizations.

Bert: Which can require a major effort.

Iva: That first challenge begins with a question, again as Phil pointed out.

> **Phil:** When I run up against a question like: "How do we build leadership capacity in the company?" I can't call everyone together and say, "OK, here are the steps. We're going to do this." It's not that simple. Finding the answer to that question is a process. It's almost a political process—and it's certainly a learning process in and of itself.

Iva: That first challenge leads to the second, much more personal challenge: How can I surrender control? For most traditional leaders the path to transformation begins with that question. The good news is that once you admit that you, the leader, don't know how to do this, that you have no formula, then, by definition, you are on the way to a new form of leadership. First you admit it to yourself, and then you admit it openly.

Bert: But if you admit that openly, you may invite danger. The organization may not be ready for a leader who doesn't know. There can be a backlash.

Iva: That shouldn't stop you—if you are really committed to this work.

Bert: That's spoken like a true visionary.

Iva: You're right, Bert. Of course that is the visionary aspect of me speaking. But don't give up on me. I really have learned some things from you, so let me be clear. I have spent the last several years engaged in a process of double-loop learning. I have had to come to terms with the fact that I can have a deep personal commitment to ideas, but my actions may have to be more pragmatic. I realize that if I'm too much of a zealot, if I push the organization beyond the limits of its tolerance, I won't be around to make change. That means I must deal with current reality as it is, on its own terms. It means that I stand on the razor's edge. I have to pick my moves carefully.

So, you are right in one sense. If I, as a leader, can't openly admit I don't know something without shaking people up or destroying my own credibility, then I must consider whether there is another way to engage others in answering the question that is more acceptable to the organization.

At the same time I must recognize that I may just be assuming that I can't admit that I don't know. It may be that a lot of people are desperate for the leader to admit that he or she doesn't know something. So I have to find some way to test my assumption. Otherwise I'm just copping out—because I'm scared or because I actually like being the leader who knows and I don't want to let go of that. We have all kinds of ways of kidding ourselves.

If we believe in this learning idea *and* we want to change our organizations for the better, we have to make conscious choices about how we're going to work within the context of the present even as we're helping to birth the emergent systems. That's not easy and it may involve compromise sometimes, but none of us should be in the business of committing career suicide because if the enlightened leaders are no longer around to lead, then this effort has no viability.

Bert: Thank you. I especially agree with the last part of what you said; the rest I'm taking under advisement. I'm just a little reluctant to say that all leaders have to undergo some kind of earth-shattering personal transformation to do this work. However, they will most likely need to learn some new skills.

Iva: Learning new skills is important, yes, but it's also more than that. Think about how Phil described his journey:

> **Phil:** For many, many years I had worked hard to have a very pronounced separation between my home life and the office. My wife and kids would be over here, but when I went out in the morning and started the car I thought to myself, "You better put your game face on, you're a different person. You're going to act differently." Then when I came home, I tried to take that face off and be another kind of person.
>
> All that is very false. In the long term, that behavior produces unacceptable strains in both places. You're not an integrated person. You're not a whole person. And if you're not a whole person it's very difficult to lead others effectively. I had to come to terms with that, and it was not easy. But, with help from some consultants in OL and other areas, I began to see that everything that happens to us has an emotional element and that to ignore the emotional aspect of things completely is not healthy.
>
> I also came to see this drive to compartmentalization within context. I began to understand why it was such a powerful drive. We have built very powerful defense mechanisms and protections because it's an area that is not well-understood, especially for the technically trained. It's much easier for us to stay

within the boundaries of Aristotelian logic and say, "Hey, you know, this is about engineering principles and economics, and so forth."

So we have this basic understanding. Most people say, "Don't go there. I don't want that because that is going to expose an awful lot of me that I don't want exposed." We collude in protecting each other from healthy personal development, and that is a very bad characteristic.

Now, of course, you don't want to overcompensate by going in the other direction. You don't want emotions out of control, with people tearing their shirts in the board room and ranting and raving, but I'm talking about the skillful acknowledgement of the emotional aspect of things. I'm talking about practicing the ability to say, "Bert, let's face it, you're making me very angry. I don't like the way I'm feeling about this. Irrespective of how logically you put your argument, I think you've got another agenda and here's why."

You can learn those skills. You can practice in small groups. I believe that these skills are essential if you're going to do anything akin to really building coherence and cohesion at top management levels. People have to be able to have those kinds of conversations.

The compartmentalization we have practiced in the business world for so long produces severe difficulties and limitations in our ability to think and act. So, in sum, I believe that this OL work is about integration. This work is about reintegrating what is segregated or separated out in our mental processes—such as separating emotion from reason and separating home from the office. That's the essence of it.

Iva: I relate to what Phil said because as I began this OL work I came to realize that something had happened to me on the road to upper management. I had adapted to what was required of me and as a result I lost touch with myself. I have come to question whether compartmentalization should be eliminated from business. In fact, I question whether it's good for business even though, at present, we accept that it is.

Bert: I understand what you are saying, but that's reality. The business environment still requires us to compartmentalize—to separate feelings from logical thought. We put them in a box. Some of that may be necessary. There is a proper role for defense mechanisms, business persona, the mask, etc. Again, it's a matter of degree.

To my mind there are two levels of integration: the integration of personal and business life and the integration of logic with emotions. With regard to the latter, my concern is that the road to integration is inherently unstable. Do we really want to take that on in the workplace? It exposes us to the risks involved with having outbursts of extreme emotion. This could undermine performance. For example, what happens when people's emotions run high? They aren't on "receive," they're on "send" only. They lose objectivity; they say things they don't mean or expect—including me. It's harder to be productive. I don't believe that good leadership lets that occur. The leader has to have a sense of when an emotional issue needs to be taken off the table and dealt with later.

I also believe that a leader has to overcome their personal emotions and doubts in order to provide the necessary leadership. When people are under a strain they look for a pillar, a rock, an anchor. That is a requirement for those who are responsible for leading people into battle. People expect their leaders to exhibit confidence and to maintain a positive demeanor. Churchill was a great example. People don't want a leader to look scattered or display too much emotion or expose their uncertainty. In fact, that's crucial to my concept of leadership.

Iva: I'm struck by the military analogy you just used. Although I agree with you, I trust that business is not war. I also agree that in the current reality of our business climates, compartmentalization is still highly valued. But during this important transition phase leaders must begin to come to terms with whether or not compartmentalization is really benefiting our organizations. Is it really making us better leaders? And, if not, what actions do we wish to take to change things? And do we have sufficient trust and commitment to begin this process?

Many will struggle with these questions because we have been so conditioned by the business culture to behave in certain ways. Just as we ourselves have had to unlearn some of these conditioned responses, so will others.

Bert: Maybe it's a question of how far you want to go with organizational learning. If you're mainly interested in improving the organization's ability to do single-loop learning, then I don't think you'll have to go as much into yourself. But if you and the organization want to practice what we're calling a deeper form of organizational learning, then that's another story.

Iva: That may be one way to think about it. Maybe there are degrees of commitment that a leader can make to organizational learning. It's a question of whether you want to commit to developing the capacity for Model II actions. If you do, then you have to be willing to go wherever that path leads you. If it requires a deeper level of questioning and personal transformation, then so be it. But if you're going to make a limited commitment to OL then I believe that you have to do so with the full understanding that your commitment is limited and you're not going to realize the full benefits.

Bert: Maybe you're not ready to make that full commitment in the beginning. But if you're willing to do *something*, that's got to be OK.

Iva: Alright, let's say that you can only make a limited commitment in the beginning. That's still going to require a major transition on the part of most leaders because we've learned that *you can't lead a learning effort in the same way you've led other kinds of efforts.*

Keeping Your Balance on the Walk Between Worlds

Bert: So you're saying that leaders may have to learn how to stop leading as they have led before.

Iva: Yes. Let's think of leadership as a continuum. At the one end we have traditional command-and-control style of leadership. At the other end we have the leadership that's necessary in order for organizations to learn. We've been calling that "collaborative leadership."

Figure 10.1
Leadership Continuum

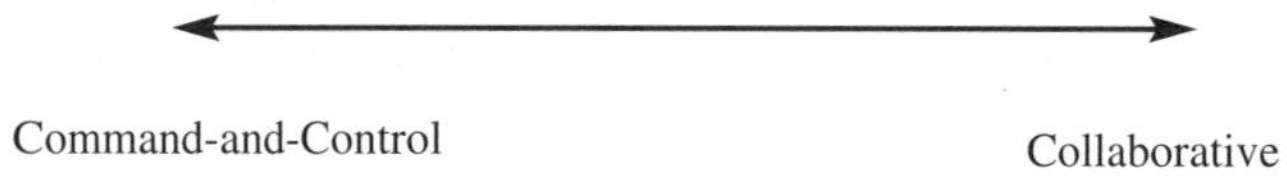

Command-and-Control   Collaborative

Bert: So, you are saying that people who want to be OL leaders must move away from command-and-control; their leadership style needs to become more collaborative.

Iva: Yes. I believe that many positional leaders, like ourselves, will understand on an intellectual level what OL leadership entails, but they will struggle with this transition, because they have been so conditioned by the business culture to behave in certain ways.

For example, there's a danger that command-and-control leaders will *suddenly* switch gears and try to act like servant leaders.[1] That will confuse the people in a traditional command-and-control organization. The people in the organization won't know whether to trust that the leader has really changed—and they won't be ready to accept more leadership responsibility themselves. That's when fear and anxiety are likely to show up because people think it's a setup.

Bert: So there's the problem of delay. As people begin to see a change in leadership it will take them time to believe and trust in the change. At the same time the leader him- or herself will go through an internally frustrating period. The uncertainty and questioning that occurs on both sides will cause these delays.

Iva: Yes, indeed, Bert, repeat behavior over time is needed before people trust that it's real. There's a delay while the leader is changing mental models and learning new behaviors. In moments of stress, there is a tendency for old habits to take over. They'll slide back to using their old command-and-control tactics. I know; I've done it.

Bert: There's also a danger that leaders who have been conditioned to be command-and-control will overcorrect and become too reluctant to act. Remember how Bill O'Brien characterized it.

> **Bill:** You asked me what kept me up at night? It was when I had to deal with poor performance. I said to myself, "If I'm going to do this I'd rather take a little more time and do it too late than do it too early because I have a human being's life here." Finally, you get signals that tell you you've waited too long. Some of your direct reports are coming to you, trying to drop hints that information technology is not working. And there are missed deadlines—a whole host of things. I erred by being too late. I was late partially by design because I wanted to minimize the fear. For the most part the fear in corporations today is very debilitating so I wanted to keep us at a very low level of fear. I would rather have a lot of other people say, "It's about time O'Brien woke up!" than having people say, "Where is O'Brien going to strike next?"

Bert: That happened to me as well. But back to your continuum. You're implying that leaders have to somehow go through a transition process that moves them on that continuum from the left to the right. I'm not sure that I believe this. I have a very different mental model of leadership.

We have a tendency in this field to take a kind of moral position against command-and-control and that's wrong. Good leadership is highly *situational*. Positional leaders have to retain the capacity to use command-and-control tactics when necessary even when they're practicing OL. Rich Teerlink gave us a good example, which we talked about in the last chapter. When he sent his two managers to resolve the problems in the plant, that was a great example of using a command style to accomplish a goal that was congruent with learning.

Iva: Rich knew just how to respond to the situation to get the most effective—and also learningful—outcome. He used his command authority to force the two managers to learn how to work together. He wouldn't let them divide up the work, which would have meant they'd come from the old reductionist paradigm. And he wouldn't let them resort to command-and-control to solve problems.

Bert: The ability to "read" a situation and to respond appropriately is a critical skill. I'm calling it "situational acuity" and I believe it's an art.

Iva: It's particularly artful because he wasn't just resorting to command, but doing so in order to promote learning.

Bert: I can see myself doing the same thing. Even though I'm committed to OL, I will intentionally go back and use command-and-control if I think I have to. Does it break me up inside? Sometimes. But it's not a question of going backwards in those cases. It's a question of making conscious choices. Many times leaders find themselves in situations where there are a lot of conflicting demands. The question is, how are you going to resolve them within the context of your management style, your values, and your inherent sense of what will work in that moment given your boss, the financials, the customer base, Wall Street, etc. One puts all that in the pot, evaluates it, and says, "I'm going to do this." That's what leadership is all about.

The Debate Intensifies

Iva: Let's hold that idea for a moment and examine it. The idea of situational leadership has been around for a long time.[2] If OL leadership is only a matter of applying a form of situational leadership, what are the implications? What, if anything, is going to be different? What's the difference between a leader who thinks they are "enlightened" but decides that they are being "situational" when they practice command-and-control—and a leader who is just being inconsistent—or who is just plain reluctant to surrender control?

Bert: You're right in the sense that this kind of situational leader has to be more sophisticated because organizational learning is now, in fact, a viable option for a situational leader. He or she has a more robust set of tools to choose from. Now it's not just a question of: Are you a Theory X or Theory Y manager? Now it's also: Do you question your assumptions?

Still, it's *not* inconsistent for leaders to go back and forth between the two. The folly is in taking one position on either extreme. If you choose to be the OL guru, then you are equally as misguided as a person who chooses to be command-and-control most of the time. When I see someone who is extreme in either direction, I get concerned because that's a one-dimensional manager. I'm also trying to get the issue of morality out of this. There is value in the heroic leader. There is a time when you have to take distasteful actions in order to get your financial bottom line aligned with expectations. You can make as much progress with command-and-control as you can with OL, under certain conditions.

Let me describe a scenario. If I come into a Greenfield situation I have more degrees of freedom than if I come into a company that's in trouble. In the latter situation, my first priority is to get us out of trouble. I may believe that I have to act quickly and decisively and don't have time to build the capacity for more participatory decision making. But say I've been hired as the new CEO of a company. Say my predecessor was let go because of poor performance and I'm coming in from a very successful company. My mission is to turn the situation around. Because of my knowledge of OL, I have a broader range of choice: I can choose to shake things up, which is what everyone expects, and lay on the formula that worked so well at my previous company.

Or, if I'm really committed to learning—and I think that I have the time and enough of the essential ingredients and I'm willing to take on the risk—I can try to bring everyone together, discuss the mistakes of the past few years, and do some double-loop learning. Based on what we discover together, I can then utilize everything I know about OL to develop a change strategy. Two choices. You make the best choice you can, given all of the circumstances. And you may *not* choose to take the learning approach even though you are committed to OL. Successful leaders will each choose their own mix of command-and-control and collaboration, so there's no formula. It's an art. That's the learning challenge: *to know when to do what in what direction.* That understanding will only be built up as more people go down this road and explore it.

Iva: Let me try to answer you by using the metaphor of a high wire. The high wire stretches across the chasm from command-and-control to collaborative leadership.

Bert: You, as a leader, are riding a unicycle on that high wire, moving back and forth between the two.

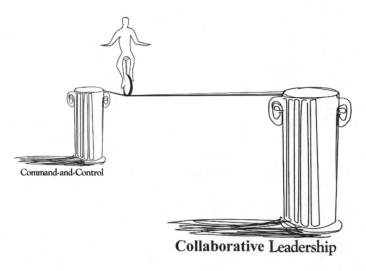

Command-and-Control

Collaborative Leadership

Figure 10.2
The Tension System

Iva: Here's where you may be missing an essential point, which is: You're not just oscillating back and forth. As Phil said, "you're moving in a general direction." *You're heading somewhere.* That means that you're heading away from command-and-control and *toward* greater collaboration. You may occasionally draw on command-and-control tactics, but in fewer and fewer situations. That ceases to be your fall-back strategy. In general, you're moving to the right, toward more collaboration.

Here's why I believe this. I believe that there is a bigger danger than the danger of throwing out command-and-control altogether and that danger is that nothing will change. Leaders have been practicing so-called situational leadership for a long time. OL changes the game. Positional leaders now must face the challenge of developing their own leadership abilities so that they can effectively practice leadership in an organization that is learning. That's different. *It has to be.*

Therefore, if we're going to use the term "situational leader" in this context we have to define what we mean by that. We have to define what it means in the context of learning. We have to bring learning into the equation. It's fine to say, "Be situational," but the meaning of situational leadership has now shifted. The ability to be situational in a learning context means that you have to take the time and develop the capacity to challenge your assumptions and reflect deeply enough to get some double-loop learning. Otherwise, you may respond to situations differently, but your response could be the result of Model I reasoning. Furthermore, we are beginning to understand that "control" as we know it now is an illusion. So we can command, but we can't really control—even in the present system. Perhaps you're struggling with the idea of surrendering control.

Bert: Let's stay with our analogy. As a leader, your job is to stay balanced on that high wire. You're in a tension system and you have to stay within the elastic zone of *your* tension system. If you exceed the boundaries of that elastic zone, something's going to change and deform permanently. You'll lose your job or you'll choose to leave. Each leader will have to figure out where those boundaries are.

Iva: And on the other side you've got the vision and values that you want to live by and enact: the principles of organizational learning.

Bert: So as you balance on the wire you're trying to balance the requirements of the present system with the ideals of the emergent system. For example, I generally make a distinction between a leader and a manager, but when it comes to this work, a leader must also be a manager. Change itself is a process that needs to be managed. So besides providing an environment where learning can occur, the leader has the responsibility as a manager to ensure that the results are forthcoming. Therefore, the decision whether and when to start a learning effort becomes a major management question. For example, the organization may need to get its financial house in order first—whatever that takes.

A leader may be able to inhabit the dual role of leading and managing the change process, but it's difficult. Leaders may have to choose to separate leadership responsibilities from operational management responsibilities. However, both are fundamental to a successful learning effort. The effort must stay grounded in present-day realities and expectations or it may lose relevancy.

Making those kinds of decisions is situational leadership to me. When you're sitting in a divisional or team meeting or in an executive committee meeting, chances are you're not expected to be sitting there as a leader of an OL process. You're going to be sitting there as a financial custodian.

Iva: You're *both* and you have to learn how to hold both, how to stay in that paradox of evolving to OL and maintaining existing performance levels. I don't think compartmentalization is the answer here. You have to be both. That doesn't mean you do it in a way that would damage you. You have to dance with it.

Bert: So you're up there trying to stay balanced. On the one side you've got all of the pressures and demands of current reality. You've got financial and performance responsibilities that you need to manage, you've got political issues, people jockeying for control and power, and maybe you've also got resistance to change. How do you stay balanced?

Balance and the Walk Between Two Worlds

Iva: Staying in balance will be a challenge—as we both know from our stories. It's a paradox again. For a lot of people who've come up through a hierarchical structure and raised themselves up on the ladder of influence, coming to OL can be like suddenly seeing the light. You think that maybe things should be done differently in order to be more successful, but abrupt change isn't going to work.

The moment you make an abrupt move, you fall. So you have to be able to stay in that conflictual space. It's very important to honor the other system, give it space to exist, because the moment you start trying to dismantle it, it's going to push back. So it's not about saying, "I've just seen the light and now we're going to do things differently. I've just been to this training course and now we're going to implement this in my organization and if you don't do what I say and want, you're not going to be able to create that which is possible." Which, of course, is what I did, in the simplest of terms.[3]

Bert: One has to remember that as a leader you're responsible for the well-being of many other people who may not yet understand the change you're trying to bring about.

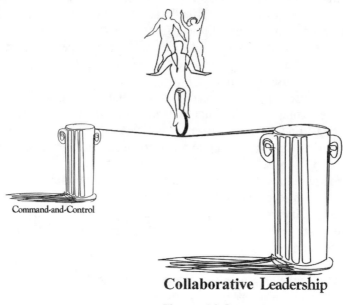

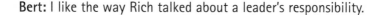

Collaborative Leadership

Figure 10.3
A Leader's Responsibility

Bert: I like the way Rich talked about a leader's responsibility.

Rich: My Dad taught me about leadership. When I became a supervisor, he said, "Richard, your whole life changes now because from now on you're not only responsible for you and your family, you're responsible for those who work with you and for you. You are the most important person in the world to them. You determine if they have a job, you determine if they get a raise. You are the decision maker about everything that's really important to them. If you have credibility with them, then they don't worry because they know you'll communicate with them about what's going on."

Iva: One has to be able to hold this vision but also recognize where others are. Most everybody else is in the current reality of the existing system so the work is to build the bridge between the two. Building the bridge involves being sensitive to the past, being sensitive to the culture you're in.

Bert: So, staying with the analogy, when you are balancing on the wheel, you're using feedback, i.e., the data that's coming back to you, very effectively. That's why you can maintain your balance. So there's one more aspect to our leadership picture. When you use feedback, you've got the equivalent of a balance beam.

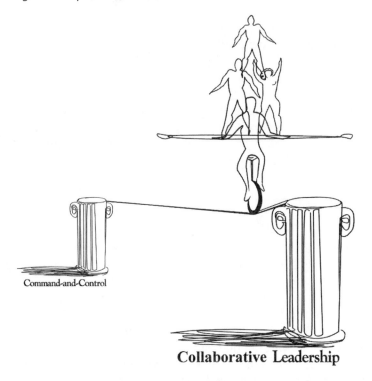

Command-and-Control

Collaborative Leadership

Figure 10.4
Using Feedback to Stay in Balance

Iva: That's why it's very important to understand and create appropriate feedback loops.

Bert: Also, we need to remember to design and pay attention to more than one kind of feedback. There's the feedback that tells you how you're doing in terms of the results you're supposed to deliver and also the feedback that tells you whether you're getting resistance. If you get feedback that tells you to stop or go slower, or take a detour, you need to listen.

Iva: Then there's the kind of feedback that tells you how you're doing in your personal transformation process. As Chris Argyris has observed, we're very likely to espouse one set of values but then operate according to another. That's when we get into trouble and create confusion for others. How does one know if one's actions are in contradiction to one's espoused values when one's employing situational leadership? Feedback will let you know. That's why it's important in the beginning to clarify the value system you want to operate by. Are you trying to develop your capacity for Model II? Because that will guide how you instruct people about the feedback they should provide. So a leader may need to find a coach.

Bert: At the very least you need to find people who will tell you the truth about yourself and about the situation. That's hard to find! In my case, I used my boss as "air cover" because I didn't trust myself to be able to read the signals. He wouldn't run interference for me, but he would tell me if I was going off-course.

Iva: While I, of course, ignored the signals that people were trying to give me. That's why there's another tool you need besides feedback. You need the capacity to reflect on the feedback you receive and the ability to learn from your reflections.

Leadership, Reflection, and Action

Bert: Reflection, let alone reflection in the midst of action, is very difficult for most traditional command-and-control leaders. We just don't have any practice in it. Personally, I resist it because I just don't think I have time for it.

Iva: Ah, that's one of those traps that we create for ourselves. Better to have a mess of short-term fixes than face the prospect of stopping for a moment to think more deeply about what we are doing.

Bert: It's very easy to say that, but in the moment the quick fix sure looks like the right thing to do. Taking time for reflection does not—even though I see the logic. It's that dual system problem again. You have to make a choice in the moment: do I go with the vision or the practical reality?

Iva: Dave Marsing has a wonderful perspective on why reflection is practical.

> **Dave:** If you don't reflect, you don't see the openings and the opportunities. Without the period of reflection, there's more and more tension and pressure put on your cognitive processes in order to be successful and to accomplish your objectives, so that sometimes you're blind to an opportunity that might be tangential.

Iva: Thinking about the importance of reflection brings up another kind of balance that leaders need to have. We need to be able to balance action with non-action. That feels like another paradox because we can't believe that we don't need to act to move the process forward.

Bert: As a Type A, I have time urgency. I have a hard time dealing with the delays involved in OL. I tend to want to act. The truth is, I run out of patience with the collaborative process and therefore I tend to revert to command-and-control, whereas Rich Teerlink seems to know instinctively how to read the situation and how to balance action and inaction. He is a real role model for me.

> **Rich:** The delay (before the effect of learning can be quantified) is longer than you would ever anticipate. But you also have to be careful of creating too high a level of expectation. That's why it's good, I think, to just talk about something. And then let it simmer and evolve a little bit.

Bert: Rich seemed to be able to balance the forces without necessarily imposing his own will. And he didn't take it all on his shoulders.

Iva: Until about two years ago, I would always revert to pushing forward when things weren't going as I felt that they should. Then I learned a powerful lesson. I saw that that behavior—which I thought was so successful—had actually caused many difficulties in my life. I could see the connection clearly. I have had so few opportunities to practice this new learning, but when I did the outcomes were great. So the only thing I long for is more opportunities to practice what I learned. The trouble is, we've created these systems that reinforce acting for its own sake. Yet, we would never agree that that is so.

Bert: The closest I've come to being able to balance action and non-action has been in cases where the problem went away on its own. I have this sixth sense that tells me when problems will fade or resolve themselves. When the sense shows up I try to listen to it, because when I override it I don't have the courage of my own convictions.

Iva: Most of us can let problems go away, at least to some degree. But letting things unfold is different. And knowing when not to act so that things will come out better than if you did act is difficult. I wish I had more practice in letting go, having faith in the flow of things, and realizing that we're not the center of the universe so we don't have to make things happen. We become so self-centered—not in self-interest, necessarily—but in believing that we alone can do it. Do we often take action in spite of the fact that we sense that we should do otherwise? Perhaps we do so because we haven't had the experience of another way of getting to an outcome.

Bert: Action pacifies anxiety. We want to get in there and do something. Yet, at the same time, management tends to be reactive. That may be why so many businesses are crisis-oriented. Until actually faced with a crisis, we tend to be inactive. A crisis gets us moving. We put ourselves in danger so that we can do something. All organizations would be learning already if we were committed to acting prophylactically rather than remedially.

Iva: Sometimes we create the crisis in order to change our behaviors, to do the right thing. I have done that even with OL. So we in business are reactive rather than creative. We are prone to action without reflection. And we are addicted to crisis. Is this what we really want? I would put this as a preeminent question.

A Question of Personal Mastery

Iva: There's one more aspect to holding the tension that I want to bring up. In order to incorporate feedback—especially criticism—and to really be reflective, we have to achieve a certain level of personal development, what Senge calls "personal mastery." Now that's a little circular, because I think that feedback and reflection can help us to achieve personal mastery. But we have to have the openness and the willingness to learn about ourselves to begin with. That takes a certain amount of self-awareness and even courage. I don't think I had that at the beginning—although I very much wanted to. So I still think that it means that organizational transformation requires starting with yourself. It always comes back to yourself.

Bert: I don't believe that OL requires that you have a cathartic approach to your life.

Iva: I can't prescribe what's right for anyone else—but I would also say that you can't preclude that if that's where your learning journey leads you—as it did in my case. If you resist the idea, you might want to consider why that's such an important boundary condition for you. Just hold that as a question. If I as a leader act in certain ways that have been accepted and forgiven or ignored because I am who I am, I have the responsibility to change those things.

Bert: I guess it depends on what your assessment of triage tells you. If you think that working on yourself will jump-start the change process for the whole organization, fine. Go ahead. If it's perceived that you are the problem, then you need the change. But my sense is that you proceed more by feeling your way together at the same time, learning to master the leadership profiles that your group both needs and is capable of delivering.

Iva: We may not agree on everything, but we do agree on the need for leaders to hold the tension characteristic of every paradoxical situation. So too for the OL leader. As you're leading you'll constantly be monitoring for feedback and then reflecting, learning, reframing, and finding another way of thinking or acting that may surprise you.

Bert: That's why Dave related it to learning a martial art. It takes practice and time to master this balance.

Iva: Maybe a lifetime.

Failure: The Leader's Learning Edge

Iva: So we're saying that if a leader wants to stay in balance, they need some tools for assessing and coping with that tension system. They'll often have to make a choice between OL values and the values of the existing system; between commanding and collaborating; between acting and nonacting; between results in the short term and the long term. The journey will require patience, preparation, and flexibility. And they will no doubt make errors because they're learning. When they make a mistake they can use double-loop learning to understand what happened.

Bert: Even then, they might fail. If so, how will they deal with that? The way we deal with so-called failure in business always makes me think of how we as parents react when a little child first begins to walk. The child usually takes a step or two and then stumbles and falls down. What do we do? We applaud, we give them all kinds of support and encouragement. That's probably the last time any of us ever experiences that kind of love and reassurance for what was, essentially, a failure. We have to change both how we define failure and how we treat failure. That's also leadership's role.

Iva: The reason we applaud when they stumble is because we acknowledge that they have taken a risk in the direction of growth. When they grow up we say we want them to take a risk, but when they stumble or fail we punish them. As a rule, today's leaders don't deal well with failure—either someone else's or their own. Dealing with failure is a *learning edge* for most leaders, a challenge that often catches us unaware. It's very hard for people who have come into the upper levels of management to deal with failure because when you're very successful and when you're creating that which you wanted and hoped for, you become more confident in your ability to master any challenge. In fact, you rarely question your mastery. Then, when something happens that is not expected—a failure—it doesn't fit into the mental model you have of yourself.

So how do we cope? Good old Model I. We look for the external influences that created the situation, we question other people's motives and abilities, we blame others. We blame circumstances. My experience in the corporate environment is that we are pros at explaining away failure, but not very good at learning from it nor at having compassion for each other when we do fail. We still have a lot to learn.

Bert: Yes, there are some people who immediately look for reasons outside themselves. They say the environment was lousy, or it was the oil crisis or something else. But when I fail I tend to blame myself first. I feel devastated personally.

Iva: That's the flip side of the same issue. In both cases we're displaying an inflated sense of our own capacities, a trait that's not uncommon in executives. The first response is like saying, "I'm responsible for nothing," and the second response is like saying, "I'm responsible for everything." If you think about it, neither one is a really centered response. When you thought you failed, Bert, what did you do differently?

Bert: I tried to learn from my mistakes. I became more reflective and I changed my approach.

Iva: But you *didn't change the way you thought about failure.* Neither did I. I believed my own story. I believed that nothing was going wrong and I certainly didn't believe that I was responsible for any of the problems I was having. So I repeated my mistakes until I really failed. I had a lot more to learn about how to create conditions so these patterns wouldn't repeat.

Bert: I like what Dave Marsing said about how to deal with failure.

Dave: I used to deal with failure very poorly—but I've learned. At this stage of my life, when those kinds of events occur I spend a lot of time reflecting on the big picture. I also spend a lot of time working through my immediate emotional reaction. I try not to take it as a personal failure

I also realize that there are a lot of times when failure is circumstantial. It's not because I had the wrong intentions or that I'm totally unskilled or a total idiot or I blew something. Instead I open myself up as much as I can to be receptive to the objective learning that lies somewhere within. And I try to get as much value out of it as I can.

Also, I'm much more concerned about the impact of the experience on those around me because most often this has been a team effort, therefore a "failure" affects more than just me. I try very hard to mitigate the suffering of the people around me and to help them work through their interpretation of what it means.

Taking the time and having the skills to be able to reflect were essential to my developing the ability to understand and cope with failure. If you don't reflect, you don't see the openings and the opportunities. Without the period of reflection, you put more and more tension and pressure on your cognitive processes in order to be successful and to accomplish your objectives. Sometimes that means you're blind to a new opportunity that the failure might be bringing forth.

Iva: If you don't know how to reflect you will not be able to do this work, and if you don't do this work, you will not know how to reflect.

Bert: That's a learning edge for me. As I look back, I was always pretty focused on getting it right instead of seeing new opportunity in the failure. That'll take some practice.

The Lonely Leader

Iva: I feel that the picture we've painted of the leader may seem rather lonely. Perhaps, because of our having been conditioned to be hero-leaders, we've forgotten that, in the end, OL leadership is about putting aside that lonely hero and enabling coleadership, shared leadership, collaboration. It's about creating networks of people who share these ideas; it's not about being a lonely martyr to the cause.

Bert: If I were being idealistic I'd say, "Absolutely, yes, you will be able to find kindred spirits and you will not have to go it alone." But if I were being realistic I'd have to say that I'm not sure that it isn't going to be lonely in practice—at least at the beginning. At the same time I'm willing to admit that I probably didn't reach out enough to people. The irony is that if I had it to do over again, I still might not know how to do that.

Iva: So there's something else we leaders need to learn more about: how to engage with and cocreate with others.

Bert: And give up the idea that we have to do it all ourselves.

What if Your Organizational Learning Effort "Fails"?

Iva: There is some risk and we have to acknowledge that not many OL leaders have been able to accomplish everything we've described.

Bert: That's true, but this is a journey. Even if you "fail" in one sense, you will have succeeded in the more important sense because you'll shed more light on the path. You'll have learned one more thing about how to bring this change about, so that others can continue.

Iva: And perhaps you'll have changed yourself.

Bert: Bill O'Brien may have said it best.

Bill: When it comes to viewing "failures," I take the long view. I think of organizational learning as part of a movement—a very positive movement. Yes, there have been some very abrupt endings to OL leaders, but for me, that isn't failure. It's the price of a movement.

Those so-called failures have been part of an enormous movement that's moving very rapidly away from the old bureaucratic, command-and-control structure. You can see the evidence. Manufacturing organizations are light years ahead of where they were ten years ago in this country both in terms of productivity and in terms of dignity and respect for the worker. They are now enlisting people's thinking capacity. Some industries, like the financial services, are behind, but it will happen there, too.

There's been enormous progress since *The Fifth Discipline* first came out, so the first casualties aren't failures, they're the price of a movement. If you want an analogy, just look at WWII. We don't say that Guadalcanal was a failure even though we lost a lot of lives. We say that that was the price of freedom.

Bert: Now that may sound like a very strong analogy, but that's really what we're talking about here. We're talking about a kind of freedom: freeing the creative potential of people in the workplace.

Can traditional command-and-control managers learn their way toward a more collaborative form of leadership? If we believe the answer is "yes," then how can they go about it? These are the questions that Bert and Iva have been wrestling with in this chapter.

As we've come to expect, Iva speaks for the vision, and Bert speaks about the practical demands that tend to define present-day management. We need to honor both of these perspectives and find a pathway that both can walk. This is our collective task. It belongs to all of us who struggle with these questions and we can only offer some thoughts here.

We think that the starting point is a deep commitment to the devolution of power. This principle applies whether one is an executive or line manager, team leader or networker. A learning leader's work is about skillfully giving away power, surrendering control, and rendering capacity for leadership in others. The word "skillful" is key here. The devolution of power involves letting go of the reins in such a way as to free the potential for self-organizing networks to emerge. Ralph Stacey writes that self-organizing networks are the structures that will enable an organization to deal more effectively with complexity. These networks can and should exist right along with the traditional hierarchical structure.

Stacey's view is that the two systems (hierarchical and network) probably should coexist simultaneously as one is good at responding to predictive situations and the other is required for dealing with the unknowable.[4]

If this holds true, then the transition we are talking about is not necessarily about moving from one system to another, but about living within and between the two, tapping into each as appropriate. This is Bert's "situational leadership" model taken to another level of understanding. Again, Bert's and Iva's perspectives complement each other. Iva speaks about living with paradox and about our ability to hold the tension that is required to stay with things that seem to be in contradiction. Bert focuses on the need to stay balanced and to seek equilibrium, however momentary, within that tension system.

How does one become skillful in devolving power? We believe that for most command-and-control managers, some degree of personal work is necessary in order to come to grips with this fundamental shift. Those who wish to embark on this journey would benefit from a broad understanding of Argyris and Schön's Model I and Model II theories-in-use.[5] With an understanding of these concepts and of single- and double-loop learning they can hopefully make some informed decisions about whether and how they want to proceed on their journey. That choice can also be informed by an understanding of their own deeply-held values. A sense of their present leadership style, perhaps informed by Rooke and Torbert's matrix, may also help to ready them.[6]

These tools can help define the territory of change. Then comes the hard part.

If managers wish to undertake this journey, they will need to seek support; it is doubly difficult for lone rangers to do this work. While they can seek some individual training in the five disciplines, the real learning—the questioning of assumptions, reframing, trying on of new perspectives and new behaviors—must happen through practice in community with others. This is true whether the purpose is to develop leadership capacity or to define a new strategy in the wake of complexity. As Stacey writes, "learning in open-ended situations has to be a group process, not a task carried out by an individual expert or visionary. No one individual is likely to possess wide enough perspectives to handle such a complex situation. Such perspectives can be developed only through a group interaction."[7]

We believe that a leader must reach out to others, must seek feedback of all kinds and shapes—often deliberately creating those feedback loops—and must work on their ability to reflect upon that feedback. The leader may seek a coach, but should not rely solely on a coach. If a leader feels too lonely in the learning process, this is probably a signal that something needs to change.

How deep does a leader's work on personal transformation need to go? The question seems unanswerable in the abstract. It can only be answered by each within the context of his or her own journey. This is a qualitatively different kind of journey for managers. As Stacey says, "in situations of open-ended change one cannot specify an intention and then identify a limited number of events and actions that will lead to fulfillment of that intention because the links between cause and effect are lost in the complexity of unfolding events."[8]

If we follow Stacey's argument, our idea of "control" changes. The locus of control shifts. Today, we tend to believe we must hold tight to the reins of control because if we don't we fear that all hell will break loose. What happens if we question that assumption? Stacey directs us to look at the evidence and to see how much in the universe dances on the edge of chaos but does not fall apart. If we can come to terms with that realization, we no longer have to hold the reins so tightly. We can make free and informed choices— sometimes choosing to control and sometimes waiting to see what kind of order wants to show up. We have set ourselves—and others—free.

Endnotes

1. Robert K. Greenleaf, *Servant Leadership* (Mahwah, NJ: Paulist Press, 1991).

2. These concepts were first introduced by Paul Hersey and Kenneth Blanchard in 1969.

3. Ralph Stacey, *Complexity and Creativity in Organizations*, (San Francisco: Berrett-Koehler, 1996).

4. Stacey, 1996, op. cit.

5. Chris Argyris, *On Organizational Learning* (Malden, MA: Blackwell Publishers, 1999).

6. Excerpted from THE SYSTEMS THINKER Newsletter article *The CEO's Role in Organizational Transformation* by David Rooke and William R. Torbert (Waltham, MA: Published by Pegasus Communications, Inc., 1999).

7. Ralph Stacey, *Managing the Unknowable: Strategic Boundaries Between Order and Chaos in Organizations* (San Francisco: Jossey-Bass, 1992), p. 112.

8. Stacey, 1992, op. cit., p. 167.

Part 4
Mapping

For organizational learning to become a viable option for businesses, we need many more practical experiments where OL principles and methods are tried out in real business environments. These practical experiments can empirically test OL's ability to bring about business results. Such experimentation can satisfy our pragmatic need to know that these ideas work and that results are replicable.

However, because organizational learning is also about helping us to move into a new paradigm, we cannot be satisfied with simple experiments designed to prove or disprove the efficacy of learning solely within the context of our old paradigm. These experiments can also help to surface and evaluate the deeply held collective assumptions that inhibit our effectiveness and our ability to learn from our experience. The visionary within us knows that assumptions can give rise to prisons of our own making, preventing us from realizing our potential. These same assumptions will also hamper our ability to learn from these experiments as well as impede the more widespread adoption of OL. If we are to break free from inhibiting and inessential assumptions we must be able to question them openly and to discuss the implications of their persistence. With more OL trials we'll have more opportunities to surface our tacit mental models. Then we can ask, Do these assumptions serve us? To what extent are they artifacts of our attempts to avoid fear and anxiety?

If we dare to experiment more, we'll also need to deeply reflect upon, compare, analyze, and then share what we are learning from those practical experiences. On the following pages we review some of the key things we learned from reflecting upon our learning journeys. We hope that they can guide you in designing your own experiments.

We think of an organizational learning experiment as a journey. For us, that learning journey seems to flow into five natural phases.

1. Inviting a Journey
2. Designing the Journey
3. Beginning the Journey
4. On the Journey
5. Journey Landmarks

In the next chapter we will try to bring those phases alive for you, offering our thoughts and reflections on the key issues that you may wish to consider at each phase. We invite you to reflect along with us, hoping our thoughts might trigger further self-discovery and further debate, urging you to adapt our thinking to your own needs.

Chapter 11

The Adaptable Map

Why embark on a learning journey? Each person begins a journey for a variety of reasons, many of which only become clear well after the journey is begun. In fact, we often make up reasons later to justify a journey, even to ourselves. Journeys beckon; we follow. Remarkably, this appears to be true even in the highly rationalized realm of organizations, as Bert and Iva can attest.

Journeys begin in the mind. As it happens, the pioneer of modern exploration, Henry the Navigator of Portugal, never himself went out on an exploring expedition. As Daniel Boorstin writes, "the pioneer explorer was one lonely man thinking."[1] So, too, a learning journey begins in the mind.

Phase 1: Inviting a Learning Journey

The OL leaders we spoke with all come to a similar conclusion. They saw that their organizations could not achieve their goals by operating in the same way as before.

That awareness led to a vision of what could be. Rich Teerlink had a vision of greater interdependence. Bill O'Brien believed that his organization could do materially better if they found a way to free the untapped human potential. Phil Carroll had a vision of a global organization based on a new structure and philosophy. Dave Marsing's vision involved responding to external demands by developing the capacity of people to tap into their own potential, to appreciate the diverse talents of others, and to work together more productively.

Much has been written on the subject of vision and we do not wish to repeat it here, other than to note a few reflections. Vision might start with one person but vision comes alive only in the process of being shared and, perhaps, changed. Vision is more a process than a thing, more verb than noun, more living endeavor than done deal. It is probably healthier to have a generative conflict about vision than to have a single vision upon which everyone *seems* to agree.

Second, we believe that vision is made more robust and energizing when it invites in practical considerations. The gap between vision and the pragmatic demands of the business may provide a rich area of inquiry. As George Bernard Shaw said, "You see things and say 'Why?'; but I dream things that never were and say, 'Why not?'" If the visionary can sit down with the pragmatist and seek to understand the "why not," creative possibilities may emerge.

Third, vision seems empty unless it is embedded in values and, as we have seen, values are at the heart of the work of OL leaders. In fact, we may even say that values precede vision in OL work. Vision is about where you want to go. Values are the context in which you are operating; values define the rules and boundaries by which you live on your journey. That's why it is so important to attempt to align organizational values with personal values, even though this is not always easy.

Bert: The danger is that we tend to see the world in terms of the values that we think are good, but does everyone in the organization share those values? For example, I remember that we used to take our construction guys out to a fancy restaurant for lunch as their recognition for doing a good job. One day one of the construction foreman stood up and told me that they were very uncomfortable. They hated it. They felt like they had to get dressed up because I was coming out. I took them out of their comfort zone.

Iva: It's so easy for us, as leaders, to think that what we value is what others in the organization value. My relationship with the factory culture taught me how important it is to value what others value. That's more important than driving toward a homogeneous set of corporate values.

Other questions we may ask include:

- Does this vision for my organization require a learning process in order to be actualized?
- If so, how can we articulate the connection so that others can see the connection clearly?

If we can answer these questions satisfactorily then vision becomes connected to learning. We have observed a tendency to adopt "the learning organization" as a vision for the organization, but we do not believe that that is ideal. The vision needs to emerge organically from the organization itself. OL seems to be used most effectively as a *means*, not an end in and of itself.

Assessing Current Reality as a Way of Inviting a Journey

Bert: It seems obvious that you'd want to start by developing an understanding of your current reality in some organized way. You could start with a SWOT analysis. A SWOT analysis can help you determine the strengths and weaknesses as well as the opportunities and threats that face your organization.

Iva: Each of the leaders we spoke to had come to some sort of assessment, though it may not have been formal. Phil Carroll's assessment of his organization gives us a brief example of what I mean.

> **Phil:** There was a lot of agreement that we had a substantial need to upgrade the financial and business acumen. There was an enormous degree of risk aversion throughout the organization. There were also obvious difficulties with the sharing of information.

Bert: I think a SWOT analysis is a good starting point because it can also help you identify the sources of leverage for organizational change.

Iva: Can you explain what you mean by "sources of leverage"?

Bert: I'll give you an example. One of the things I thought about when I was leading a learning effort was, How does change happen around here? I came up with an assumption: Change had to be either data-driven or champion-driven. Those were the two fundamental levers for change in our culture. Then I asked myself: What makes a change sustainable? The answer was that it had to have a financial impact. So my advice to others is that you have to know what your culture values are and start there because there's got to be a good fit between the OL project you begin and the existing culture.

Iva: I can see how identifying those sources of leverage could help because you have to be artful about how much tension you introduce into the system. If you don't find those leverage points you run the risk of rejection right away. I can also see that if you do a SWOT analysis you'll come up with some assumptions. Those assumptions might be useful in the beginning, but they also need to be open to question and revision as you go.

Bert: That's true. A SWOT is a strategic tool—so obviously I have an underlying assumption that you need to strategize organizational learning, at least to some extent, in the beginning. You need to be savvy about the political climate in your organization and you need to think about how you are going to play in that arena.

Iva: That's very practical, but I'm thinking of the other side. You could also start your assessment of current reality with Chris Argyris's work. You could start by asking whether your organization supports learning. Do people in the organization operate according to Model I or Model II values? Are there defensive routines in place? Are people able to openly admit to and discuss mistakes and failures?

Bert: You can use some of the OL tools, such as systems thinking and habits of mind like inquiry, to begin assessing your organization's culture. For instance, you might ask, How are decisions made here? You may hold the belief that decisions are being made through consensus, but when you start looking at how a decision was actually made, you may find that decisions aren't really being made by consensus at all.

Iva: As a guideline, you could use a framework like the one developed by Joseph and Jimmie Boyett where they contrast a culture that supports learning with one that doesn't. (See Table 11.1.) This framework is based on Ed Schein's extensive research.[2]

Table 11.1
Cultures that Enhance and Inhibit Learning

A Culture that Inhibits Learning	A Culture that Enhances Learning
• Task issues take precedence over relationship issues.	• Leaders balance the interests of all stakeholders—customers, employees, suppliers, the community, and stockholders.
• Management is sorted into the "hard" things and "soft" things, and the "hard" things are considered to be more important.	• Schein says that in a learning organization, "No one group dominates the thinking of management because it is recognized that any one of these groups can slow down and destroy the organization."
• Leaders pay attention to the hard things—data, money, bottom lines, payoffs, production, competition, structure, and so on.	
• Everyone pays lip service to the "soft" people things and relationship stuff but the real work of management is seen as that which can be quantified.	
• People viewed by managers as another resource to be used and manipulated like capital and raw materials.	
• Leaders and managers are engineers and technocrats who are preoccupied with creating and maintaining systems that will be free of human foibles and errors.	• Leaders and managers believe that their people can and will learn, and value learning and change. Schein notes: "It takes a certain amount of idealism about human nature to create a learning culture."
• A key theme of the culture is designing humans out of the systems rather into them.	
	• That idealism exists in full measure.
• People in the organization are reactive rather than proactive. They change only in response to outside forces that are seen as threats.	• People hold the shared belief that they have the capacity to change their environment and that ultimately they make their own fate.

- People focus on solving problems' rather than creating something new.

- This may be a necessary assumption for learning. After all, writes Schein, "If we believe that the world around us cannot be changed anyway, what is the point of learning to learn. Relax and make the best of your fate."

- The organization is preoccupied with short-term coping and adapting.
- Being "lean and mean" dominates the thinking of leaders and managers.
- The idea of "slack" is unthinkable.

- The organization makes time for learning.
- Some "slack" time is not only allowed but desired so that it can be used for learning.
- Schein says, "Lean and mean is not a good prescription for organizational learning."

- Work roles and tasks are compartmentalized and separated from family and self-development.
- "Walls" and "chimneys" separate functions.
- In solving problems people believe that the best approach is to break the problem into its components, study and fix each component in isolation, and then synthesize the components back into the whole.

- People in the organization have a shared belief that economic, political, and socio-cultural events are interconnected and that this is true inside the organization as well as in the environment.
- There is a shared commitment to learning and thinking systemically and to understand how things work and especially the consequences of actions over time.

- Managers are presumed to have a "divine right" to information and prerogatives.
- Financial and other information is kept from all those who do not have a "need to know."
- Position and access to information confer status and power.
- People sit on relevant information, put a spin on things to protect their power position, and sometimes actually lie to put themselves in a better light.

- Managers and employees have a shared commitment to open and extensive communication.
- The organization has spent some time helping people develop a common vocabulary so that communication can occur.
- People have a shared commitment to tell the truth.

- Individual competition is perceived as the natural state and the proper route to power and status.
- There is a cultural bias toward "rugged individualism."
- The lone problem solver is seen as a hero.
- Teamwork is viewed as a practical necessity but not something that is intrinsically desirable.

- People share the belief that trust, teamwork, coordination, and cooperation are critical for success.
- Individualistic competition is not viewed as the answer to all problems.

- Leaders and followers assume that leaders are supposed to be in control, decisive, certain, and dominant.
- Leaders are not allowed to acknowledge their vulnerability

- Leaders acknowledge their own vulnerability and uncertainty.
- The leader acts as a teacher and steward of change rather than a charismatic decision maker.

This table is reprinted courtesy of John Wiley & Sons, Inc. It first appeared in *The Guru Guide: The Best Ideas of the Top Management Thinkers* by Joseph Boyett and Jimmie T. Boyett (published by John Wiley, 1998).

Cultural Analysis

Bert: Whatever framework or method you use, the goal is to come to some understanding of how your organization can benefit from learning.[3] Then the goal is to work with others to make that happen successfully. So, it's a two-part assessment.

Iva: I don't think we've paid enough attention to culture in this work up to now. Edgar Schein has done ground-breaking work in organizational culture, but we seem to be resisting doing the work to deeply understand the culture of our organizations. If we want to take Senge's approach and think in terms of the five learning disciplines, a cultural assessment is critical because some of the five learning disciplines are going to be more compatible with some cultures than with others. I've learned the hard way that all five disciplines are necessary in order to develop the capacity for organizational learning, but more technical environments will respond better to Systems Thinking, for example, whereas others will want to begin with Dialogue. A cultural analysis will help you to become sensitized to such things. Then you're more prepared to consider how you can introduce the disciplines in a balanced manner without introducing too much tension into the system. The question is: How do you do a cultural assessment so that it's both robust and generative, rather than just accepting your own or others' untested assumptions about your culture.

Bert: I have to say that it's difficult to understand your culture when you're inside of it. You tend to have a blind spot; you don't see what you don't see.

Iva: Yes, that's a challenge, but I'd like to suggest that this is where collaboration becomes key. A cultural analysis is no small task. First, you have to understand what "culture" means and what attributes you are going to use to define your culture and its various subcultures. It won't be easy and most likely you'll need help, particularly if you're an executive leader. Despite the best intentions, it's very difficult for executive leaders to really understand the current reality of their organizations. It's hard for them to get in touch with how people think and feel about difficult issues and challenges. I can attest to that. Therefore, it's important that this isn't a solitary assessment; you need to enlist skillful, experienced, trustworthy help. Still, as a leader, you have to make sure that that reflective mirror is being held up to the organization.

I don't have a formula for how to come to that understanding, but I can at least suggest that people who are considering leading a learning effort spend some time with the following questions:

- How is your culture likely to enhance or inhibit learning? What are the strengths and weaknesses of your culture?

- How will your culture affect how you implement a learning effort?

- Are you concerned with multiple subcultures? How do they differ and how do they relate to one another?

- How might you go about this up-front analysis? What resources are necessary? Who should be involved?

Timing: A Question of Readiness

Bert: I want to suggest that before you start you need to ask the simple question: Is the timing right for a learning effort? Answering that question is going to call upon your pragmatic side. You have to determine whether there is, in actuality, an opportunity for learning. Is the organization really ready? If the answer is no, then you have to stop for now.

Iva: That's going to be tough, especially if you've already formulated a vision. How do you suggest we evaluate whether the timing is right?

Bert: Ask yourself, Is this the right time to introduce change? If you're bleeding, fix things first. If you're about to get a new manager or a new boss, it's not the right time. If the leadership is under total review, it may be too big a risk. If you have just reorganized, be careful. If you have new networks and relationships, establish your networks first because you'll need them to be in place before you take on a learning effort.

You can assess whether the timing is right by asking a series of questions such as the following:

- What is the relative financial health of your organization?

- Is there a climate of openness and a receptivity to change?

- Is there an opportunity for change such as a burning platform or a Greenfield?

- What is the natural heartbeat of the organization?

Iva: Can we discuss why you put "relative financial health" as your first question?

First Things First: The Debate

Bert: My argument is that you have to have good financial results before you can begin an organizational learning effort. Without good financial results, you don't have the luxury of beginning an OL-based transformation effort.

Iva: Why do you believe that?

Bert: The OL leaders we interviewed said that if they didn't have financial results, they'd be shut down. I'm drawing the conclusion that if you're in financial trouble to start with, the first thing you do is triage and stop the bleeding.

Iva: This is like a chicken-and-egg argument to me. Which comes first? You're saying that if financial results are good that means I can go into a process of introducing OL. But there is an alternative premise that says that OL is supposed to help us get better results—financial and otherwise. In fact, certain units are obtaining better results with OL such as the Electrical Fuel Handling Division (EFHD) of Ford, which subsequently became part of Visteon. They were able to obtain improvements in quality, cost, timing, and profitability.[4]

Bert: There are certainly situations where it seems that applying OL methods and tools has led to financial results, but it's not clear to me that we're able to prove to the vast majority of management that these results can be attributed to OL methods and tools. It's a question of attribution.

Iva: I agree that attribution is a challenge. It's a particular challenge in the case of OL because cause (the application of OL tools and methods) and effect (financial results) will be separated in time and space. That makes direct attribution difficult. But, there's a subjective aspect to all objective measures: how results are being evaluated depends upon who is measuring and for what purpose. Organizational politics and other issues can affect how certain results are interpreted and attributed.

Measurement and attribution are probably the most difficult issues that proponents of OL face. They constitute a significant obstacle to this work, but we won't be able to continue pursuing OL as a way to create future results if businesspeople don't take that risk.

Bert: That's exactly what I'm saying.

Iva: But this has a lot more to do with how goals and measures are set and who sets them than it does with OL *per se*. What measures really tell us that a company is *alive*? Until we have that, OL will have a hard time.

Bert: I think we are in agreement on that. If Wall Street doesn't think well of the company, or your division president doesn't think well of your division it's risky to introduce OL. And so far that depends on how well you're doing according to traditional measures.

Iva: So as an OL leader one of your first jobs should be to determine what the "vital signs" of your organization are. In my view, the vital signs are the aspirations or values that guide actions in the organization much more than the financial results.

For example, in his book *The Living Company* Arie de Geus talks about learning as the primary competitive advantage. He discovered that companies that have longevity—remarkable longevity as it turns out because some companies are 700 years old—have certain characteristics. They are sensitive to environment in order to learn and adapt; cohesive, with a strong sense of identity; tolerant of unconventional thinking and experimentation; and conservative in financial policy in order to retain the resources that allow for flexibility.[5] Companies with those features are the ones that live. The rest just come and go. If Wall Street would understand those factors and start thinking about how results are produced in a different way than they do today, things would change.

Bert: But that's not current reality and if we are going to make OL sustainable, we have to respect our current reality. I agree that OL will help a firm in perpetuity, but I also believe that if you have a survival issue on your hands, forget the perpetuity stuff. For me it's a question of prioritization and sequence. I'm not excluding either; it's a threshold issue and a question of timing.

Iva: But then how do you get to survival?

Bert: You don't do it with OL because there are time delays. You do it with the tried-and-true methods of command-and-control in terms of getting your house in order.

Iva: I think that's a critical paradox of all of this work. Is it possible that this is a pragmatic decision but one that immediately sets up an internal conflict? Perhaps it is precisely because the potential of the people has not been unleashed—because you have a command-and-control organization—that you're in a dire financial situation.

Bert: That could be, but that's reality. In reality, how many options do you have? I'll go further. If you are doing OL work and your performance falls, the first thing that would be stopped is this type of work.

Iva: But isn't that the tragedy of it?

Bert: Oh, it may be very tragic if you're committed to this work.

Iva: It's a catch-22! You can't embark on the things that would help you improve because you're not there already.

Bert: There's no point in trying to save the life through remedial surgery if you don't first stop the bleeding.

Iva: So when you say, "Get the results in order," you could be talking about downsizing?

Bert: Whatever it takes.

Iva: So there is going to be a cost to innocent people that you're going to have to live with before you can say, "OK, now I can care about people again."

Bert: If you're being hobbled in some way, you have to at least begin standing on both feet before you can start a learning effort. If that means that your budget is in crisis and you're going to have to cut people to get within budget constraints, then that's what you do. Stop the bleeding before you look at the rest.

Iva: Rather than risk embarking on an OL journey with the conviction that it will yield the results? If I have a difficult financial situation that requires the engagement of people to resolve, I think a better process is to give the people some tools to help them be more creative. That's much better than standing on top saying, "You're in; you're out because you didn't make your financials."

Bert: I agree with that. It *is* a better strategy. But my question is, If you're in financial trouble, can you afford to take that road? Can you really afford to take that risk? Or are you first going to have to do something precipitous to stop the leak?

Iva: I am saying that the risk of doing something precipitous is no more or less than the risk of attempting to integrate the people and their thinking into the process of creating the results you all want.

Bert: I disagree. Remember the conversation we had with Dave Marsing about how you can put only so much tension into the system?

Dave: I have loads of compassion for my boss. I put my boss through absolute agony! Because I get the results, I have a lot of latitude, but there are limits. That is why the immune system analogy is really important. Because you need to know what the threshold of tension is in the organization. How much can it tolerate before you begin to trigger automatic responses?

Bert: Right. So you know when to back off.

Dave: It's not so much that you back off because then you're not making any progress. You have to fine-tune how much tension you knowingly put into the system. If you want to make a change, the system needs a certain amount of tension because it stimulates growth and learning. You just need to be a good judge of how much tension the system can tolerate before it automatically rejects you.

I keep up constant tension in multiple dimensions, but I don't do it at a pace that cramps people. And what's great is that in different networks within the organization, people's tolerance for my tension has grown over time. They get used to it. Then the energy level that they've been operating at begins to subside because they've adapted to that level of tension. And then you "up" it a notch.

Bert: I submit that embarking on an OL effort when you're bleeding financially puts too much tension into the system.

Iva: I acknowledge that I introduced too much tension into the system at Philips when I was doing OL work. That had less to do with OL itself than it did with my lack of understanding at the time about how to work with the systemic nature of change. So I certainly agree that you must be mindful of the amount of tension you put into the system. You have to introduce tension very artfully. But I submit that you *also* put intolerable tension into the system when you make arbitrary decisions, such as the decision to downsize in response to financial problems.

Bert: But you have to remember that to the outside world, the decision to use OL as a remedy actually seems much more arbitrary and risky than a decision to downsize. With OL we're trying to institute a change. Instituting a change in an organization that's in financial turmoil is similar to trying to apply consensus decision making when you're in a theatre that's on fire.

Iva: So we resort to so-called proven methods. As you say, there is as yet no real compelling case that proves OL creates the path towards reversing downsizing.

Bert: My point exactly. I agree that you can't reach your potential unless you use OL and we do have some evidence that supports that. We have pockets of people who have demonstrated that they have been able to think out-of-the-box better and handle the vertical ramp-ups better because they had OL. So I think there's demonstrable proof of that. But that doesn't constitute critical mass.

That's why you first have to take care of business—in terms of known methodologies such as downsizing or product redefinition. It's very dangerous to adopt a significant departure from normal values in the culture to fix a problem when in fact you're in a state of financial uncertainty. It's dangerous for you and it's dangerous to the future life of OL. It's like in WWII: If you open up too many fronts and you're not consolidated on any of them, you're going to lose. So you better consolidate one or two, or you'll be shut down.

But then remember to take off the tourniquet, because if you leave it in place, you're going to get gangrene. Similarly, if all you care about are your financial results, you're not going to have sustainability down the road. To sustain your organization long term, you also need to develop the infrastructure for OL.

Iva: Do you recall how Dave Marsing helped us put this debate in perspective?

Dave: You're both right. OL is both a dessert topping and a floor wax. Let me tell you what I mean by that. It is absolutely essential to achieve the results that the Board of Directors and the stockholders expect and assume. It is, however, not sufficient to only do that. To ensure that you have a future, you have to be able to anticipate opportunities and be agile enough to capitalize on them when they're there. To do that you have to do some things better than just being the best in the world at reacting. In other words, you have to be able to learn.

Bert: People have to evaluate their own situation and decide what their risk factors are.

Iva: As they're evaluating their situation, I think they need to ask themselves a different set of questions than just the usual. Why not ask:

- Why are we getting these results that we don't want?
- What are the systemic causes of these results?
- Are we thinking about the future or just reacting to the present?

These questions may prove to be fruitful and maybe they could lead people out of the usual mess we create with our "quick fixes"—but asking these questions takes some courage.

Portals for Learning

Bert: Assuming that you've been able to answer the questions above, then you can move on to address some of the other kinds of timing issues. You can look for obvious openings, or portals, where a new approach can be most easily introduced.

Iva: Probably the most ideal condition for an OL project is a Greenfield, but even in Greenfield situations the culture is not necessarily completely open. For example, even newly hired people will have preexisting assumptions. Leaders need to set the context and then train and orient people to the learning environment.

Bert: A burning platform can be another great opportunity for learning. A burning platform is created when people don't know what to do and are searching for solutions.

Iva: So you have almost an existential crisis in that the old way doesn't work anymore.

Bert: There is now a vacuum that something has to fill. That creates an opening for a credible idea, a credible leader, or sometimes even a prophet who comes forth and says, "Let me give you the word."

Iva: In my mind, we're back to the financial question again. Couldn't a problem with financial results constitute a burning platform? In other words, a financial crisis for which there is no obvious proposed solution could be conducive to OL. Do you agree with that?

Bert: Yes I do, but only if certain conditions are met. The proposed solution has to have credibility. Now, the leader can provide that credibility if people trust the leader and respect the leader. The other source of credibility is the proven track record of the method. People either trust the method or they trust the leader.

Iva: So you're saying that a burning platform could provide a way to introduce OL even though it's unclear that OL has that proven track record?

Bert: It depends on whether the OL leader is credible.

Iva: Which might be tough to find in an organization where the only experience is having gone through one crisis after another.

Bert: But remember what Bill O'Brien said about leaders needing to be forged out of the suffering of the organization?

> **Bill:** The conclusion that I've come to is that the people who are going to do the leading ought to emerge out of the suffering of the organization. "Suffering" could be too strong a word, but certainly leaders need to have experienced firsthand the frustrations of dealing with the politics, the bureaucracy, the inconsistencies of today's business organizations. And then, the miracle is that rather than becoming cynical or defeated, through some kind of internal alchemy they've turned that frustration and pain into a *constructive* frustration.
>
> That's the transforming energy that's going to help us make profound change in our organizations. It's generative energy and it's informed by both experience and compassion.

Iva: One final thought, if I may. As leaders we have to do some deep thinking about what kind of thinking caused us to get to the burning platform in the first place. Secondly, if you're a leader in an organization that has a burning platform your credibility may be in jeopardy. If you don't think that OL has credibility yet, then you might not be motivated to take a risk with it. That's if you want to play it safe. But there's another side to the coin. Surely we don't want to just keep replicating the same thinking that created our problems. We may not have the luxury of waiting for proof. We may have to take a calculated risk and in order to create a different future.

Can You Hear the "Natural Heartbeat" of the Organization?

Bert: This concept comes to us by way of Dave Marsing at Intel. Dave realized that he had to take a "stealth" approach to organizational learning work.

> **Dave:** Topmost in my mind—and this is really key to both my philosophy and strategy—is that I want to do this work in such a way that the transformational aspect is not obvious. So I map out the key change points, problems, and issues that I anticipate coming down the pathway. Then I think about how each one of those can nudge OL another step further.
>
> I very subtly use this method as an ongoing practice. The idea is to expose people gradually so that eventually it's automatic and happens so easily and naturally that they don't even know they're "learning."

Bert: Dave discovered that there was a natural rhythm or "heartbeat" in his organization. There were some patterns to the way things worked. Once you discern the pattern you can see that there are some obvious and natural opportunities for learning.

Iva: We should share the story Dave told us about Boeing. He provides us with a good example.

Dave: We had a joint effort with Boeing in which we tried to help the people at Boeing design ways to leverage learning given the pace of their business. This was within the context of both the introduction of new models and the introduction of significant redesigns and subsystems into planes.

The folks at Boeing were getting frustrated because they were pushing against a very set cadence in that environment. So we tried to get them to start thinking about what I called the natural heartbeat of the organization through observing the cycles involved in production. There are transitional periods in the production cycle and if you're prepared to launch learning initiatives at those times, you'll be working *with* the organization's natural heartbeat rather than against it. And most companies have those kinds of natural rhythms.

Bert: Many of our TQM projects failed because we didn't choose projects that were meaningful to the organization. Hopefully, we all learned that lesson. Now here's an opportunity to learn a lesson about how to determine the appropriate timing and pacing for a learning effort. All organizations operate according to their own rhythm. The skill for us as leaders is to develop the capacity to observe those rhythms, to hear the "natural heartbeat" of the organization, and then capitalize on it.

Iva: So we're saying that you need to look for the portals, the natural windows of opportunity when the organization is ripe for change. If you understand the rhythm of the organization you'll have a better sense of when those portals are likely to show up. You'll know when learning efforts can be inserted organically into the pulse of the organization such that they will enhance the flow more than disrupt it.

Bert: Right, thus minimizing the possibility of initial rejection. If you're looking for a portal, the following questions might help:

- If you are involved in product development phases, do the periodic changeovers to a new product represent a portal?

- Are there opportunities during the budget process? For example, are there quarterly/periodic reviews to readjust the budget to see how it compares with the forecast?

- Does your performance review process include agreements with employees about their personal development? Is the company or division reviewing its training curriculum?

- When you do employee surveys, are there meetings to determine what you're going to do about the results?

- Are there TQM or other local initiative forums where new ideas are fostered and tried? Many companies have Quality audits, which provide an opportunity to question assumptions. What processes do you use to engage employees in openly sharing their ideas? Would OL tools and methods be helpful in that process?

Is the Leader Ready?

Bert: Thinking about leadership readiness reminds me of something I heard John Naisbitt talk about. He talked about a "Want Ad" looking for people to volunteer for a job. The ad said that the job would involve travel, but it was going to be cold and miserable. When you return, probably nobody would recognize what you had done. It was even possible that you may never come back alive. The ad was for a trip to climb Mt. Everest. Despite that Want Ad description, about 360 people volunteered to take the trip.

At this stage, an OL effort is like that. First of all, leaders have to think that it's worth doing on its own merit. So you have to think about what's driving you. If it's ego, ego falls away quickly as soon as resistance comes. Ego assumes power, but you're not going to have power when you're trying to bring in new ideas and you find that some people are fighting you. You're going to be standing alone a lot.

Iva: I see the issue of power a little differently. It's about how you use power with those ideas. If you use your power from the old paradigm, it will bite you back. The more you push, the more resistance you'll encounter and yes, you will become a lonely leader. One of the reasons you can be lonely is because people are afraid of the way that you might use your power. So you have to let go of power and ego at the very beginning, but there's a built-in paradox. You can't do this work without devolving power, and you can't learn how to devolve power without doing this work. So while you're trying to make that transition there are going to be difficult moments for both yourself and the organization until you reframe and are truly seen as a leader that is not using their power in the old ways. This is where the need for collaboration comes in, because you will need other people to make this transition successfully. As a leader, you have to be humble and accept that you do not have all the answers. You have to acknowledge that you do not *know* and be willing to be vulnerable, but you also have to be strong and very committed.

Bert: If you want to do this kind of work—if you want to transform an organization—I'd go so far as to say it's going to be a rough road. You have to like solving puzzles and problems, dealing with people, and valuing differences. You must understand that that which is worthwhile may take some time and a great deal of effort, so you have to like solving puzzles and problems, dealing with people, and valuing differences. You have to understand that you'll probably feel real low and also very much alone sometimes. It's almost—I hate to go this far—it's almost heroic. On the other hand, you have to have a very practical mind. If you get too heroic, you become ineffective. And if you get to a place where you're becoming too crusading in your attitude—and I did become almost evangelistic—you tear yourself apart. As somebody very eloquently said, "The soft stuff is the hard stuff." Trying to create a learning organization is the hard stuff. So you have to be certain that you are willing to take on the task, including the risks and possible reversals that may be experienced as you lead a learning effort. In other words, you have to be sure that the timing is right not only for the organization, but also *for you.*

Iva: So the question is: Is the leader ready? Although this seems like a simple question, we think it is extremely important. Senge has written that organizational transformation begins with personal transformation. Argyris's work underlines that idea, emphasizing the interdependent relationship of personal and organizational change. Neither one of us knew enough to do a more formal self-assessment when we began. However, we're now both certain that it's a good idea.

Bert: I did not do any kind of in-depth self-assessment. However, I did my own sort of personal SWOT analysis. I said to myself: Make sure this is not an ego trip. If you have a lot of ego be prepared to be humbled. If you feel that you're at all vulnerable in your job, don't do this! Go back to basics contingent to your bottom line.

Iva: I did not do this kind of reflecting until much later, and then I wanted to go much deeper. I wanted to really know myself, to learn how to be introspective, and to understand more how I impact the world instead of just focusing on how things impact me.

Bert: Phil Carroll gave us another perspective when he described the kind of personal reflection that he engaged in just after he learned that he would become the next CEO of Shell Oil.

Phil: I didn't go through an experience like St. Paul on the road to Damascus, but I did a lot of reflecting and thinking. I spelled out in my own mind what changes I thought were necessary and desirable.

For example, as I reflected back on my own managerial experience, I saw that we had a pretty effective model of management at Shell, but it was based on a certain understanding of the employee contract. The contract went something like, "I am the company; I am the management. You get security, protection, and largesse from me, and what I demand is loyalty and willingness to follow my orders." That was the model for the most part. It was a royalist model as opposed to a democratic model. As you get into this new world, however, that model just isn't going to cut it, so we all have to change.

Bert: As I listened to Phil I had an insight into my own motivations. The employee-firm implied social contract that Phil talks about seems less prevalent today. Companies used to offer security in exchange for loyalty, but that contract has given way as people now want jobs that offer creativity, excitement, and opportunities for personal growth and rewards on multiple levels. Underlying those expectations I see a need for congruence between people's values and the firm's mission.

This shift in the contract has affected me personally. When I began my OL work, my driving personal concern was not to lose my job. I can see now how that affected the decisions I made. Having gone through that experience and thinking about it further, my new requirement is to find a meaningful way to contribute and make a difference.

Iva: So I think we're agreeing that some degree of self-assessment is absolutely necessary, but the depth of the self-assessment you're able to do will depend upon what you're ready for and how much support you have.

Areas of Inquiry for the Leader

As Senge et al. have so clearly articulated, change is a kind of dance. Leading change is even more demanding, since leaders are, in many ways, summoning forth the music. The leader is not scoring the music, as a command-and-control leader would do. In this case, the score is being written by many. Rather, the leadership is enabling the notes to come together in harmonious progression. Leading change requires the deft orchestration of balancing and reinforcing forces. Leadership must be more collaborative; in other words, more adaptable and fluid. That fluidity shows up in a number of ways. Specifically, Senge has also identified three types of leaders who are important for a learning effort: executive, line leader, and networker.[6]

Iva: I would like to expand this view a bit. Ideally, the OL leader needs to understand all three and also be capable of embodying all three. This is in my view the most difficult task for any leader who has grown up in a command-and-control environment, like Bert and I did. I have a lot of hope that leaders that are coming after us will be better prepared for it, and I hope we will contribute to it. Speaking for myself, I can say that learning how to embody that which I want to create is the most important and learningful part of the journey I am on.

Through our interviews we have learned that OL leaders seem to manifest these qualities:

- A balance of pragmatic and visionary perspectives
- A commitment to values
- The ability to design effective strategies and tactics
- A commitment to greater collaboration and the skillful devolution of power that will make collaborative leadership possible
- A commitment to steward learning
- A commitment to be learners themselves
- A commitment to defining their own unique pathways

As we reflected on these qualities, they seemed to lend themselves to questions that we might ask ourselves before embarking on a learning journey. The questions seemed to fall into six areas as shown in Figure 11.1.

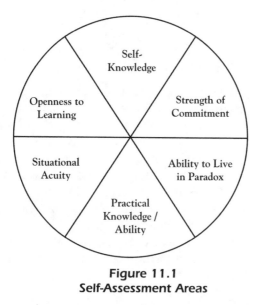

Figure 11.1
Self-Assessment Areas

The first three areas—self-knowledge, strength of commitment, and the ability to live in paradox—all address the inner territory, the starting place for the inner journey. Openness to learning and situational acuity both address the ability to sense emergent forces, to reflect, and to learn through our reflections on action and practice. The area of practical knowledge and ability should help us to realistically assess to what degree we have the skills and resources to begin the journey.

In the pages that follow we offer our reflections on each of these six areas and offer questions that you might wish to ask yourself as you invite your own learning journey. From these snippets of our reflective conversations you'll observe that we don't always see things in the same way or even agree on the depth of self-assessment that is required of OL leaders. We hope these differences stimulate and enrich your inquiry. Again, there is no single path; yet, at a deep level, there is fundamental agreement.

Self-Knowledge

Iva: One's ability to design strategy and follow one's own path seems to flow directly from self-knowledge. Dave Marsing seems to be a terrific example.

> **Dave:** My work with Human Dynamics helped me to understand the way that I deal with things and the way I process information. I know my strengths and weaknesses better and I'm less likely to attempt things that are not in tune with my particular dynamic. For example, I realized that things come together for me visually, in a very integrated, organic kind of way. If I try to force my thinking into a linear, mechanical structure, I create more problems than when I let my thinking follow its natural path.

> **Bert:** I think what's important is not so much "knowing yourself" in the broad sense as it is to understand the leverage points of your strengths and weaknesses, knowing how others view you, and having a clear sense of your ability to shepherd this work in your organization. Here's an example. Say you're a leader known for being very pragmatic and results-oriented. If you embrace OL then you'll bring your credibility to this work, which would be an interesting and very, very desirable event. However, if you have a reputation of pursuing every flavor-of-the-month fad, you're not going to be able to bring credibility to the table and that will be a significant disadvantage. What do you do, then, to build credibility? Here's where you might do a kind of personal SWOT analysis.

Iva: You're saying that self-knowledge is about knowing yourself in the context of the journey: Are you the appropriate person to lead this?

Understanding your strengths and weaknesses is necessary but I would still suggest that's not sufficient.

Questions to Help Your Self-knowledge Assessment

- Do you resonate with the qualities we have found in other OL leaders?

- Do you have a clear sense of why you want to embark on this journey? Where has that clarity come from?

- Ask yourself whether you have the strength of character to define your own pathway. Is your ego strong enough—but not too strong?

- Locate your level on the Rooke Torbert grid. Are you a "strategist?" What are your strengths and weaknesses vis-à-vis a learning effort? What skills might you need to develop?

- Do you have the ability to communicate and network successfully within the existing hierarchy and across functions?

Strength of Commitment

Bert: Phil Carroll gave the best description of how I feel about commitment.

> **Phil:** If you're going to go into this as the leader, you have to have an intensity of belief in what you're doing that is very high. You have to honestly say to yourself that if I cannot do this—if the organization rejects my efforts to make change—then I have failed. If leadership above me will not support it, if my boss or whatever key support I need won't let me do this, then I'm better off out of here.
>
> If you're not willing to say that and really mean it, then you probably should not take this on. I say that because this is not a comfortable, easy thing to do. It requires enormous amounts of energy to keep it going, both psychic as well as physical. If you're not deeply committed, you shouldn't begin. That's why I feel so strongly about emotion playing a part. There is no way you can *reason* to sufficient commitment to logically undertake this. You have to have very strong feelings.
>
> We all have times of doubt and concern—meetings where you think, "that was terrible"; times when you think people are not getting it; or times when business starts going bad and you have particular problems. You worry about it and question

whether or not you are right. But if you entertain those doubts for very long, you'll lose your ability to go on.

Iva: For Bert and myself it was important enough to put ourselves in jeopardy. Upon reflection I realized that my commitment was coming not just from a concern for profits, but from a deeper place. If you are able to have clarity regarding the source of your motivation, this will help you channel your commitment and effort. You'll also be freer to make informed choices.

Bert: The question is, where's your bottom line? What constitutes for you an inability to continue? I accepted certain boundaries because I had a fear of losing my job.

Questions to Help You Assess the Strength of Your Commitment

- What is your experience with making commitments?
- Are you prepared to conduct (several) experiments, reflecting and challenging your assumptions?
- Can you make a commitment without knowing what the outcome will be?
- How important is this work to you? Are you willing to put your job on the line?

Living with Paradox

Iva: Sometimes it seems as if people in the business world constantly encounter paradox. We want contradictory things and there does not seem to be a solution. Whether we go in one direction or another, the outcome does not seem satisfactory.

Bert: I can see where management in particular can be torn by priorities that seem to contradict each other. We care about people but we have to lay off people to reduce cost. Is that what you mean?

Iva: I think both of us have experienced being in paradox without realizing it. I believe we're caught in those contradictions because we're living in between two systems. On the one hand we have the hierarchical, command-and-control way of being that we were brought up in; on the other hand we have this new system that's trying to be born, a new system that is emergent, connected, and based on relationships.

Bert: I think a lot of us have dealt with that tension through compartmentalization.

Iva: The problem with compartmentalization is that you deny the tension rather than hold it. If you compartmentalize, the long-term consequence is that you tend to become more disintegrated as a person and you don't find real solutions—you reach for a "quick fix" instead because you want to make the tension go away. Ideally, we resolve paradox by questioning assumptions and reframing the situation, but that's not instantaneous. The only way to accomplish that is to hold the tension. Holding tension puts us in a place that feels very unstable—yet it isn't. I think we're finding that if we can learn to hold that tension we can discover a way to reframe and then solutions begin to show up unexpectedly.

Questions to Help Assess Your Ability to Live in Paradox

- Can you both hold and live with creative tension?
- Do you have the ability to live with (and within) two systems, helping to build the bridge between them?

Situational Acuity

Bert: I think that the ability to "read" a situation and to respond appropriately is a critical skill. I'm calling it "situational acuity" and I believe it's an art. Rich Teerlink gave us a good example when he wouldn't invest his two managers with command-and-control authority when he sent them to resolve the problems in the plant.

Iva: Rich knew just how to respond to the situation to get the most effective—and learningful—outcome. He used his command authority to force the two managers to learn how to work together. He wouldn't let them divide up the work, which would have meant they'd come from the old reductionist paradigm. And he wouldn't let them resort to command-and-control to solve problems.

Bert: That's very artful.

Iva: It's particularly artful because he wasn't just resorting to command, but doing so in order to promote learning.

Questions to Help Assess Your Situational Acuity

- What is your model of leadership?
- Is your leadership style flexible? How do you know?
- How might you develop your situational acuity?

Openness to Learning

Iva: How do you assess your openness to learning? You have to accept that you don't know everything.

Bert: And that answers can come from anywhere in the organization.

Iva: And you have to be prepared to give up things that you really believed were true. I believe that this also involves an openness to learning from so-called failure, unlearning and changing your views, and developing an appreciation for diversity.

Questions to Help Assess Your Openness to Learning

- Are you prepared to learn from your mistakes, examining your assumptions?
- Can you let go and move on or do you tend to dwell on the past?
- Can you show vulnerability, admit to others that you don't have all the answers?
- Do you value and seek out diverse viewpoints? Do you think that good ideas can come from virtually anywhere?
- Are you interested in nurturing the potential of others?
- Have you reached out for appropriate help in making these appraisals of yourself?

Practical Knowledge and Ability

Bert: There are a number of different aspects to the practical knowledge you need. For example, you need the ability to assess your organization whether you choose to perform a SWOT analysis or a cultural assessment.

Iva: It's important that this isn't a solitary assessment—but as a leader you do have to see it most clearly and make sure that that reflective mirror is being held up to the organization. I would also offer that you need a very good understanding of the systemic nature of change.

Questions to Help You Assess Your Practical Knowledge and Ability

Assess your understanding of the systemic nature of change as described, for instance, in *The Dance of Change* by Senge et al. Will you be able to identify strategies for weakening the balancing processes? Also, assess your practical ability to lead change: your knowledge of the systemic nature of change as well as your political capital.

- How well do you understand the systemic nature of change? Will you be able to identify strategies for weakening the balancing processes?
- Can you recognize—and resist—your organization's defensive routines?
- Do you have the practical ability to lead change? What is the status of your resources, the strength of your network, and

the courage of your allies? Do you have enough influence and credibility to execute? What is the measure of credibility in your organization? Do you have both the support and the political capital you need?

- What are your strengths and weaknesses vis-à-vis leading a learning effort? Based on this overall assessment, how would you describe your learning edge?

Designing the Adaptable Map

Once you have invited a journey, you'll want to design your strategy for bringing learning to life within your organization. The caveat is that we cannot approach this task in the same way that we have approached other strategy efforts. We are turning to a different kind of thinking about strategy. We used to take a very reductionist, analytical, linear, and structured approach to strategy. We'd design strategy starting with knowing what we want. We'd develop the arguments to support what we want. Then we'd go through a linear process of policy deployment, delineating the steps in between where we were currently and where we wanted to be, dividing the tasks and measuring our progress along the way. The emphasis was on analysis (not synthesis), central planning, a formal strategy document, and formal presentations. The danger is we'll proceed to "do organizational learning" in that same way, but *this kind of map cannot be designed that way.*

We are coming to a new understanding of strategy, seeing it as an organic, emergent process. Stacey defines "emergence" as a process by means of which the business system as a whole can create order out of chaos. When he says that strategy is an emergent process he means that strategy does not emanate from a preordained central vision. Rather, strategy arises out of what managers do—and, consequently, what they learn as they do it. Strategy is dynamic and it emerges from the "ongoing, spontaneous, and self-organizing processes of learning and political interaction." Therefore, the work of leaders is not to define strategy in the rarified air of a meeting room, but to create the context in which it can emerge by entering into the "mess" of the organization. They create a context that enables strategy to emerge by "continuously developing agendas of issues, aspirations, challenges, and individual intentions."[7]

Since OL journeys involve ventures into new territory, we believe that they are best planned with this sense of strategy in mind. Learning journeys are best traveled using adaptable maps: maps that sketch out the journey beforehand but which we can also update and change frequently as new things are learned about the territory and how best to navigate the terrain.

Phase 2: Mapping a Learning Journey

We will use this understanding of strategy as a backdrop to our suggestions. At this point you have thought about vision and values, perhaps you have done some cultural and SWOT analyses and self-assessment. What's next?

Taking Dave Marsing's advice, we suggest that you map out the key change points, problems, and issues that you anticipate coming down the pathway, thinking about how each one of those can nudge OL another step further. As you begin to map the journey, consider the best strategic approach for you to take given what the people in the organization value, the possible vision that seems to call to your organization, and your assessment of the organization's culture and learning needs. Think about what assumptions or theory of change underlie your initial approach and how you will test those assumptions publicly. (The process of surfacing assumptions creates opportunities for double-loop learning.) Think deeply about whether your organization needs to begin with single-loop learning or if it is ready to move into a deeper form of OL. If the latter, you need to think about how that dialectical process can be supported. Consider how you might begin building the capacity for learning within yourself, your team, and your organization. Reflect on how you'll design your map such that it is adaptable, allowing you to learn your way into the strategy as you go.

Iva: I'd like to offer my thoughts on strategy. We have learned in our journey that awareness is only a spark; to light the fire more is needed. The selection of the methods and the consultants (capacity builders) that can provide the initial support is an important step. There are various consultants who can bring the ideas of OL to life through their specific tools and methods. Most of these respected consultants deal with all the relevant disciplines, though most of them have their own specific entry into the learning process. For example, there are those who focus on Systems Thinking, those who enter into this field through action science, those who focus initially on human behavior, those who use Dialogue as the entry point, etc. What criteria will you use to decide how you are going to start?

Bert: I think the most important starting place is to look for a way to align the corporate goals and values with the goals and values of the people in the organization. Then build a bridge between those goals and values and success in the marketplace.

We believe that your initial map should also include a consideration of the following:

- Links to results;
- Links across system boundaries;
- Effective use of feedback;
- Assessment;
- Sustainability.

Linking to Results

Bert: Can you translate your learning pilot into a financial outcome that is good for the firm? You may not be able to directly translate the benefit of learning into dollars, but you have to at least have a conceptual link to financial performance. That's what you're in this for. Don't misunderstand.

Iva: It's certainly important to make the link between learning and business results, but it's an open question as to whether those results must be strictly financial. Of course, learning should translate into financial results in the long term, but thinking this way in the short term can also get us into trouble. We can talk ourselves out of doing some foundational work upon which our long-term success depends because we can't immediately attach a dollar benefit to it. I also recognize that you can't ask a whole organization to take a leap of faith. Your reasoning has to be thought through and it has to be open to challenge.

Bert: For example, you could make a very clear argument such as the following: If I build the capability of people in this way, they will be uniquely qualified. If they are uniquely qualified, their efforts will generate product ideas that will shape the marketplace. If we shape the marketplace, we will be able to charge high margin prices because we have the first mover advantage in the marketplace. Then we'll have extreme profitability. You can take a scenario like that around to people and see if they want get behind it or challenge it.

Iva: I agree that you need to link learning to specific results, but let's not forget also that when people start to realize results on the personal level that creates energy that sustains learning.

Linking Learning to Results

- Have you defined the results you expect from your learning effort? What kinds of personal results can people expect to experience? Have you discovered what results are meaningful to the organization?

- What measures will allow you to assess the impact of learning on results?

- When do you expect to see results? Does the timing of anticipated results jibe with the rhythm of the organization? If not, will the organization be able to tolerate the delay? What you can do to help the organization manage that tension?

Define the Boundaries and Linkages of the System

From the beginning, think of the group you will be working with as a system, a system with boundaries and linkages to other systems. It is also a subsystem within a larger system. By thinking in these terms you can begin to anticipate how learning and change within your system may affect other systems. Since the systems are inherently interconnected, your unit can't really go about its learning process in isolation. The assumption that you can do so has contributed to the perception that OL pilot groups are cultlike. New things often need nurturing incubators in the beginning, but they cannot be isolated from the rest of the world for too long or they can become "cultural islands" within the larger context.

The learning initiative described by George Roth and Art Kleiner in their book *Car Launch* provides a good example of what can happen when we don't realize that we need to manage these linkages. Organizations need to have a common understanding of what numbers mean in order to effectively coordinate action. In that case, however, the learning team was using certain key indicators in a new way. This led to a rise in the reporting of errors—actually a sign of increased learning. As you might imagine, these numbers were interpreted in an entirely different way by management in other functional areas and by the senior management of the larger system. This led to confusion and conflict.[8]

Understanding the boundaries of the learning system, managing the interconnections, and engaging the larger system all require skills that may be new to us. They also require significant communication skills. Research by Argyris and Schön has indicated communication difficulties associated with hierarchies and cross-divisional relationships comprise one of the major threats to organizational learning.[9] Therefore this kind of communication represents a learning edge for most managers. Rather than following our Model I tendency of trying to convince others that we are right we must practice holding tension and learn how to engage others as we go.

Questions to Help You Consider the Boundaries of Your System

- Have you defined the boundaries of the system you are working with? Are you working at the team level? The unit level? The organizational level?

- How does the system you're concerned with interconnect with other systems? If learning changes how your team or department works, will there be an impact on other subsystems?

- When and how will you engage the larger system? (Remember that waiting until you have results to show is most likely a poor strategy.)

Using Feedback Effectively

In systems thinking terms, feedback loops are always present. Feedback informs how the system responds to the larger environment. Scientists have observed that because of their ability to use feedback, systems can exist in a state of bounded instability; they can constantly change without disintegrating or descending into turmoil. Human beings may realize the same benefits from feedback; however, they may need to develop their capacity to see, interpret, and use feedback. In human terms this means that we may need to actively seek out sources of feedback and link into them.

Bert: Feedback can help with issues of pacing and timing that can tend to trip up a learning effort. If you get good feedback you'll be better able to remap in midstream.

Iva: We need feedback not only to help with our strategy, but also to guide our personal transformation. We need to reach out for help in the form of coaches, trainers, and/or truthful, courageous supporters who will tell us whether we are "walking our talk" and living in accordance with our espoused values. We cannot do this work as the lonely, heroic leader because we can never really see ourselves objectively. We need to question and test our assumptions and practice new ways of being in collaboration with others, in communities of practice.

Bert: So if we're really committed to getting good feedback we may have to create new structural elements or make some personnel changes.

Iva: Right, you may need to spend valuable time developing a supportive network before you can begin. Furthermore, if you want to be able to use the feedback you get, you may need help with building your own reflective capacity or that of the organization. Particularly, if we're trying to create a Model II-based organizational learning system, we must create the opportunity for a dialectical learning process to occur. You may seek out a qualified facilitator, coach, or a reflective analyst.[10]

Questions to Help You Use Feedback Effectively

- Have you found and developed a supportive network? Have you found people you trust who will give you honest feedback? To what degree are you open to coaching?

- Have you created the necessary structural elements that enable feedback for your organization, such as a reflective analysis or an after-action review? Will feedback be communicated—both to the team doing the work and to those as yet uninvolved?

- Is there coaching support provided for others in your organization?

Assessment

Assessment is one of the toughest assignments. If possible, identify multiple measures in order to have the fullest possible picture. In the very beginning, identify some interim measures or indicators that you can use to assess whether your learning effort is on track—especially if you anticipate delays. Define both qualitative and quantitative measures. Find out who has to agree on the measures and get agreement. Prepare the ground so that a perceived "failure" to meet some early yardstick can become an opportunity for learning rather than a reason to pull the plug. One of the keys will be to find the ability to back off from time urgency that so characterizes command-and-control type leaders and many organizations. Learning both creates and requires delays.

Bert: One of the ways we can apply what we learned from TQM is to get agreement with the relevant parties on the terms of assessment ahead of time. Get agreement that if things appear to get worse in the beginning they won't just pull the plug. In fact, we need to give ourselves the space to make that agreement and find the time for the results to show up.

But it's not only the issue of time that needs to be understood. One also needs to have a clear understanding of how results in an OL context will differ from previously published norms. I'm thinking of the *Car Launch* example. Just as the history of TQM shows us, a new approach generates very different kinds of results, which may not match expectations. Unless the ground is prepared, these results will most likely be misinterpreted.

Iva: The key is to initiate generative conversations up front so that the proper assessments are in place thereby minimizing the potential for knee-jerk reactions to those different results that learning projects tend to produce. But that's also a bit of a catch-22 because in order to be successful in those conversations one has to be skilled in the practice of having those conversations—and most of us are not. Furthermore, you may need to unveil your concerns, reveal what you don't know. In other words, you may need to practice OL in an environment that may not be quite ready for that approach.

Bert: The larger question is: How do you launch OL if the organization doesn't believe in it yet? You do what you believe will work in the situation. Certain environmental conditions may allow you to proceed without as much agreement—although perhaps with increased risk. This may involve some political savvy on the leader's part because this is a political process. For example, you have some political capital that you can spend or if you have some established credibility and strong allies you can work the political process. For example, if you've got a portal because you're in charge of a Greenfield you have latitude. If you've got a portal and you're certain that you can deliver on the expected results without a time delay by doing OL work, then you can take Dave Marsing's "stealth" approach.

Iva: So we need to be politically savvy even as we practice the art of generative conversation.

Bert: Right. Again, we've got to take a "two systems" approach.

Iva: Would it be appropriate to say that the most difficult thing to project and assess is the delay? How is the delay created? What is the structure of the delay? We can retrospectively define what the delay was and how it influenced the outcome—system diagrams do that very well. But can we forecast it?

Bert: The issue of delay needs to be understood, and it's very complex. If initiatives don't yield results within certain timeframes and expectations they are pulled. This potentially results in a self-fulfilling prophecy. Detractors of OL say, "You see, it didn't work." Then there is the potential for the OL people to use excuses, "Well, you didn't give me enough time and that's why it didn't happen." This is a complex area, fraught with potential problems, so several things need to be considered.

Consider the challenge of attribution. When we first embarked on Quality efforts the results actually got worse in the beginning. We were unprepared for that. Later, we learned that was a normal part of the journey. The reason things *seemed* to get worse was that people started to focus their attention on it. OL seems to be following the same pattern as the *Car Launch* example demonstrated.[11]

Iva: There's also our personal sense of time urgency, which affects how we're able to deal with delays.

Bert: Since many of us leaders are "Type A" personalities, we can all learn from what Phil said.

Phil Carroll: We're all impatient. We all would like to see things accomplished faster. But I believe that there is an inherent pace to things. There's a pace that is unique to the company and the industry. The pace of our business is going to be geared differently than the pace of things in a Silicon Valley startup or in Ford Motor Company.

A sense of urgency, a desire to move quickly is a strong, positive trait, but you can't have the expectation that learning is going to happen miraculously overnight. You have to build capability, you have to erect a learning infrastructure within an organization through processes that reinforce it. All of that takes time.

Questions to Help You Plan for Assessing Your Learning Journey

- Who needs to agree on the terms of assessment? Are you collaborating with them?
- How should your learning effort be assessed? Should there be qualitative as well as quantitative measures? Can you define interim indicators of progress?
- In what timeframe can you expect to see results? What if there is a delay?
- How might you capture what you are learning along the way—without sanitizing out the missteps and "failures"?
- How will you diffuse what you are learning?

Sustainability

Even before a learning effort is brought to life, think about what energies, what currency will keep it going. Perhaps thinking about this topic will lead you to do some things differently even at the very beginning.

Bert: People tend to associate any kind of movement with the person who is most prominent. It's a natural tendency, but it gets in the way of change, as Phil Carroll pointed out.

Phil: When it became obvious that my time was coming to an end and I was going to leave, I got a lot of questions at various meetings. People asked, "What's going to happen to all this?

Why should I commit to this thing if you're going to be gone in another 12 to 14 months and this will all go away?" I said, "If I leave and the transformation process goes away, then you were not transformed. You never were really with it. You were just sort of an interested observer on the outside."

Iva: How does the leader create conditions for transitional change without creating a legacy that other people will shy away from? How do you design yourself out so the change doesn't depend on you?

Bert: After you've done all the right things, the important question to ask yourself becomes, How much have I involved other people in taking the leadership position? Have I let other people stand up in front of groups? It's important to wean yourself out of the process, just like succession planning.

Iva: You also have to know *when* to do that, because if you do it too soon, they might think you don't care. They think, let's wait this out.

Bert: You start by building the capacity, then you feather it down, and then you almost work yourself out of a job. That's why it's like succession planning. If the movement is more important than you are, then you drive for improvement in the movement, but then you don't leave the movement in the lurch. You make sure that succession planning is part of what you do.

Iva: As a leader you also have to come to terms with how that's going to feel. Leaders have pretty big egos—but to plan for sustainability you're going to have to let go. That's not always comfortable, as Rich Teerlink told us.

> **Rich:** I would say that I was too wrapped up in myself and too worried about my value to society. You ask: Was it all worth it? How do you define "worth?" I'm a very wealthy man. But wealth is not the scorecard. It's more about, How do you feel? Do I feel that I made a difference? It's not about everyone else recognizing the difference. It's that *I* recognize it. But when you're leaving the organization the fear is that no one will recognize it.
>
> You've got to step back and say wait a minute. We tried this and we tried that. Some things worked; some didn't. There was a lot of frustration. But if I look at where the company is today and what's going on inside the company, I know I was part of that. And if that lives on, what more can I ask for? Do I have to have my name associated with it? That's ego, and that's wrong. You know, we started OL and I had a part in it, but it was a whole bunch of people and I was one of many. There were a lot of good things that happened that I wasn't part of.

And OL did make a difference. You see, that's the conclusion that I evolved to. I know it made a difference and the hell with everything else. And I'm going to tell people that they can make a difference in their companies.

Questions to Help You Design in Sustainability

- Will you "leave it better than you found it"? Will the effects be significant and long-lasting?
- Is your learning effort "personality dependent," or have you created conditions such that the learning will continue if and when you leave?

Phase 3: Beginning the Journey

As you begin the journey, you will encounter a major challenge: How will you engage the organization? The way in which you go about involving the organization in a learning effort is very important because the way in which you engage people tells them how serious you are about learning. It also tells the organization how serious the leadership is about collaboration and the devolution of power. If people see that they are being asked to be contributors, they will be more likely to engage. If you "roll out" a learning effort you deliver a very different communication than if you engage people in a dialogue about where you all think the organization should go and why. A roll-out can turn people off immediately, just as a vision statement that comes down from the hierarchy generates little interest. As Stacey writes "the role of top management is not to invent and preach simple, clear aspirations but rather to create a context favorable to complex learning from which challenges may emerge."[12]

A dialogue on the state of the organization can have mutual benefits. Visioning may begin as a solitary practice, but clarity about the vision and values comes with communication. Vision needs to be shared. If a dialogue can be open and honest, it can help clarify the vision and the values as well as the perception of current reality. Of course, the problem is that the organization may be predisposed against such honesty. It may be operating according to Model I values—even while espousing Model II values. These situations are common. The question is: Are these barriers anticipated, planned for, and worked through as artifacts of the transformation process?

The engagement process itself may be a learning journey. Leaders may have to work hard at developing new skills: particularly, the ability to listen.

Bert: There is a tendency for executive leaders to remain aloof, to be too busy to listen, to not be as approachable as one would like.

Iva: Listening takes time. It takes energy. It takes skill.

Bert: The reason for that aloofness is that executives are fearful and people are fearful. I remember a time when I asked a colleague why he never let anyone ask him a question. His response was, "Well, they might ask me a question that I don't know the answer to."

Iva: Not having the answer is such a frightening experience for leaders.

Bert: Sometimes leaders rhetorically ask, "Are there any questions?" I usually count the number of seconds the executive waits. If it's less than five, I know they don't want questions. In that sense, you need the skill of listening, but you also need the skills of self-awareness and overcoming imagined fears—because they really are imagined more than real.

Iva: You've got to break the frame of a command-and-control culture where people have learned to wait for the leader to tell them what to do. That's going to be tough and awkward.

Bert: If you want to tear that barrier down, you have to take a hard look at the artifacts of management in your culture that create that sense of distance: the clothes, the Power Point slides, the seating arrangements—

Iva: The leader needs to tear down those barriers because they become the barriers to truth-telling and communication. You need to provide enough time and space so that communication can be enabled.

Bert: And put people at ease so they'll tell you the truth. Whether I was in a technician's truck or in an executive meeting, I felt that people believed that they could tell me what they thought—but the problem was that I wouldn't always hear them.

Iva: Are you really sure that people felt that they could tell you what they thought? You might have thought they really trusted you, but if you didn't hear them they probably held back. Communication needs to be symmetrical. Once you've lost trust it's very difficult to gain it back.

Bert: You could be right. You don't know what you don't know.

Iva: There may have been a disparity between your espoused values and your theory-in-use. That's exactly what Rich Teerlink said.

Rich: People were always willing to tell management what they thought, but the problem was that sometimes we didn't listen to what they said! As leaders we want to say, "Let's talk about this. Let's look at the world a little differently." We have good intentions but then we often end up being the kind of leader who says, "Let's look at the world differently and here's what *I'm* thinking." We leaders have to learn how to keep our mouths shut!

Questions to Help You with Engaging the Organization

- Have you found a way to align personal and organization goals as much as possible? Have you translated your vision, values, and strategy into terms that people can engage with?

- Are you driving change from the top? Do you appear to be doing so?

- Are you creating a "listening environment," an organization that values inquiry and listening to others? Are you engaged in dialogues about important things versus "rolling it out"? Are people telling you honestly what they think? Are these learnings shifting your awareness? Have you been able to tap into the inherent commitment in your organization?

- Are there signs that the organization is engaged? Is the larger system engaged?

- Are your supportive networks and early adopters growing—or are you the lonely (and "heroic") leader?

Phase 4: On the Journey

Those in the midst of the journey will face such questions as: How do they know if what they're doing is working, if they're on the road to success or failure—or oblivion? How do they know that they have adequate feedback? Have they taken time for sufficient reflection?

As you go through a change process, you need to keep your feet on the ground. Because of our bias toward action and our tendency to avoid reflection, we can sow the seeds of our own destruction. Ironically, it is when we are deeply committed to what we believe are high ideals that we become most intractable and therefore most prone to failure. We can do this in many ways: by being in denial, by feeling incredulous that others don't see the value of these ideas, or by overreacting to negative feedback.

The Benefits of Reflection

Developing the capacity for reflection is one of the most important aspects of the learning journey. We often use the excuse of time, but that is most likely a rationalization. Many leaders rarely question their assumptions. They believe their assumptions are sacrosanct, it is the implementation that is flawed. If one develops the capacity to reflect in the midst of action one will be better able to:

- Detect "biological rejection phenomenon" in the culture and respond accordingly.
- Center yourself as you experience the highs and lows that go along with this journey.
- Respond to the inevitable challenges that arise.
- Recognize different types of feedback and how to act accordingly. For example, what are the warning signs that things are not going well? Or going *too* well?
- Intuit the correct pacing and timing of things, thus enabling you to effectively balance action with nonaction.
- Anticipate learning from mistakes and failures.
- Attend to your own personal development and transformation. As a leader of change, you need to find the means to deal effectively with your blind spots, your fears, personal weaknesses, and insecurities because they will most likely be triggered and are likely to affect the way you manage change.

Questions to Help You Design in Reflection

- Have you found ways to nurture reflection in both yourselves and others?
- Have you found ways to build both individual and collective reflection (and double-loop learning) into the organizational environment?
- Are you getting feedback on how well you seem to be balancing action with non-action?
- What is your response to feedback and challenges, mistakes, and failures? Are you using them as opportunities for reflection and double-loop learning?
- Do you notice that you tend to avoid reflection—particularly questioning assumptions?
- Are you reaching out for support?
- Have you considered who defines success and failure for you?

Phase 5: Journey's Landmarks

As the journey progresses, look for landmarks.

Questions to Help You Recognize Landmarks

- Note the results you are experiencing. Are your results tangible if not quantifiable? Are the results surprising you? Are there significant delays? If so, are there interim signals that indicate that results are forthcoming?

- What are you learning?

- Is learning occurring at both the individual and team level? What kind of learning (single- or double-loop learning) is occurring? What assumptions are changing? How will that learning translate into organizational learning?

- Is the learning transferable? How?

- Is the larger system engaged? How do you know?

- Are there signs that the learning is self-sustaining?

We've summarized the guiding questions at each phase in Table 11.2. This list is not meant to be exhaustive and we hope that as you learn you will be inspired to challenge and improve this list.

In this chapter we have tried to offer some considerations to help you map your own learning journey. We offer them not as prescriptions, but rather as perspectives derived from our collective reflection on our experiences and the experiences of four other leaders. Through this period of reflection we have come to believe that both we and our organizations would have benefited if we had asked these questions as we mapped our own journeys.

At the same time, we recognize the fallibility of maps. As Herman Melville wrote, "True places are not found on maps." The purpose of the journey is not to follow the maps, but to find those "true places." It is in this spirit that we offer these questions and reflections to others.

Table 11.2
Mapping the Journey

Phases of the Journey	Suggested Areas of Inquiry
Phase 1: Inviting a Journey	• Does this vision for my organization require a learning process in order to be actualized? • If so, how can we articulate the connection? Can others see the connection clearly?

Questions to Help with Cultural Analysis:
- How is your culture likely to enhance or inhibit learning?
- What are the strengths and weaknesses of your culture?
- How will your culture affect how you implement a learning effort?
- Are you concerned with multiple subcultures? How do they differ and how do they relate to one another?
- How might you go about this up-front analysis? What resources are necessary? Who should be involved?

Timing—A Question of Readiness:
- What is the relative financial health of your organization?
- Is there a climate of openness and a receptivity to change?
- Is there an opportunity for change such as a burning platform or a Greenfield?
- What is the "natural heartbeat" of the organization?

Finding Portals for Learning:
- If you are involved in product development phases, do the periodic changeovers to a new product represent a portal?
- Are there opportunities during the budget process? For example, are there quarterly/periodic reviews to readjust the budget to see how it compares with the forecast?
- Does your performance review process include agreements with employees about their personal development? Is the company or division reviewing its training curriculum?
- When you do employee surveys, are there meetings to determine what you're going to do about the results?
- Are there TQM or other local initiative forums where new ideas are fostered and tried? Many companies have Quality audits, which provide an opportunity to question assumptions. What processes do you use to engage employees in openly sharing their ideas? Would OL tools and methods be helpful in that process?

Burning Platform:
- Why are we getting these results that we don't want?
- What are the systemic causes of these results?
- Are we thinking about the future or just reacting to the present?

Leadership Readiness—Questions to Help You Assess Your Self-knowledge:
- Do you resonate with the qualities we have found in other OL leaders?
- Do you have a clear sense of why you want to embark on this journey? Where has that clarity come from?
- Ask yourself whether you have the strength of character to define your own pathway. Is your ego strong enough—but not too strong?
- Locate your level on the Rooke Torbert grid. Are you a "Strategist?" What are your strengths and weaknesses

vis-à-vis leading a learning effort? What skills might you need
to develop?
- Do you have the ability to communicate and network successfully within the hierarchy and across functions?

Questions to Help You Assess Strength of Commitment:
- What is your experience with making commitments?
- Are you prepared to conduct (several) experiments, reflecting
and challenging your assumptions?
- Can you make a commitment without knowing what the
outcome will be?
- How important is this work to you? Are you willing to put
your job on the line?

Questions to Help Assess Your Ability to Live in Paradox:
- Can you both hold and live with creative tension?
- Do you have the ability to live with (and within) two sys-
tems, helping to build the bridge between them?

Questions to Help Assess Your Situational Acuity:
- What is your model of leadership?
- Is your leadership style flexible? How do you know?
- How might you develop your situational acuity?

Questions to Help Assess Your Openness to Learning
- Are you prepared to learn from your mistakes, examining
your assumptions?
- Can you let go and move on or do you tend to dwell on the
past?
- Can you show vulnerability, admit to others that you don't
have all the answers?
- Do you value and seek out diverse viewpoints? Do you think
that good ideas can come from virtually anywhere?
- Are you interested in nurturing the potential of others?
- Have you reached out for appropriate help in making these
appraisals of yourself?

Questions to Help You Assess Your Practical Knowledge and Ability
- How well do you understand the systemic nature of
change? Will you be able to identify strategies for weakening
the balancing processes?
- Can you recognize—and resist—your organization's defensive routines?
- Do you have the practical ability to lead change? What is the
status of your resources, the strength of your network, and
the courage of your allies? Do you have enough influence
and credibility to execute? What is the measure of credibility
in your organization? Do you have both the support and the
political capital you need?
- What are your strengths and weaknesses vis-à-vis leading a
learning effort? Based on this overall assessment, how would
you describe your learning edge?

**Phase 2: Designing the
Adaptable Map**

Questions to Help Link Learning to Results:
- Have you defined the results you expect from your learning
effort? What kinds of personal results can people expect to
experience? Have you discovered what results are meaningful to the organization?
- What measures will allow you to assess the impact of learning on results?

Table 11.2 (*continued*)
Mapping the Journey

Phases of the Journey	Suggested Areas of Inquiry

Phase 2: Designing the Adaptable Map (*continued*)

- When do you expect to see results? Does the timing of anticipated results jibe with the rhythm of the organization? If not, will the organization be able to tolerate the delay? What can you do to help the organization manage that tension?

Questions to Help You Consider the Boundaries of Your System:

- How have you defined the boundaries of the system you are working with? Are you working at the team level? The unit level? The organizational level?
- How does the system you're concerned with interconnect with other systems? If learning affects how your team or department works, will there be an impact on other subsystems?
- When and how you will engage the larger system?

Questions to Help You Use Feedback Effectively:

- Have you found and cultivated a supportive network? Have you found people you trust who will give you honest feedback? To what degree are you open to coaching?
- Have you created the necessary structural elements that enable feedback for your organization, such as a reflective analysis or an after-action review? Will feedback be communicated both to the team doing the work and to those as yet uninvolved?
- Is there coaching support provided for others in your organization?

Questions to Help You Plan for Assessment:

- Who needs to agree on the terms of assessment? Are you collaborating with them?
- How should your learning effort be assessed? Should there be qualitative as well as quantitative measures? Can you define some interim indicators of progress?
- In what time frame can you expect to see results? What if there is a delay?
- How can you capture what you learn along the way? How will you diffuse what you are learning?

Questions to Help You Design in Sustainability:

- Will you "leave it better than you found it"? Will the effects be significant and long-lasting?
- Is your learning effort "personality dependent"? Have you created conditions such that the learning will continue if and when you leave?

Phase 3: Beginning the Journey

Questions to Help You with Engaging the Organization:

- Have you found a way to align personal and organization goals as much as possible? Have you translated your vision, values, and strategy into terms that people can engage with?
- Are you driving change from the top? Do you appear to be doing so?
- Are you creating a "listening environment," an organization that values inquiry and listening to others? Are you engaged in dialogues about important things versus "rolling it out?"

- Are people telling you honestly what they think? Are these learnings shifting your awareness? Have you been able to tap into the inherent commitment in your organization?
- Are their signs that the organization is engaged? Is the larger system engaged?
- Are your supportive networks and early adopters growing— or are you the lonely (and "heroic") leader?

Phase 4: On the Journey

Questions to Help You Design in Reflection:
- Have you found ways to nurture reflection in both yourself and others? Have you found ways to build both individual and collective reflection (and double-loop learning) into the organizational environment?
- Are you getting feedback on how well you seem to be balancing action with non-action?
- What is your response to feedback and challenges, mistakes, and failures? Are you using them as opportunities for reflection and double-loop learning?
- Do you notice that you tend to avoid reflection—particularly questioning assumptions? Are you reaching out for support?
- Have you considered who defines success and failure for you?

Phase 5: Journey's Landmarks

Questions to Help You Recognize Landmarks:
- Note the results you are experiencing. Are your results tangible if not quantifiable? Are the results surprising you? Are there significant delays? If so, are there interim signals that indicate that results are forthcoming?
- What are you learning?
- Is learning occurring at both the individual and team level? What kind of learning (single- or double-loop learning) is occurring? What assumptions are changing? How will that learning translate into organizational learning?
- Is the learning transferable? How?
- Is the larger system engaged? How do you know?
- Are there signs that the learning is self-sustaining?

Endnotes

1. Daniel Boorstin, *The Discoverers* (NY: Random House, 1983), p.159.

2. Edgar H. Schein, *Organizational Culture and Leadership,* 2nd ed. (San Francisco: Jossey-Bass, 1992).

3. Edgar. H. Schein, *Organizational and Managerial Culture as a Facilitator or Inhibitor of Organizational Learning* (1994, working paper available at www.sol-ne.org/res/wp/10004.html#one).

4. David Berdish, "Learning for Operational Excellence: A Manager's Story," *Reflections: The SoL Journal,* 1999, Vol. I, No. 1.

5. Arie de Geus, *The Living Company* (Boston: Harvard Business School Press, 1997).

6. Peter Senge et al., *Dance of Change: The Challenges of Sustaining Momentum in Learning Organizations* (New York: Doubleday, 1999), pp. 10–21, 565–568.

7. Ralph Stacey, *Managing the Unknowable: Strategic Boundaries Between Order and Chaos in Organizations* (San Francisco: Jossey-Bass, 1992), pp.146–147.

8. George Roth and Art Kleiner, *Car Launch: The Human Side of Managing Change* (New York: Oxford University Press, 2000), pp. 109–110.

9. Chris Argyris and Donald Schön, *Organizational Learning* (Reading, MA: Addison-Wesley, 1978).

10. Marty Castleberg has done ground-breaking work in helping teams within Harley Davidson develop their capacity to reflect upon their collective experience and turn that reflection into more thoughtful action. In his role as a reflective analyst (RA) Marty has pioneered tools and methods, such as reflective notes (RNs), which provide meaningful (and sometimes confrontational) feedback to the teams. The feedback helps team members to think more systemically and critically, challenge their assumptions, and draw value from diverse perspectives. As one team member put it, "It has given our team a perspective or way of looking at ourselves that we otherwise would not have had."

    The reflective feedback is structured such that it is available to the team both in real-time and overtime so that they can map their progress. At key moments, the feedback is combined with individual ad hoc coaching—another aspect of the RA's role. As a consequence of having access to an agent of reflection, the HD teams have developed their capacity to learn collaboratively and make better, more informed choices. If you would like to contact Marty for more information, he can be reached at his e-mail address: martberg@execpc.com.

11. Roth and Kleiner, 2000, op. cit., pp. 149–176.

12. Stacey, 1992, op. cit., p. 141.

Chapter 12

A Call to Action

The Call

Bert: I would like us to close with a call to action. In order to have more sustainable organizational learning projects we have to have more *attempts* at sustainable projects. We have to have more people trying, even if they fail, so we can all learn.

Iva: We have acknowledged that there are perceived barriers to businesses' adopting organizational learning. For example, we've acknowledged that we do not have sufficient proof that these tools and methods will yield specific financial results—particularly in the short term. But we are also saying that we cannot provide this proof until we have more businesspeople who are willing to engage with organizational learning. In other words, they have to be willing to take a risk.

Bert: The theoreticians have raised the flag; they have been carrying the banner. Businesspeople have not been carrying the banner because of all of the things that we have been discussing. Nonetheless, this is a call to action for businesspeople—with a heavy dose of reality thrown in.

Iva: When businesspeople *have* taken up the standard, when they have tried to implement these learning ideas in their organizations—as we have tried to do—that's when all the difficulties have arisen.

Bert: And therein lie all the learnings.

Iva: We're certainly talking about paradox here. On the one hand we don't have proof that OL will lead to improved financial results. On the other hand we won't get that proof until we try. We're asking businesspeople to engage with paradox.

Bert: Yes, it is a paradox of sorts, but that's the only way the theory can be tested. It's the only way we can find out what works and what doesn't. It's the only way we can figure out how to change things. I recognize that this can seem pretty intimidating because the process of change is still largely unknown to us. It seems complex, chaotic, and not easily observable, except historically.

Iva: But you can see how that presents a dilemma to most people in the business world. They cannot safely or reliably use the ideas and tools until the bridge is built from here to there.

Bert: We have incomplete knowledge, but when in the business world did we ever act with complete knowledge? That's the essence of entrepreneurialism. I also say that we will never have that knowledge without more experiments in the real world. We need to find better ways to measure and capture the impact that learning can have on an organization. We need better ways of anticipating and dealing with delays so that we don't shut down good ideas too soon. We won't be able to learn how to do that unless businesspeople accept the risks and engage with those questions.

If we in the business world don't accept this call to action and create those experiments, then we are accepting the limitations of the structure that we find ourselves in. We are accepting that we cannot get there from here. I disagree strongly. I think we can.

Iva: We do not know enough yet about *how* to change our organizations—we only know that we must. So, we must begin.

Bert: Despite my continued support of the notion of a heroic leader, I also have to acknowledge that businesspeople can't do this alone.

Iva: We need to learn in community with one another. The kind of learning we're talking about is not a solitary endeavor. Transformative learning requires other people. That means we still have more to learn about how to support each other's learning journeys.

Bert: It's time for the businessperson's dilemma to become *everyone's* dilemma: academics, consultants, and businesspeople. There has to be compromise on the other side as well. The strong advocates of organizational learning are going to have to balance their optimism with an acceptance—maybe even appreciation—of the cynicism of many businesspeople. Even the people who go to organizational learning seminars have something to learn about the importance of acknowledging current reality. They are going to have to temper the exuberance and somewhat honeyed version of the world that you get when you go to these training courses with a solid understanding of just how difficult the transition to learning is going to be for most organizations.

Iva: You are asking the visionaries to come closer to the pragmatists. What do you ask of the pragmatists?

Bert: It is time for people in the business world to discuss the things we usually never discuss. First and foremost, we must come to terms with the fact that we are all part of a system. If we accept that—and we must—there are implications. People in the business environment are very comfortable with taking things apart and understanding the parts. We might be able to understand one part in detail very well, but we still are not able to create the opportunities for the firm to actualize its purpose. For example, suppose you are the head of manufacturing. You have a problem: your costs are too high. So you fix your cost problem by changing your supplier, a solution which, in turn, creates a new set of operating and quality standards for the company. This apparent "fix" of your problem in your area then ripples throughout the entire organization. It complicates training, selling, and repair. It even potentially has an impact on the effectiveness of your product from a customer point of view.

Iva: When we do things like change suppliers we're only concerned with reducing our costs, but our actions don't only have an impact inside the firm. They also have an impact on the outside world. We just don't think about that impact. We think that the impact is for other people to worry about, because that's the nature of business, right? But if we stopped and looked we would see how our actions might, through connections in the marketplace, not only affect others but also impact us negatively. For example, if that supplier that we drop goes out of business, the cost of materials can go up and that could, eventually, raise our costs again. We do not pay attention to how all this connected. It's the Beer Game on a much larger scale, and we tend to disregard it.

Bert: Unless we also take responsibility for understanding the relationship of the parts to the whole and the relationships between the parts, it is unlikely that we can actualize the potential of the firm.

Iva: And, unless we commit to that understanding, the business world will not be able to take actions that contribute to the greater good even though there's increasing demand for more accountability.

Bert: Therefore, we must also engage in conversations that help create greater awareness of the larger systemic context in which business operates including the human element and the environment and the assumptions that we hold to be as true as gravity, but which are only assumptions. That's a big difference from traditional strategic planning.

Of course, as a pragmatist I want these conversations to be both generative *and practical.* They have to link organizational learning to the real-world problems that businesspeople face. These conversations have to have action-oriented outcomes.

Iva: I agree that that would be ideal for most businesspeople, but I'm not certain that such conversations can be both generative and practical at the same time. I'm not sure that we can go directly from awareness to action. We may need to proceed more slowly—which will try the patience of both pragmatists and visionaries.

Business has such enormous power today to shape what happens in a community or a country, yet it isn't clear what responsibility business has to society. However, organizational learning has started in the business domain. Business could take the lead by applying what they have learned to other domains, to help ameliorate conflict and resolve social problems.

That's why the call to businesspeople, especially line managers, who have the responsibility to create wealth is so important. The more people who are responsible for the bottom line become knowledgeable about all of this, the better chance we have of moving forward.

Bert: The more we ply the philosophy that reinforces the importance of learning, collective learning, learning as the principal means of operating, the more likely we are to be able to change the system. If everybody were learning it *would* change our system.

Iva: At its core, the whole idea behind organizational learning is that there is hope. Organizational learning provides a glimpse of hope that we can indeed create win-win situations for each other even though we have different mental models, different racial or ethnic backgrounds, different political affiliations. There *is* a way if we begin to think differently about who we are and how we act and what we want to create. That's what organizational learning can offer us. Despite—and also because of—everything we've said, I'm still convinced of that.

Bert: At the same time, I want us to be realistic about what we can accomplish in what time frame. Recall Bill O'Brien's message: We're part of a movement, part of a shift that's been in the process of becoming for a thousand years.

Iva: So we're on a journey. Learning how to navigate that winding road with all the pain and bumps is not easy. Of course, we want it to be easy. We want the risks and barriers removed. We want the formula, the silver bullet, the single path, but this is a journey. We have to be willing to leave that longing behind—

Bert: And get on the road.

So the journey comes full circle. Business organizations are poised at a transition point. Organizational learning has emerged as an alternative to the thinking that has traditionally guided business leadership and management. Can we embrace this new alternative? What will it take to do so?

Throughout this book we have shown the tension that exists between what we have termed the pragmatist and the visionary orientations. Through this dichotomy we have reflected upon the inspiration that pulls many toward organizational learning and the vision that is embedded in its potential. We have also honored the forces that hold us back, tethering the majority quite firmly to current reality.

But one of the tenets of organizational learning is that we must dispense with the tendency to dichotomize, therefore we must come to terms with this dichotomy. So another way to view the seeming polar opposites of pragmatist and visionary is to see them not as binary choices but as aspects of a greater whole and therefore, as reflections of each other. Each, when taken to the extreme, can become a closed system. Pragmatism taken to its extreme becomes impractical. As we have seen with Argyris's Model I, attempts to be consistently rational can become irrational and a determination to "win" can translate into rigid learning systems built upon self-defeating defensive routines. Mental models that cannot be questioned become fodder for the jokes of tomorrow.

Born out of a rejection of grand ideological schemes, pragmatism taken to an extreme can lead to the out-and-out rejection of ideas not because they are impractical, but primarily because they are ideas—particularly if they threaten the status quo. While it has been said that "nothing is as practical as a good theory," pragmatists can refuse ideas until they are proven safe, making the window of opportunity for change very small indeed.

Likewise, the visionary can stumble. The visionary runs the risk of becoming the "true believer," who is so convinced of the vision that his or her vision also solidifies into unquestioned ideology. To be gifted with vision is to be given the ability to see possibilities. However, convinced of his or her vision, a visionary can become a *knower* who then ceases to see clearly and who does not inquire into nor seek to understand or learn from the sources of resistance. It requires deftness and skill to sort through when and how to urge a vision forward and when to hold back, revisit, rethink, and readjust.

Neither the visionary nor the pragmatist is all right or wrong. Both have much to learn from each other and, together, they can create a potent, mutually reinforcing learning system out of which could emerge a new, less illusory and more fulfilling reality.

The pragmatists can teach the visionaries much about what is needed in order to build the bridge from our current, practical business reality—however illusory—to something better. If the visionaries are able to inquire deeply and sensitively enough, the pragmatists can teach them much about the power of fear. From the pragmatists, the visionaries can learn how fear often comes disguised as an unquestioned need for control and how, ironically, the visionaries can trigger a fearful response in the pragmatists. The visionaries can learn to see what the pragmatist sees and understand the practical requirements for turning visions into tangible realities.

From the visionaries, the pragmatists can learn a sense of possibility. As they begin to become open to the greater sense of the systemic perspective, they can begin to expand their sense of what is in the best interests of business. They can begin to see that their bedrock beliefs are mental models of an increasingly illusory sense of reality. They can begin the painful process of acknowledging what they have had to give up for those beliefs. In time, they can begin to reclaim the closed-off parts of themselves, relearning how to aspire and create.

The visionary and the pragmatist represent two sources of wisdom. And, just as a walk to a new place requires two feet, so does our journey require these two sources of wisdom. But the visionary and the pragmatist do not constitute the whole. As Paula Underwood has written, it is those who see both possibilities who truly sustain a people.[1] It follows, then, that this transition lies in the hands of those of us who can appreciate both wisdoms.

To be effective in this time of transition we must honor both perspectives and develop the capacity to live within the tension between them for as long as it is necessary. There are few things that will be harder to do because we will be driven to reduce the tension. We will be pulled inexorably toward one end or the other. We may tend to oscillate, causing confusion in others and discordance within ourselves. When the pragmatist within perceives a threat to the bottom line, this will trigger a tendency to disengage with learning, to see it as superfluous to getting the job done. At that same moment the visionary tendency will be to push harder, urging the pragmatist to let go of the old rules.

Once we have awakened to this tension we must remind ourselves that at each moment we have the option to respond either reactively or creatively to that tension. Of course, most of us have been conditioned to respond reactively to circumstances; most corporate cultures reinforce this reactive behavior. We may not yet know how to break the cycle of conditioned response. We may not yet be able to reframe so that we can perceive the reality from a different perspective and, in the process, change our perceptions.

There are no easy answers. We will not be able to create this transition to learning if we believe that we must first resolve all of the demands of pragmatism. Nor can we get there by sheer force of vision. The simplest thing that can be said is to begin to notice when we are being pulled toward one extreme or the other. At that moment, stop and ask questions such as: What is going on? Why is this moment triggering me to move back to my safety zone? What am I afraid of? What can I learn by staying with this moment? How can I inquire into it? Can I respond in a more creative way to this situation?

The transition will come down to these moments and to our individual and collective responses to them. To live in this tension and to address it creatively—in each moment—is the challenge to pragmatist, visionary, and those who value both.

Endnote

1. Paula Underwood, *The Walking People: A Native American Oral History*, (San Anselmo, CA: A Tribe of Two Press, 1993). Paula Underwood is an author, a lecturer, a trainer, and a consultant in education, cross-cultural understanding, and organizational methodologies based on lifelong training and experiences in a Native American philosophy.

Index

Page references with "t" denote tables

A

Accidental learning, 48–49
"Action-logics," 176–177
Adaptable map, 256–257,
    271t–272t
"Air cover," 76, 95, 101, 170
Analysis, SWOT, 74–75, 235
Argyris, Chris, 43, 48–52, 59,
    101, 104, 144, 157–160, 177,
    221, 229, 248, 259
Aspirations, 145–146
Assessment, 261–263, 272t

B

Beer Game, 6–9
Beliefs, 153–154
"Biological rejection" phenom-
    enon, 81, 166–167, 268

C

Carroll, Phil, 185–186, 188,
    189, 191–192, 195–198, 201,
    208–212, 235, 248–249,
    252, 263–264
Change, 43, 98–102, 141–142,
    144–145, 147–148,
    156–158, 249
Commitment, 252–253
Creative tension, 40–41
Culture, 236t–237t, 238–239

D

de Geus, Arie, 21, 28, 240
Devolving of power, 229
Dialogue, 59t, 148–150, 156
Diffusion of innovation,
    150–151
Dixon, Nancy, 47–48

D (continued)

Double-loop learning, 49–50,
    53, 163–178
Downsizing, 15–17, 27t

F

Fazio, Phil, 112, 125–127,
    133–137
Fear, 152–153
Feedback, 260–261, 272t

G

Governing variables, 51–52

H

Hamel, Gary, 29
Heil, Gary, 28, 87

I

ISO 9000, 14–15

J

Journeys, 63–92, 111–139

K

Kim, Daniel, 69, 124
Knowledge
    practical, 255–256
    self-knowledge, 251–252
Kolb, David, 44

L

Ladder of inference, 58t
Leaders, 247–256
Leadership, 106–108, 181–230
    situational, 172, 215–218

Butterworth–Heinemann Business Books . . . for Transforming Business

Innovation Strategy for the Knowledge Economy: The Ken Awakening,
Debra M. Amidon, 0-7506-9841-1

Innovation Through Intuition: The Hidden Intelligence,
Sandra Weintraub, 0-7506-9937-X

The Intelligence Advantage: Organizing for Complexity,
Michael D. McMaster, 0-7506-9792-X

Intuitive Imagery: A Resource at Work,
John B. Pehrson and Susan E. Mehrtens, 0-7506-9805-5

The Knowledge Evolution: Expanding Organizational Intelligence,
Verna Allee, 0-7506-9842-X

Large Scale Organizational Change: An Executive's Guide,
Christopher Laszlo and Jean-Francois Laugel, 0-7506-7230-7

Leadership in a Challenging World: A Sacred Journey,
Barbara Shipka, 0-7506-9750-4

*Leading for a Change: How to Master the 5 Challenges
Faced by Every Leader*
Ralph Jacobson, 0-7506-7279-X

Leading Consciously: A Pilgrimage Toward Self Mastery,
Debashis Chatterjee, 0-7506-9864-0

Leading from the Heart: Choosing Courage over Fear in the Workplace,
Kay Gilley, 0-7506-9835-7

Learning to Read the Signs: Reclaiming Pragmatism in Business,
F. Byron Nahser, 0-7506-9901-9

Leveraging People and Profit: The Hard Work of Soft Management,
Bernard A. Nagle and Perry Pascarella, 0-7506-9961-2

Marketing Plans That Work: Targeting Growth and Profitability,
Malcolm H.B. McDonald and Warren J. Keegan, 0-7506-9828-4

A Place to Shine: Emerging from the Shadows at Work,
Daniel S. Hanson, 0-7506-9738-5

Power Partnering: A Strategy for Business Excellence in the 21st Century,
Sean Gadman, 0-7506-9809-8

*Putting Emotional Intelligence to Work:
Successful Leadership is More Than IQ,*
David Ryback, 0-7506-9956-6

Resources for the Knowledge-Based Economy Series

The Knowledge Economy,
Dale Neef, 0-7506-9936-1

To purchase any Butterworth–Heinemann title,
please visit your local bookstore or call 1-800-366-2665.